State Aid and Public Procurement in the European Union

Editors:
Sarah Schoenmaekers
Wouter Devroe
Niels Philipsen

State Aid and Public Procurement in the European Union

Lifelong Learning Programme
Maastricht Centre for European Law
Maastricht University

intersentia

METRO

Ius Commune Europaeum

Editors:
Sarah Schoenmaekers
Wouter Devroe
Niels Philipsen

State Aid and Public Procurement in the European Union

Intersentia Ltd
Sheraton House | Castle Park
Cambridge | CB3 0AX | United Kingdom
Tel.: +44 1223 370 170 | Email: mail@intersentia.co.uk

ISBN 978-1-78068-274-7
D/2014/7849/144
NUR 828

Cover image: © Ruzanna Arutyunyan – Dreamstime.com

British Library Cataloguing in Publication Data. A catalogue record for this book is available from the British Library.

PREFACE

This book contains a collection of essays written by academics and practitioners who contributed to the elective Masters course on 'State Aid and Public Procurement in the European Union' at Maastricht University, and to two conferences on State aid and public procurement organised in Maastricht in 2013 and 2014, respectively.

In 2011 the European Commission's Education, Audiovisual and Culture Executive Agency (EACEA) decided to support the 'State Aid and Public Procurement in the European Union' course by recognising it as a Jean Monnet European Module (Lifelong Learning Programme).

First of all, the course aims to provide stakeholders – students, but also practitioners, civil servants, and consumers – with a thorough knowledge of EU public procurement law and State aid rules. But the course also addresses the largely unexplored links and interfaces between these two legal fields, which both aim to complete the internal market and to prevent the distortion of competition. These fields share common concepts, while observance of public procurement rules may limit the risk of individual transactions being qualified as State aid (as the *Altmark* case law and Commission packages illustrate).

The Jean Monnet Module grant enabled us first of all to invite a series of distinguished speakers, who shared their knowledge, experiences and views on State aid and public procurement law and their underlying relationship. Guests included the academics *Prof. Dr Phedon Nicolaides* (College of Europe, Bruges), *Dr Hanna Schebesta* (Wageningen University; European University Institute Florence), *Ms Rita Beuter* (European Institute of Public Administration), as well as the legal practitioners *Mr Bert Lejeune* (Paulussen Advocaten) and *Mrs Len Broeders* (Broeders Advocaten).

Secondly, lectures and tutorials were provided by members of the Law Faculty of Maastricht University, including the undersigned. During tutorials, participants learnt to apply theory to concrete cases by using an interdisciplinary (law and economics) method and a problem-based approach. They learnt to analyse specific public contracts that were granted on the basis of a public procurement procedure and to determine if these contracts conferred an advantage on certain undertakings in breach of EU State aid rules. Participants thus learnt to determine whether the procurement framework can provide an ultimate safeguard to prevent the award of a public contract from constituting state aid.

Thirdly, the Jean Monnet Module made it possible for us to organise two conferences on 'State Aid and Public Procurement in the European Union', on 23 May 2013 and 27 May 2014. These conferences attracted a wide audience of specialised academics, practitioners, supervisors and students. The most recent conference was opened by *Mr Vincent Verouden* (DG Competition, European Commission; Brussels School of Competition). Other speakers included *Prof. Dr Doris Hildebrand* (Free University of Brussels; EE&MC), *Prof. Dr Pieter Kuypers* (Radbout University Nijmegen; Dutch Commission of Public Procurement Experts; AKD), *Dr Laura Parret* (Houthoff Buruma), *Prof. Dr Raymond Luja* (Maastricht University), *Mr Georg Glavanovit* (Ernst and Young), *Prof. Dr Caroline Buts* (Free University of Brussels), *Prof. Dr Wouter Devroe* (Maastricht University; KU Leuven; Allen & Overy; Belgian competition authority), *Dr Stefan Weishaar* (University of Groningen), *Mrs Len Broeders* (Broeders Advocaten), *Prof. Dr Steven Van Garsse,* (Antwerp University; Flemish Knowledge Center on PPS) and *Mr Bert Lejeune* (Paulussen Advocaten). Their illuminating and thought-provoking presentations often led to lively debates on the path to follow towards European integration in the fields of State aid and public procurement and the development of the internal market. The Jean Monnet Module has most certainly fostered interaction between the worlds of theory and practice and has provided opportunities for all categories of stakeholders present to work together, to learn from each other's experience, and to broaden horizons. We hope that the conferences have thus made a small but genuine contribution to the development of the European Union as an advanced knowledge society.

The present book contains a selection of (conference) papers written by those who were involved in the course and in the conferences.

We want to express our sincere gratitude to EACEA for the support and co-financing which proved crucial in developing the course – which attracts more participants every year – and in organising the conferences, which will also continue to be organised on a yearly basis.

Sarah Schoenmaekers, Wouter Devroe and Niels Philipsen

CONTENTS

Preface v
About the Editors xi

Modernisation of State Aid Rules in the European Union. Application of Economic Concepts and Principles
Doris Hildebrand. 1

1. Introduction 1
2. Economic Concepts and Principles in State Aid. 2
   2.1. Refined Economic Approach in the 2005 State Aid Action Plan 2
   2.2. 2012 State Aid Modernisation Programme (SAM). 3
   2.3. The Balancing Test 8
      2.3.1. Market Failures 9
      2.3.2. Structure of the Balancing Test 11
3. Modernised State Aid Guidelines 12
   3.1. 2013 Regional Aid Guidelines 12
   3.2. 2014 Environmental Protection and Energy Guidelines 13
   3.3. *Ex Post* Evaluations. 14
4. Conclusion 16
References 16

Defining the Scope of State Aid. How Tax Cases Affect the State Aid Framework
Raymond H.C. Luja. 19

1. Introduction 19
2. What is the Advantage of Indirect Aid?. 20
3. Do Directives Give Carte Blanche?. 23
4. The GBER as a Procedural Nightmare 25
5. *Ex Officio* References by National Judges. 26
   5.1. Tax Courts Invoking State Aid. 26
   5.2. National Tax Authorities Invoking State Aid in Court 28

6. How Does an Analytical Taxation of Royalties Fit within the State Aid Framework? 29
7. Looking Forward: Taxation of Public Enterprises 31
8. Concluding Remarks 32

Ex Post **Evaluation of State Aid**
Caroline Buts and Marc Jegers 33

1. Introduction 33
2. The Evolution of Economic Analysis and the Emergence of *Ex Post* Evaluation in State Aid Control 34
3. Literature Review 36
4. Existing Practices and Methodological Guidance 37
5. Possibilities for Multi-Criteria Analysis 40
6. Conclusion 43
References 44

The Evolving Treatment of Services of General Economic Interest under EU Law
Wouter Devroe and David Gabathuler 47

1. Context 47
2. What is an SGEI? 49
 2.1. Provision of a Service in the General Interest 49
 2.2. Existence of a Market Failure 51
 2.3. Universal and Compulsory Nature of the Service 52
3. The Present: Altmark, SGEI Package and Member State Reporting 52
 3.1. Background (Altmark) 52
 3.2. 2011 SGEI Package 55
  3.2.1 'Altmark' Communication 55
   3.2.1.1. Key State Aid Concepts 55
   3.2.1.2. Altmark Criteria 58
  3.2.2. *De minimis* Regulation 60
  3.2.3. Commission Decision 61
  3.2.4. Framework Communication 62
 3.3. Reporting 64
4. Sectoral Application of the Rules on SGEI 68
 4.1. Introduction 68
 4.2. Energy 68
  4.2.1. Legal Framework 68
  4.2.2. Commission Practice 69
 4.3. Environment and Waste 73
5. Conclusion 75

Compensation for the Net Extra Costs of Public Service Obligations
Phedon Nicolaides ... 77

1. Introduction ... 77
2. Clarifications: (i) Altmark vs. market economy investor principle, (ii) Altmark vs. compatible State aid, (iii) Altmark vs. Article 106(2) TFEU ... 78
3. What Constitutes a Genuine SGEI? ... 80
4. Under-Provision by the Market ... 81
5. Pre-Determined Parameters of Compensation and No Over-Compensation ... 84
6. Conclusions ... 85

To Procure or Not to Procure? That's the Question!
Sarah Schoenmaekers ... 87

1. The Notion of 'Contracting Authority' ... 88
   1.1. The Status of (Dutch) Health Insurance Companies ... 90
   1.2. The Status of (Dutch) Housing Cooperatives ... 92
      1.2.1. Current Regime ... 92
      1.2.2. Future Regime ... 96
2. Thresholds ... 98
3. Conclusion ... 99

2014 Procurement Reforms and Bid Rigging: Mixed Blessings or Our Happily Ever After?
Stefan E. Weishaar ... 101

1. Introduction ... 101
2. Competition Law and Bid Rigging ... 102
   2.1. Fines ... 103
   2.2. Criminal Sanctions ... 104
   2.3. Public Enforcement ... 104
   2.4. Private Enforcement ... 106
3. Public Procurement and Bid Rigging ... 108
   3.1. Lowering Bidders' Costs ... 109
   3.2. Small and Medium-Sized Enterprises ... 110
   3.3. Deterrence ... 111
   3.4. Most Economically Advantageous Tenders ... 112
4. Conclusion ... 113

Concessions and Public Procurement
Steven Van Garsse ... 115

1. Introduction ... 115
2. The Concept of the Public Works and Services Concession is a Loaded One ... 116
3. Concessions versus Public Contracts ... 118
4. Written Contract for Pecuniary Interest ... 119

5. Execution of Works or Provision of Services 121
6. Operating Risk 123
7. The Legal Regime in the New Concessions Directive 126
8. Closing Considerations 127

EU Green Public Procurement Policy Modernisation Package, Eco-Labelling and Framing Measures
Hanna Schebesta 129

1. Introduction 129
   1.1. Environmental Considerations in EU Public Procurement 129
   1.2. Early Case Law Driving the Development of a Green Procurement Policy ... 130
2. Green Public Procurement and Directive 2014/24/EU 132
   2.1. Technical Specifications (Article 42, Annex VII) 132
   2.2. Qualitative Selection Criteria (Articles 57–64) 133
   2.3. Award Criteria (Articles 67–69) 133
   2.4. Contract Performance Criteria (Article 70–73) 134
3. Use of Eco-Labels 135
   3.1. The Dutch Eco-Labels Case in the Light of the Procurement Modernisation Package ... 136
   3.2. Explaining the New Approach of Directive 2014/24/EU 137
4. Eco-Labels and their Significance for Green Public Procurement 138
   4.1. Content Level Considerations 138
   4.2. Governance and Legitimacy 140
   4.3. Influence of Public Procurement on Private Purchases 141
5. EU Green Public Procurement Framing Measures 141
   5.1. Analysis of the Framing Measures 142

Transparency Obligations for Parking Services
Len Broeders 145

1. Introduction 145
2. History 145
3. The Court of Justice and the Transparency Obligation 147
4. The Judicial Procedure in the Netherlands 149
5. Conclusion 150

ABOUT THE EDITORS

Sarah Schoenmaekers studied law at the European Law School of Maastricht University. She has been a practising lawyer in Belgium (Omnius advocaten) since 2006. In 2010 she obtained her PhD at Maastricht University. From 2009–2012 Sarah Schoenmaekers worked as a lecturer at Maastricht and Hasselt Universities and since 2013 she has been an Assistant Professor at Maastricht University (specialisations: public procurement law and substantive European law). Since 2013 she has also been working as a post-doctoral researcher at the Open University of Heerlen. She is a scholar of the Maastricht Centre of European Law, the Institute for Transnational Legal Research (METRO) and a member of the Ius Commune Research School. She is a project manager of several research projects.

Wouter Devroe is Professor of Competition Law at Maastricht University, Professor of Law and Chair of the Economic Law Department at KU Leuven, attorney in Brussels (Allen & Overy), and Assessor at the Belgian Competition Authority. He previously clerked at the European Court of Justice and was a member of the adjudicating branch of the Belgian competition authority. He studied law in Leuven (lic. jur. 1990, summa cum laude), Heidelberg (Ruprecht-Karls Universität; Erasmus) and Chicago (LLM Northwestern University; Fulbright Grant). His PhD concerned privatisation, corporatisation and public service law. His teaching and research focus on European and economic law.

Niels Philipsen is Associate Professor in Law and Economics at Maastricht University. He graduated in economics (specialisations: microeconomics and antitrust policy) at the School of Business and Economics of Maastricht University and obtained his PhD in 2003 at the Maastricht Institute for Transnational Legal Research (METRO). In 2003 Niels Philipsen worked at the European Commission (DG Competition) in Brussels. In summer 2005 he was a visiting scholar at the University of Illinois in Urbana-Champaign (USA), and in spring 2007 he was a European Visiting Professor at Peking University in Beijing (China). Since 2004 he has been working as a Senior Researcher and project manager for many different research projects. He teaches courses in law and economics, competition law, business economics and State aid. In 2013 he became Vice-Director of METRO.

MODERNISATION OF STATE AID RULES IN THE EUROPEAN UNION APPLICATION OF ECONOMIC CONCEPTS AND PRINCIPLES

Doris Hildebrand*

1. Introduction

Since the modernisation of EU antitrust law in 2003 – initiated by Regulation 1/2003[1] – a general tendency of the European Commission (Commission) to withdraw from its 'direct' duties can be seen.[2] The 2012 State aid modernisation (SAM) programme (European Commission, 2012(a)) is another example in this development. By identifying common principles, e.g. for assessing compatibility of State aid with the internal market, and by revising, streamlining and consolidating guidelines, the Commission limits its direct involvement. Whereas such an approach is reasonable in principle, the actual implementation is a demanding task. This task requires a clear vision of the Commission (upfront) how the economic concepts and principles related to State aid work and how these principles can be applied in practice. This article first discusses the Commission's vision about these principles and secondly, whether these principles are introduced properly in the new State aid legislation. The article concludes with an appraisal of whether national administrations in the Member States and, in the case of litigation, whether national judges have enough guidance to perform their tasks with respect to the EU State aid rules.

* Prof. Dr. Dr. Doris Hildebrand is Managing Partner of EE&MC-European Economic & Marketing Consultants. Bonn*Brussels*Vienna, www.ee-mc.com and Professor at the Department of Applied Economics of the Free University of Brussels. Address for correspondence: Doris Hildebrand, Adenauerallee 87, D-53113 Bonn. E-mail address: DHildebrand@ee-mc.com.

1 Council Regulation (EC) 1/2003 of 16 December 2002 on the implementation of the rules on competition laid down in Articles 81 and 82 of the Treaty, OJ L 1, 2003.

2 Council Regulation 1/2003 has contributed to stronger enforcement of antitrust rules at national level within the EU. The Regulation put an end to the previous notification system, under which companies notified agreements to the Commission for approval under the antitrust rules.

2. Economic Concepts and Principles in State Aid

State aid rules are important since they ensure that competition principles, which are indispensable for the functioning of the internal market, are also applied to Member States. State aid is defined as an advantage in any form whatsoever conferred on a selective basis to undertakings by national public authorities. The Treaty on the Functioning of the European Union (TFEU) generally prohibits State aid unless it is justified by reasons of general economic development (European Commission, 2014 (d)). The Commission is in charge of guaranteeing that the State aid rules are respected within the European Union. One of the critical rules[3] is that State aid measures granted by Member States to undertakings must be reported to the Commission for prior approval. When certain criteria are met, State aid is compatible with the TFEU. State aid legislation specifies exemptions in this respect: Member States may grant state aid without prior notification and approval by the Commission. An exemption is possible when the State measure is found to be a State aid in accordance with Article 107(1) TFEU and the criteria of Article 107(3) TFEU apply. This requires an assessment of the positive effects of aid (in terms of contributing to a well-defined common interest objective) as compared to its negative effects (i.e. the resulting distortion of competition and trade) (the 'balancing test'). Furthermore, the aid must be necessary and proportionate to the particular objective of common interest to be compatible with the Treaty. Based on the Commission's experience in the past, the Commission defines categories of aid and conditions under which aid measures can benefit from exemptions under Article 107(3) TFEU. The Commission block exempts, via a General Block Exemption Regulation (GBER), State aid measures that are considered unproblematic. The GBER is applied directly by numerous national administrations in all Member States including, in case of litigation, national judges. In the following, the modernisation of EU State aid rules is discussed.

2.1. *Refined Economic Approach in the 2005 State Aid Action Plan*

A first State Aid Action Plan (SAAP) was launched during the tenure of Commissioner Kroes in 2005.[4] With the SAAP, the Commission intended to regroup all existing block exemption regulations into one general BER (GBER). The SAAP was also the initial step towards the implementation of the 'refined economic approach' in State aid (Friederiszick, 2007): economic analysis should be refined and used as a tool for reform. Like in antitrust and mergers, the Commission developed and enhanced the economic tools used to analyse State aid cases. The 'refined economics' was supposed to support the wider policy objectives of the Commission. In particular the SAAP aimed at pro-active use of subsidies to support growth and jobs, by improved targeting aid at the market failures to be corrected, through horizontal instruments like R&D and innovation aid, risk capital aid, or targeted support for SMEs. The refined economic analysis should help identify real

3 Except for aid of a very low amount.

4 The SAAP was the flagship project of N. Kroes, then Commissioner for Competition Policy (N. Kroes, 2007(a)).

market failures and then assess the actual effects of a measure, both in terms of its positive impact and concerning its negative effects on competition and trade (Kroes, 2006). More precisely, from an economic point of view, the newly introduced assumption by the SAAP was that if aid does not change the behaviour of the recipient, then that aid cannot help to reduce the market failure or reach the objective of common interest which it is supposed to address. Re-formulated in a more legal manner: if the aid does not change the behaviour of the subsidised companies, then the aid cannot contribute to the furthering of Community objectives, as set out in Article 107(3) TFEU. In such a case, the aid would be incompatible with the common market (Nyssens, 2007, p. 4).

The major element of the refined economic approach is a balancing of the positive and the negative effects of State aid under Article 107(3) TFEU, also known as the 'balancing test'. This balancing exercise is quite similar to the economic assessment under Article 101(3) TFEU. Considering the 'more economics-based approach' in EU competition law, the antitrust rules were already modernised in 2003. Regarding State aid, the assumption at that time was that a similar economic framework can be developed by applying the lessons learnt from antitrust (Hildebrand & Schweinsberg, 2007, p. 449). Then Commissioner Kroes pointed out in 2007: 'More work and time will be needed to fully reap the benefits of enhanced economic reasoning in EU state aid procedures.' Both at a national and European level, the political mandate has since then been in favour of 'less and better targeted state aid'. This objective should help the EU and the Member States deliver high levels of employment, productivity and social cohesion (Kroes, 2007(b)).

The 2012 State aid programme launched by then Vice-President Almunia is the next wave in this modernisation exercise. This wave is supposed to implement the economic principles as identified by the balancing test into actual legislation.

2.2. *2012 State Aid Modernisation Programme (SAM)*

In the light of Europe 2020 the Commission published its next comprehensive State aid reform programme – also known as SAM – in May 2012. Modern State aid policy should focus (again) on facilitating well-designed aid targeted at market failures and objectives of common European interest. The SAM programme was summarised by then Vice-President Almunia as follows: 'Economic forecasts currently indicate that growth in the EU will remain low for some time. In this environment, Europe must tap the full potential of a competitive internal market and, in a context of fiscal consolidation, governments must focus their spending on growth-enhancing priorities. I expect our state aid reform to help public authorities make more efficient use of scarce public resources and design public support to firms so that it helps achieve the EU's growth objectives while limiting competition distortions' (European Commission, 2012(b)). Similar to the 2003 modernisation exercise in antitrust law, SAM should limit competition distortions that could undermine a level playing field in the internal market. The Commission linked three main objectives to this mandate: (1) more with less; (2) rules clarification and procedures improvement; and (3) simplification and targeting of the rules. Thus, the goal of SAM is to promote effectiveness in public spending which means that State aid should only be used where it represents real added value from an economic perspective. A concrete definition of the market failures that are addressed by State aid and a greater scrutiny of the incentive effect are the key features of this reform (discussed further below) (European Commission, 2012(a)). Both features relate to economic principles. The economic concepts applied are unique in this matter: the main aim of SAM is to ensure value for money and to avoid competition distortions.[5] In order to identify the best set of State aid rules, the Commission started with an analysis of actual State aid expenditures.

In 2011, EU Member States granted €784 bn of State aid. Worsening economic conditions in the second half of 2011 prevented most EU Member States from phasing out State aid support to the financial sector (European Commission, 2012(c), p. 28). Thus State aid expenditures remained high due to the additional support given to the financial sector.[6] That is why 'crisis state aid' and 'temporary aid' still amount to up to 92% of all State aid provided in 2011 (€720 bn). The following figure, based on the Commission's State Aid Scoreboard,[7] illustrates the expenditures granted by EU Member States in 2011 through existing aid measures which fall within the scope of Article 107(1) TFEU.

Figure 1. Overview of State aid amounts in 2011

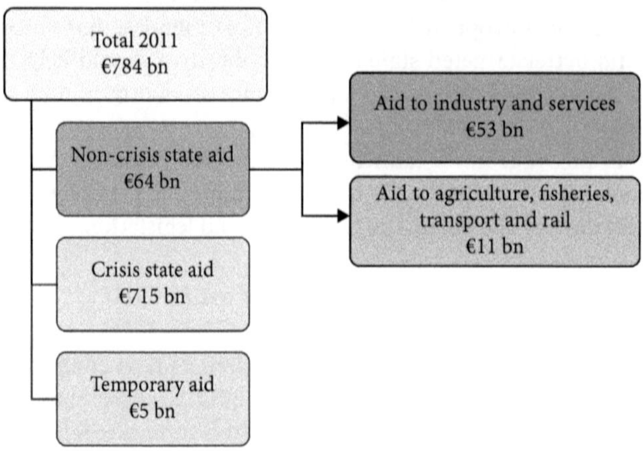

Source: European Commission, 2012 (c), pp. 8–9.

5 On top of that, rules in place were too complex and applied equally to smaller and bigger cases. In addition, a number of key State aid instruments were due to expire before the end of 2013 (European Commission, 2012(a)).

6 In the period from 1 October 2008 to 1 October 2012 the Commission approved aid to the financial sector for an overall amount of €5,058.9 billion (40.3% of EU GDP). The bulk of the aid was authorised in 2008 when €3,394 billion (27.7% of EU GDP) was approved, mainly comprising guarantees for banks' bonds and deposits. After 2008 the aid approved focused on the recapitalisation of banks and impaired asset relief rather than on guarantees, while more recently a new wave of guarantee measures have been approved mainly by those countries experiencing an increase in their sovereign spreads, such as Spain and Italy.

7 The State Aid Scoreboard is an instrument for providing a transparent and publicly accessible source of information on the State aid expenditure in the EU and the Member States.

'Non-crisis state aid' accounts for just 8% (€64 bn). Within this segment, aid to 'industry and services' represents 83%. 17% of 'non-crisis state aid' goes to aid in the agricultural, fisheries, transport and rail sectors. These numbers make clear that the focus of the SAM initiative should be on aid to 'industry and services'. The two following figures illustrate the distribution of aid to industry and services in value and volume terms (Koopman, 2013(a)).

Figure 2. Distribution of non-crisis State aid to 'industry and services'

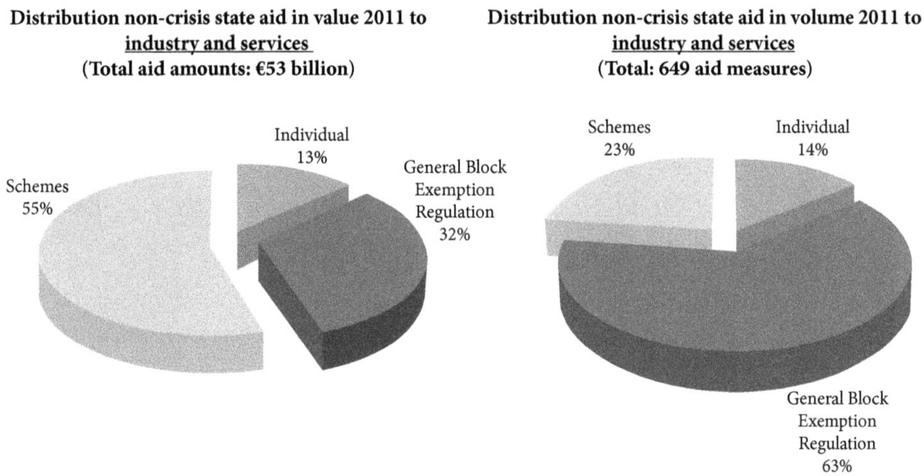

Source: European Commission, 2012 (c).

In value terms, 87% of the aid is not individually examined by the Commission, but is granted because of previously approved aid schemes[8] or block exemption regulations (BERs and GBER). The corresponding share in volume terms is 86%: 63% of all State aid measures are granted under the GBER and 23% under schemes. Based on these numbers, the conclusion is that the GBER is a crucial element within SAM. Within the block-exempted State aid measures, different types of aid turned out to be more important over time. As illustrated in the figure below for the period 2006–2011, aid for regional development (green) and environmental protection (red) increased in particular. In total, the increase in block-exempted State aid measures for industry and services in the period 2006–2011 was 394%.

8 An aid scheme is any act on the basis of which, without further implementing measures being required, individual aid awards may be made to undertakings defined within the act in a general and abstract manner and any act on the basis of which aid which is not linked to a specific project may be awarded to one or several undertakings for an indefinite period of time and/or for an indefinite amount.

Figure 3. Trend in the block-exempted state aid expenditure for industry and services, EU-27, in € million, 2006–2011 (increase 2006–2011: +394%)

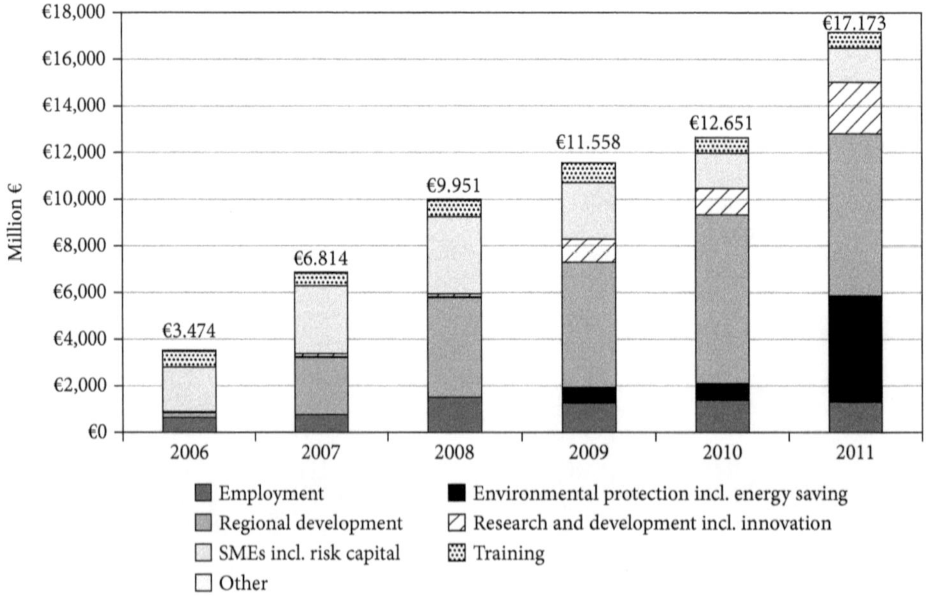

Source: European Commission, 2012 (c).

Thus, the block-exempted measures related to 'regional development' and 'environmental protection' are the most important measures within the 'non-crisis state aid' segment. Because of these analyses, the Commission proposed to increase thresholds and categories within the current State aid rules. Based on a revised Enabling Regulation[9] the Commission added new categories for exemptions.[10] By pushing the block-exempted area up to 80–90% of the aid measures and by introducing a new *de minimis* threshold, the Commission identified the pillars in the new State aid architecture as outlined below.

9 (Council Regulation (EC) 733/2013 of 22 July 2013 amending Regulation (EC) 994/98 on the application of Articles 92 and 93 of the Treaty establishing the European Community to certain categories of horizontal State aid, 2013).

10 New categories include aid for local, broadband, research and energy infrastructures, innovation clusters, regional urban development funds, culture and heritage conservation, audio-visual works, sports and recreational infrastructures and aid to make good damage caused by certain natural disasters.

Figure 4. Overview of new architecture: GBER and *de minimis*

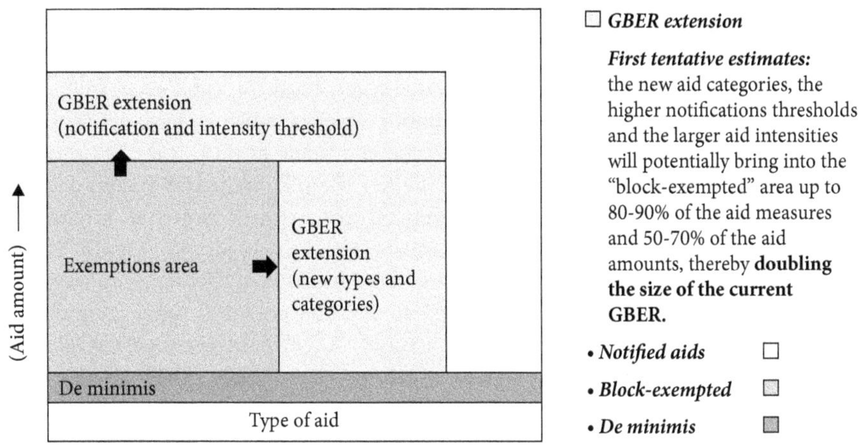

Source: Koopman, 2013(a), p. 17.

This new architecture also requires a shift from *ex ante* scrutiny towards *ex post* control, thereby incorporating more responsibilities for the Member States. The Commission itself wants to focus in the future only on large, potentially more distortive State aid cases (Koopman, 2013, p. 2). Thus, again the Commission is – as with the EU antitrust rules – withdrawing from direct duties, and focusing on policy-making and large (and potentially most distortive) cases only.

The two measures of the new architecture – the GBER and the *de minimis* Regulation – are discussed in the following section. The other aspect of the reform, namely the revision of selected State aid guidelines is elaborated further below. Several guidelines, including guidelines for regional aid, environmental aid, R&D and innovation, risk capital and broadband, have been aligned. This revision should promote more effectiveness in public spending (use of State aid only where it represents real added value), a clearer definition of the market failures that need to be addressed and greater scrutiny of the incentive effect.

In 2014, the Commission extended the scope of exemptions from prior notification of State aid via a revised General Block Exemption Regulation (GBER).[11] Member States are now able to grant more aid measures and higher amounts without having to report them to the Commission for prior authorisation. The Commission's estimate is that about 75% of State aid measures and some 66% of aid amounts are block exempted under the revised GBER. More aid measures could be exempted if Member States design their aid 'schemes' in accordance with the possibilities offered by the GBER. This means that up to 90% of all aid measures could be exempted from prior notification and approval by the Commission. National public registers of individual aid awards should ensure peer

11 Commission Regulation (EU) 651/2014 of 17 June 2014 declaring certain categories of aid compatible with the internal market in application of Articles 107 and 108 of the Treaty (2014) OJ L 187/1, 2014.

review and greater accountability. In particular, companies can check whether aid granted to their competitors is legal. This transparency also facilitates enforcement for national and regional authorities by increasing awareness of aid granted at various levels (European Commission, 2013(a)).

Monitoring and *ex post* evaluations are other tools in this new architecture. Evaluations should clarify to what extent public support schemes have achieved their purpose and what their impact on markets and competition was. In particular, evaluations should focus on: (1) assessing whether the scheme is effective in achieving the direct objective for which it was introduced (for instance regional development, environmental protection, etc.); (2) assessing whether the scheme provides for indirect effects on the objective of interest (e.g. the positive spill-overs of R&D expenditures); and (3) detecting negative indirect effects, in particular the potential aggregated effect of large schemes on competition and trade (for instance, foreclosure of markets or relocation out of poorer regions). All those elements require economic analyses as already introduced by the SAAP in 2005.

The Commission also adopted a revised *de minimis* Regulation[12] in December 2013. Small aid amounts are exempted on the grounds that these are deemed to have no impact on competition and trade in the internal market at all. More specifically, measures that fulfil the *de minimis* criteria do not constitute 'State aid' in the meaning of EU rules and therefore do not need to be reported to the Commission for approval before they are implemented. The *de minimis* amount of up to €200,000 per undertaking over a three-year period remained unchanged under the new rule. Companies experiencing financial difficulties are no longer excluded from the scope of the Regulation. In addition, subsidised loans of up to €1 mn may also benefit from the *de minimis* Regulation if certain conditions are met (European Commission, 2013(b)).

In the following section, the main element of the 'refined economic approach' in EU State aid law, namely the balancing test in Article 101(3) TFEU, is discussed. The balancing test entails the main economic principles and concepts related to State aid.

2.3. *The Balancing Test*

State aid compatible with the internal market is specified in Article 107(2) TFEU, whereas Article 107(3) TFEU mentions aid which *may* be considered to be compatible with the internal market.[13] To qualify for an exemption under Article 107(3) TFEU, economic

12 Council Regulation (EC) 1407/2013 of 18 December 2013 on the application of Articles 107 and 108 of the Treaty on the Functioning of the European Union to de minimis aid (2013) OJ L 352/1, 2013.

13 Article 107(3) TFEU: (a) aid to promote the economic development of areas where the standard of living is abnormally low or where there is serious underemployment, and of the regions referred to in Article 349, in view of their structural, economic and social situation; (b) aid to promote the execution of an important project of common European interest or to remedy a serious disturbance in the economy of a Member State; (c) aid to facilitate the development of certain economic activities or of certain economic areas, where such aid does not adversely affect trading conditions to an extent contrary to the common interest; (d) aid to promote culture and heritage conservation where such aid does not affect trading conditions and competition in the Union to an extent that is contrary to the

principles and concepts are applied. The test in Article 107(3) TFEU – weighing the positive effects of a State aid measure, e.g. risk capital measures or aid for research and innovation, against potential crowding-out or other negative effects on competition and trade – is known as the balancing test. The economic argument is that State aid should address and correct market failures and thereby restore competition again. In this analysis, several types of market failures are relevant, as illustrated below.

2.3.1. Market Failures

Externalities are the most frequently discussed type of market imperfection in the context of State aid policy. An externality exists whenever one individual's actions affect the well-being of another individual, whether for the better or for the worse, in ways that need not be paid for, according to the existing definition of property rights in the society. Externalities – of either the 'positive' or the 'negative' sort – create a problem for the effective functioning of the market. The external portions of the costs and benefits of producing a good will not be factored into its supply and demand functions because rational profit-maximising buyers and sellers do not take into account costs and benefits they do not have to bear. Hence a portion of the costs or benefits will not be reflected in determining the market equilibrium prices and quantities of the good involved. Accordingly, aggregate supply and demand for goods that entail positive externalities is too small. On the contrary, goods that entail negative externalities may encounter demand above the socially optimal level (Fritsch & Ewers, 1996, p. 81).

The term public good is used to describe goods that are characterised by non-rivalry and non-excludability (Samuelson, 1954). Public goods cannot practically be withheld from one individual consumer without withholding them from all ('non-excludability') and for which the marginal cost of an additional person consuming them, once they have been produced, is zero ('non-rivalrous consumption'). Consequently private production of the good is unprofitable, and the good may not be provided at all by the free market (Musgrave & Kullmer, 1990, pp. 55–56). National defence is an example of a public good.

A market failure can also arise through differently distributed information. Information asymmetry models assume that at least one party to a transaction has relevant information whereas the others do not. If the buyers are less informed than the suppliers of a good, this might be exploited by suppliers in terms of providing products with reduced quality and thus at lower costs, which the buyers do not realised due to their information deficit. The consequence is a so-called 'adverse selection': worse products drive out qualitatively better products.

Markets may also not function efficiently when there is a coordination problem between market actors. This aspect plays a key role in standards setting. Another aspect is market power. Notably, market power leads to prices that are too high from society's point of view, thereby not achieving efficiency (Friederiszick, 2007, p. 634).

common interest; (e) such other categories of aid as may be specified by decision of the Council on a proposal from the Commission.

The economic objective of state aid in correcting a market failure can be explained by the use of the graph below. In this graph, it is assumed that a private domestic supply and demand curves for health services exist. These are expressed as S_0 and D_0 respectively. Consequently, with a world price of P*, equilibrium quantities of health services provided and consumed domestically are Q_0 and Q_d.

Figure 5. Demand and supply of health services

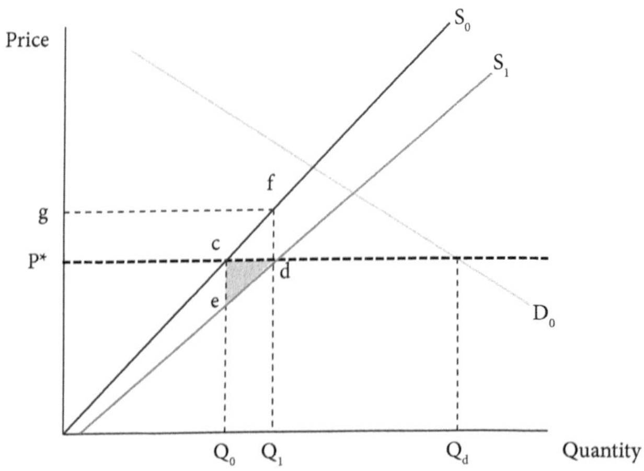

Now, suppose that there is a positive externality in the provision of health services. This might be relevant to the case of health services: private treatment for contagious diseases could provide a considerable benefit to others, for which they do not pay. Consequently, the initial supply curve is not representative of the benefits of the provision of health services. In fact, the social costs of providing each unit of the health service would be lower than what is portrayed by the supply curve S_0 below which only displays private costs. If externalities are taken into account, the new supply curve would be S_1, which indicates a lower unit cost of health service provision.

If the world price and the demand curve D_0 are assumed to reflect the true social costs, then the domestic provision of health care services at Q_0 would be less than the socially optimum level of provision Q_1. The cost to society of this under-provision would be the area *cde*. To see this, assume a total State subsidy of the amount *dfgP** is granted, which expands the amount of health service to Q_1. The total cost of the imports being replaced as a result of the subsidy is Q_0Q_1dc, but the total cost to society from providing the incremental service would be Q_0Q_1de. The difference is the area *cde* – shaded in the graph above. The conclusion is that, if a positive externality in the provision of health care services exists, a State subsidy could be used to increase welfare.

Thus, the aims of State intervention and implementation of State aid are to correct these market failures because State aid is more efficient and welfare-enhancing than market solutions.

In the event of an identified market failure, the Member States can calculate the net benefit caused by the state intervention. Aid can and should be granted where that net benefit is positive: the benefits outweigh the costs. Because of these economic considerations, a thorough economic analysis is necessary to disclose the real intention and the justification for a State measure. The balancing test transfers these economic considerations in a legally practicable mode.

2.3.2. Structure of the Balancing Test

The structure of the balancing test is straightforward. The test has three steps: the first two steps address the positive effects of State aid whereas the third step deals with the negative effects by balancing the positive and the negative effects.

First, the aid needs to address a well-defined market failure or a well-defined objective of common interest (e.g. growth, employment, cohesion, and environment). Objectives of common interest can be divided between those targeting efficiency (increasing wealth in the economy) and those targeting equity (better division of the wealth between stakeholders, notably to reflect social and regional cohesion).

The aid must be well targeted. This means that the aid needs to be well designed to deliver the desired objective. However, it is not sufficient for State aid just to target a market failure. The aid also needs to involve a change in firms' behaviour in order to be justified. This behavioural change is tested by the 'incentive effect'. From the economic perspective, it is important that the incentive effect generates benefits for the consumers as a result of the State measure. Without an incentive effect, a firm's behaviour does not change and consumers are not affected either. The aid would be a simple transfer from taxpayers' money to the firms. In this sense, the consumer standard (as operationalised by the incentive effect) is a safeguard against windfall profits to firms (Friederiszick, 2007). By means of a counterfactual analysis, important findings on the incentive effect are gained: the incentive impact is expressed as the difference between two scenarios comparing a situation with and without the State measure. In its guidance paper on a common methodology for State aid evaluation, the Commission qualifies the analysis of the incentive effects as direct impact of the aid on beneficiaries (European Commission, 2014(a), p. 6). The guidance paper continues with the description of the indirect impact of the aid scheme, which in fact relates to the last step in the balancing test – namely to the effects on competition and trade.

The proportionality of the aid measure is another major element in the balancing test. The question to answer is whether the same change in behaviour can be obtained with less aid. According to established case law, the amount and the intensity of State aid must be limited to the necessary minimum (*Schmitz-Gotha Fahrzeugwerke GmbH v Commission of the European Communities*, 2006). Thus, before resorting to State aid, which is in general only the 'second best' option to achieve an optimal allocation of resources, it should be verified whether other less distortive measures could remedy the market failure or reach the common objective. This assessment entails an analysis of whether there are other, better-placed instruments, which are either more effective or less costly in reaching the objective chosen. Therefore, alternative instruments, which are considerably milder while still having the same effect as the chosen one, are examined. If the result of this analysis is that the desired objectives cannot be achieved with a lower intensity and the impacts involved, the conclusion can be drawn that no milder instrument solves the market failure: the chosen measure is therefore necessary. Thus, by analysing the incentive effect and proportionality, State aid is tested as to whether it is an appropriate policy instrument and whether it is designed in such a way that it effectively solves the market failure.

The final step is the analysis of whether the distortions to competition and trade resulting from the State aid measure are limited so that, on balance, the aid is compatible with the State aid rules. The Commission calls this assessment the 'indirect impact' of a State aid measure. If the positive effects dominate the negative effects, an exemption under Article 107(3) TFEU is likely.

The next section discusses whether the Commission was successful in implementing these basic economic principles to SAM guidelines and frameworks. Since regional aid and environmental protection and energy are the most important non-crisis state aid measures, these two are discussed in the following section.

3. Modernised State Aid Guidelines

One of the main objectives of the SAM is to revise, streamline and consolidate State aid guidelines to make them consistent with common economic principles to assess the compatibility of aid with the internal market. As a result, the Commission modernised a set of horizontal rules, which set out the Commission's position on particular categories of aid. Two of the new revised guidelines are tested whether they are coherent with the legal and economic State aid rules.

3.1. 2013 Regional Aid Guidelines

The 2013 Guidelines on regional aid define how Member States can grant investment aid to companies in order to support the development of disadvantaged regions in Europe between 2014 and 2020.

In the outermost regions and sparsely populated areas, the possibility for Member States to grant operating aid to companies is maintained. The maximum levels of aid remain unchanged for the least developed regions. Anti-relocation provisions are strengthened. Regional aid that has caused the same or similar activity to relocate within the European Economic Area (EEA) are not allowed. In line with the general reform, more aid categories are exempted from the obligation of prior notification to the Commission. The overall share of regions where regional aid can be granted increases slightly as well.[14]

However, large aid measures are still subject to in-depth assessments of their incentive effect, proportionality, contribution to regional development and effects on competition. In this respect, the guidelines adopt a *stricter* approach on aid for investments made by large enterprises in the more developed assisted areas. Evidence shows that large

14 From the current level of 46.1% to 47.2% of the EU's population.

companies' decisions to invest in a given region are prompted by factors such as the cost and availability of production factors (workforce, land, capital, etc.) and the general economic context (taxes, business environment), rather than by State aid. Granting aid in such a context, where a large company would have invested in any event, amounts to handing out 'free money' that merely reduces the company's ordinary operation costs which its (local) competitors have to meet without aid. This leads to a waste of taxpayers' money and to competition distortions in the internal market. Therefore, aid to large enterprises in these areas is only allowed for investments that bring new economic activity, for initial investments for the diversification of existing establishments into new products or for new process innovation. The aim is to make sure that it is more likely that these investments are carried out thanks to the State subsidy (European Commission, 2013(c)).

The Commission defines the common assessment principles in paras. 25–29 of the Regional Aid Guidelines (European Commission, 2013(d), p. 25). In the assessment of whether a notified aid measure is compatible with the internal market, the design of the aid measure should be in such a way that the positive impact of the aid towards an objective of common interest exceeds its potential negative effects on trade and competition. This general statement is in line with the basic economic principles of the balancing test described above. The Regional Aid Guidelines continue by identifying seven criteria which should be scrutinised: (1) contribution to a well-defined objective of common interest in accordance with Article 107(3) TFEU; (2) need for state intervention: a State aid measure must be targeted towards a situation where aid can bring about a material improvement that the market cannot deliver itself, for example by remedying a market failure or addressing an equity or cohesion concern; (3) appropriateness of the aid measure; (4) incentive effect: the aid must change the behaviour of the undertaking(s) concerned in such a way that it engages in additional activity which it would not carry out without the aid or it would carry out in a restricted or different manner or location; (5) proportionality of the aid (aid to the minimum); (6) avoidance of undue negative effects on competition and trade between Member States; the negative effects of aid must be sufficiently limited, so that the overall balance of the measure is positive; and (7) transparency of aid. To conclude, the assessment criteria identified in the 2013 Regional Aid Guidelines are coherent with the economic principles identified in the balancing test above. The only new criterion is the 'transparency of aid' criterion. This criterion is required to exercise *ex post* control of the rules. As with the EU antitrust rules it is now the responsibility of the actors to make sure that the legal/economic rules are applied in accordance with EU law. On top of that, the Commission added a new tool: *ex post* evaluations. The new tool is discussed further below.

3.2. 2014 Environmental Protection and Energy Guidelines

The 2014 environmental Guidelines aim to support Member States in reaching their 2020 climate targets, while addressing the market distortions that may result from subsidies granted to renewable energy sources (European Commission, Guidelines on State aid for environmental protection and energy 2014–2020, 2014(b)). To this end, the guidelines promote a gradual move to market-based support for renewable energy. They also provide criteria on how Member States can relieve energy-intensive companies that are particularly exposed to international competition from charges levied for the support of renewables. Furthermore, the 2014 guidelines include new provisions on aid to energy infrastructure and generation capacity to strengthen the internal energy market and ensure security of supply. To increase cost effectiveness and limit distortions, the 2014 guidelines also foresee the gradual introduction of competitive bidding processes for allocating public support, while offering Member States flexibility to take account of national circumstances. The guidelines also specify the gradual replacement of feed-in tariffs by feed-in premiums, which expose renewable energy sources to market signals. The guidelines allow reducing the burden for a limited number of energy intensive sectors defined for the whole EU too. In particular, the 2014 guidelines include criteria for supporting energy infrastructure, focusing on projects that improve cross-border energy flows and promote infrastructure in Europe's less developed regions. Another new feature is to permit aid to secure adequate electricity generation when there is a real risk of insufficient electricity generation capacity. This will allow Member States to introduce so-called 'capacity mechanisms', for example to encourage producers to build new generation capacity or prevent them from shutting down existing plants or to reward consumers to reduce electricity consumption in peak hours (European Commission, 2014(d)).

With respect to the common assessment principles, the environmental guidelines include in paras. 26–29 the same seven criteria as stated above concerning the regional aid guidelines (European Commission, 2014(b)). Market failures which should be addressed by the State aid are mentioned in para. 35, namely negative externalities, positive externalities, asymmetric information, and coordination failures. A further novelty is that State aid should only be directed at residual market failures, that is to say the market failure that remains unaddressed by other policies and measures (para. 36).

The general statement in the Environmental Protection and Energy Guidelines is in line with the basic economic principles of the balancing test described above. Again, from an economic perspective the new element in these guidelines is the *ex post* evaluation.

3.3. *Ex Post Evaluations*

Up to now, the State Aid Scoreboard has performed monitoring. In general, today no proper evaluation of the impact of aid schemes on the markets takes place. Aid schemes are approved *ex ante* based on pre-defined criteria on the assumption that their overall balance will remain positive. However, the new SAM guidelines and frameworks foresee the possibility to require evaluations for aid schemes with large aid budgets, containing novel characteristics or when significant market, technology or regulatory changes are foreseen (European Commission, 2014(c), p. 2). Such an *ex post* evaluation of aid has the goal of providing analysis on the effectiveness and efficiency of an aid measure and suggesting improvements and lessons to be learnt (European Commission, 2013(e)). The GBER for example requires evaluation of large aid schemes with an average annual State aid budget of at least €150 mn in specific fields. This concerns large aid schemes in the fields of regional aid, aid for SMEs and access to finance, aid for research and development and innovation, energy and environmental aid and aid for broadband infrastructures. Results should be available within four years of the start of a scheme. The mandatory evaluations should be carried out by independent experts and are in principle based on the common economic methodology described above.

Evaluation is particularly relevant for regional aid since the bulk of this aid is granted under these schemes. The Commission intends to review them in the first half of 2017 (European Commission, 2013(f), p. 9). Environmental protection and energy aid is another important area since a distortion of competition and the identification of market failures is a tricky task with respect to environmental issues. The evaluation exercises should in particular make it possible: (1) to verify that the assumptions underlying the approval of the scheme on the basis of an *ex ante* assessment are still valid; (2) to assess whether the scheme is effective in achieving the direct objective for which it was introduced; and (3) to cater for unforeseeable negative effects (European Commission, 2013(g), p. 84).

In performing *ex post* evaluations, different methods depending on the availability of data and time constraint are available (European Commission, 2013(h)). In May 2014, the Commission published a guidance paper which outlines the evaluation plan and the selection criteria for aid schemes (European Commission, 2014(a)). A first review of this guidance paper shows that whereas the economic concepts and principles of State aid are addressed in principle in this paper, the selection criteria presented in this guidance paper are not thoroughly linked to the economic concepts and principles of State aid measures under Article 107(3) TFEU. The section on selection criteria in the guidance paper refers to the technical appendix on relevant methods to identify the causal impact. However, the Annex itself discusses methodologies and techniques for assessing the direct effect of policies *in general*. The link of these methodologies and techniques to competition economics – defined in the guidance paper as indirect effect – can be improved. Member States need more guidance on this topic. As stated correctly by the Commission in the guidance paper, measuring the direct and indirect effects of a policy normally requires the use of different tools. The last decades have seen an important development of methodologies and techniques intended at assessing the direct effect of policies on their beneficiaries. The techniques presented are: Differences-in-Differences, Regression Discontinuity Design (RDD) and Instrumental Variables (IV). These methodologies derive their validity from different assumptions and the best choice is normally driven by the context of the policy and the availability of data (European Commission, 2013(h), p. 21). In this respect, some basic competition economics concepts, like the use of a counterfactual analysis, are talked through and the critical elements in such an analysis are mentioned (random experiments vs. natural or quasi-experiments). The reminder of the document presents the most common methodologies used to assess a *direct* policy impact in general without making explicit reference to the evaluation questions related to the *indirect* impact of the aid measure as defined in paragraph 3.2 (p. 6) in the same document. Also, the examples given in the guidance paper (pp. 32–34) do not relate to the 'indirect' lag of the balancing test/evaluation questions raised.

4. Conclusion

In value terms, 87% of State aid is not individually examined by the Commission, but is granted because of previously approved aid schemes or block exemption regulations (BERs and GBER). Analyses show that the block exempted measures related to 'regional development' and 'environmental protection' are the most important measures within the 'non-crisis state aid' segment. Our analysis shows that the economic concepts and principles used in the regional aid and environmental guidelines are coherent with the balancing test developed under Article 107(3) TFEU. The Commission remains consistent in its policy shaping.

On the subject of the *ex post* evaluation required by the Commission as a new tool, national authorities (and courts) need more guidance on the last section of the balancing test, namely the actual balancing. Such detailed guidance is necessary since national authorities might face conflicting interests in respect of self-policing the conformity of their projects with the State aid rules. The rule is that distortions to competition and trade resulting from a State aid measure need to be limited so that, on balance, the aid is compatible with the EU State aid rules. The guidance paper on *ex post* evaluation published by the Commission is not persuasive on this aspect. Whereas a counterfactual analysis provides useful insights on the direct effects of a State aid measure, State aid needs to pass the whole balancing test – including the proportionality, appropriateness and final balancing lags. If the Commission also goes for a success story with respect to SAM, the Commission is well advised to train Member States on *ex post* evaluations with programmes similar to the training programmes for national judges as done after the antitrust modernisation in 2003. However, this would require the Commission itself to have a clear picture of how these *ex post* evaluations are implemented in practice.

References

Commission Regulation (EU) 651/2014 of 17 June 2014 declaring certain categories of aid compatible with the internal market in application of Articles 107 and 108 of the Treaty, OJ L 187/1 (26 June 2014).

Council Regulation (EC) 1/2003 of 16 December 2002 on the implementation of the rules on competition laid down in Articles 81 and 82 of the Treaty, OJ L 1 (4 January 2003).

Council Regulation (EC) 1407/2013 of 18 December 2013 on the application of Articles 107 and 108 of the Treaty on the Functioning of the European Union to *de minimis* aid, OJ L 352/1 (18 December 2013).

Council Regulation (EC) 733/2013 of 22 July 2013 amending Regulation (EC) 994/98 on the application of Articles 92 and 93 of the Treaty establishing the European Community to certain categories of horizontal State aid (22 July 2013).

European Commission (2012(a), 8 May), EU State Aid Modernisation (SAM), Communication from the Commission to the European Parliament, the Council, the European Economic and Social Committee and the Committee of the Regions, COM/2012/0209 final, Brussels.

European Commission (2012(b), 8 May), State aid: Commission launches major initiative to modernise state aid control, IP/12/458.

European Commission (2012(c), 21 December), State aid scoreboard 2011, Commission Staff working document 'Facts and figures on state aid in the EU Member States', SEC(2012)443, 21 December 2012, Brussels, available at http://ec.europa.eu/competition/state_aid/scoreboard/index_en.html

European Commission (2013(a), 18 December), State aid: Transparency and evaluation in the draft General Block-Exemption Regulation, European Commission MEMO/13/1175.

European Commission (2013(b), 18 December), State Aid: Commission adopts revised exemption for small aid amounts (*de minimis* Regulation), IP/13/1293.

European Commission (2013(c), 19 June), State aid: Commission adopts Guidelines on regional aid for 2014–2020, IP/13/569, Brussels, available at http://europa.eu/rapid/press-release_IP-13-569_en.htm

European Commission (2013(d), 23 July), Guidelines on regional State aid for 2014–2020, OJ C 209, 23 July 2013, Brussels.

European Commission (2013(e), 12 April), Evaluation in the field of State aid, Issues Paper, available at http://ec.europa.eu/competition/state_aid/modernisation/evaluation_issues_paper_en.pdf

European Commission (2013(f)), Executive Summary of Impact Assessment Report, SWD(2013)215, Brussels.

European Commission (2013(g)), Impact Assessment Guidelines on regional state aid for 2014–2020, SWD (2013) 214, Brussels.

European Commission (2013(h), November), Evaluation in the field of State aid, Draft Methodological Guidance Paper, available at http://ec.europa.eu/competition/consultations/2013_state_aid_modernisation/draft_guidance_paper_en.pdf

European Commission (2014(a), 28 May), Common methodology for State aid evaluation, SWD(2014)179 final, Brussels.

European Commission (2014(b), 28 June), Guidelines on State aid for environmental protection and energy 2014–2020, OJ C 200, pp. 1–55, Brussels.

European Commission (2014(c), June), 'You can't improve what you can't measure: State Aid Evaluation', Competition Policy Brief, Issue 7, Brussels.

European Commission (2014(d), 21 August), available at http://ec.europa.eu/competition/state_aid/overview/index_en.html

European Commission (2014(d), 9 April), State Aid: Commission adopts new rules on public support for environmental protection and energy, IP/14/400, Brussels.

M. Fritsch and H.-J. Ewers (1996), *Marktversagen und Wirtschaftspolitik: Mikroökonomische Grundlagen staatlichen Handelns,* Verlag Vahlen.

H. Friederiszick (2007), 'European State Aid Control: an economic framework' in Paolo Buccirossi (ed.), *Advances in the Economics of Competition,* MIT Press, pp. 1–58.

D. Hildebrand and A. Schweinsberg (2007), 'Refined Economic Approach in European State Aid Control - Will it gain momentum?' *World Competition*, vol. 30(3), pp. 449–462.

G.-J. Koopman (2013(a), November 12 (1)), 'State Aid Modernization – An Update', *Presentation,* Brussels.

G.-J. Koopman (2013(b), November 12 (2)), 'State Aid Modernization: What remains to be done? An update', *Concurrences*, pp. 1–4.

N. Kroes (2006, 21 September), *The refined economic approach in state aid law: a policy perspective* (Speech/06/518, Performer), College of Europe Conference, Bruges.

N. Kroes (Interpret) (2007(a)), *Two years into the SAAP – State of Play and prospects*, EStALI Conference, Speech/07/316.

N. Kroes (Interpret) (2007(b)), *The Law and Economics of State aid control – a Commission Perspective*, Germany Joint EStALI/ESMT Conference, Berlin.

R.A. Musgrave and L. Kullmer (1990). *Die öffentlichen Finanzen in Theorie und Praxis*, Stuttgart, UTB.

H. Nyssens (2007, 15–16 November), *Economics in State Aid: soon as routine as dentistry*, available at http://ec.europa.eu/competition/speeches/text/sp2007_14_en.pdf

P.A. Samuelson (1954), 'The Pure Theory of Public Expenditure', *Review of Economics and Statistics*, pp. 387–389.

Schmitz-Gotha Fahrzeugwerke GmbH v Commission of the European Communities, Case T-17/03 (Court of First Instance (Fourth Chamber, extended composition) 6 April 2006).

DEFINING THE SCOPE OF STATE AID HOW TAX CASES AFFECT THE STATE AID FRAMEWORK

Raymond H.C. Luja*

1. Introduction

The definition of State aid as included in Article 107(1) TFEU is a general one. As the Court of Justice rightly pointed out in the 1960s,[1] it makes little sense to apply State aid provisions to traditional subsidies only, while leaving open the option to grant financial benefits by other means, for instance via the tax system.

So, in essence, the general State aid framework does apply to a broad range of tax benefits as well. In this contribution I am not going to address the many complexities that arise in interpreting these general rules when confronted with taxes. What I will do is point out how some of the peculiarities in decisions and judgments concerning fiscal aid may affect the State aid regime in general.[2]

For this purpose I have selected a few issues that will be briefly addressed. In section 2 I will go into the treatment of indirect aid, and in particular the discrepancy that may exist between the financial advantage enjoyed by an aid recipient and the amount of resources given up by the State. In section 3 I will focus on the attribution of State aid to governments in light of compliance with EU directives. Section 4 will briefly cover the renewed General Block Exemption Regulation (GBER), and the procedural nightmare it may become for diligent taxpayers. *Ex officio* references to the ECJ by national judges will

* Prof. Dr. Raymond H.C. Luja is Professor of Comparative Tax Law at Maastricht University, fellow of the Maastricht Centre for Taxation and the Ius Commune Research School and member of the EU Tax Law Team of Loyens & Loeff NV as a specialist in fiscal State aid and harmful tax competition. This contribution is based on a lecture given on 27 May 2014 at the Maastricht Conference 'State Aid and Public Procurement in the European Union'; developments after that date have not been taken into account. The author can be contacted at Raymond.Luja@maastrichtuniversity.nl.

1 Case 30/59, *De Gezamenlijke Steenkolenmijnen in Limburg v High Authority of the European Coal and Steel Community* [1961] ECR 3.

2 Given the nature and purpose of this chapter, items in part reflect issues that have been the subject of more single-issue or tax-focused publications by the author. References to those publications will be provided at the heading of each paragraph.

be addressed in section 5, in the context of such judges being asked to rule on the awarding of subsidies or tax benefits in domestic proceedings. Then, as an intermezzo, in section 6 I will address one 'hot' issue from a tax perspective, namely that of analytical versus synthetic taxation and its place within the general State aid framework. Royalties will serve as an example here. An outlook follows in section 7, where I will single out one developing issue in particular: the treatment of public enterprises as profit-pursuing market participants. Some concluding remarks will follow in the final section.

2. What is the Advantage of Indirect Aid?[3]

In recent tax-related judgments we have seen a development in the treatment of indirect aid, in particular in the determination of the financial advantage (also known as the actual 'aid') that results from such indirect tax benefits.

In the *FINECO* case, the (then) Court of First Instance had to deal with a number of tax benefits given both to investment funds that specialised in small and medium-sized enterprises and to their investors. The Commission found that, *inter alia*, the tax benefit provided made it more attractive for third parties to invest in these funds. This led to indirect aid, as the additional investment would lead to an increase in the entry and management fees that the funds and/or their managers would receive in turn. So the issue was raised whether the entire sum of tax benefits given to the investors was to be recovered from the investment funds, or just an amount equivalent to the sum of additional fees received:

> '[T]he applicants argue that, under the contested decision, the specialised investment vehicles or the fund managers which manage them are required to give back something which is entirely different from the advantage which, according to the Commission, they had derived. They would have to repay an amount corresponding to the tax relief of which they are not the direct beneficiaries, whereas, according to the Commission, their advantage consists in an increase in their entry and management fees. The principle of proportionality is therefore infringed.'[4]

The CFI then held:

> 'In their capacity as taxpayers, the specialised investment vehicles or the fund managers which manage them are the only possible interlocutors for the Italian Republic in the context of proceeding with recovery of the unlawful aid. The restoration of the previous situation, which would have prevailed if the operations in question had been carried out without the tax reduction, accordingly calls for the recovery from those bodies of the difference between the

3 See footnote 2 and R.H.C. Luja, 'Indirecte fiscale staatssteun: over de (bij)rol van investeerders, crediteuren en werknemers' in A.C.G.A.C. de Graaf, S.J.C. Hemels and J.C.M. van Sonderen (eds.), *'k Moet eerlijk zeggen: Vriendenbundel Henk van Arendonk*, SdU, Den Haag, 2013, pp. 217–227, para. 4, and R.H.C. Luja, 'The Selectivity Test: The Concept of Sectoral Aid' in A. Rust and C. Micheau (eds.), *State Aid and Tax Law*, Wolters Kluwer, Alphen aan den Rijn, 2013, pp. 107–118, at para. 7.03.

4 Case T-445/05, *Associazione italiana del risparmio gestito and Fineco Asset Management SpA v Commission of the European Communities (FINECO)* [2009] ECR II-289, para. 199.

> standard tax and the reduced tax resulting from the measure at issue, even though they always have the option of subsequently effecting recovery in turn from their investors or even from the State, in accordance with the provisions of national law.'[5]

No appeal was filed in respect of this judgment. In respect of recovery the judgment raises two main issues. First, could the investment funds (or their management) even be required to pay back all tax benefits if they were allowed to recapture those benefits from others? Would it not have sufficed merely to recover the financial advantage that was received on balance? More importantly, the Commission did establish that the indirect financial advantage (the aid) consisted of the increase in fees. If this is so, then what should happen if the actual increase in fees is lower than the amount given up by the State to convince investors to engage in this kind of specialised investment? From my perspective, it should have been the financial advantage indirectly enjoyed by the funds that is the proper basis for recovery and not the amount given up by the State.

A somewhat similar issue came up in *Électricité de France (EDF)*. In this case, France argued that it gave up a tax debt as part of an alleged capital contribution to a government-held entity. The ECJ held:

> 'The intention underlying Article [107(1) TFEU] and the private investor test is thus to prevent the recipient public undertaking from being placed, by means of State resources, in a more favourable position than that of its competitors. [...] However, the financial situation of the recipient public undertaking depends not on the means used to place it at an advantage, however that may have been effected, but *on the amount that the undertaking ultimately receives*. Consequently, when considering whether the private investor test was applicable, the General Court did not err in law by focusing its analysis, not on the fiscal nature of the means employed by the French State, but on *the improvement* [...] *in EDF's financial situation* and on the effects of the measure in question on competition.'[6]

What we can see here is that the amount of aid is to be determined along the lines of the financial advantage enjoyed by the company involved and not by the means used by the government to come to that result. In this case, the main questions were whether a tax debt could be forfeited by the government as a means to improve the capital position and whether any investment of capital – whether by means of cancelling a tax debt or otherwise – should have been in line with the private investor test. The latter would require, *inter alia*, an *ex ante* analysis of the French government's economic reasoning and of the expected return on investment, which seemed absent.[7] Despite this specific setting, the ECJ is very clear in what advantage is relevant for the State aid analysis, an aspect of the *EDF* case that is often overlooked. In light of this judgment, the outcome of the *FINECO* case would likely have been different in the event the actual increase in fees would have

5 Ibid, para. 201.

6 Case C-124/10P, *EDF* [2012] not yet reported, paras. 90–91 (emphasis added). For ease of reading, all Treaty references have been updated in this chapter.

7 As its previous decision was partly annulled, the Commission had to reinvestigate the PIT application. A second formal investigation has been opened (OJ C186/73, 28 June 2013).

amounted to only a part of the taxes given up by the State (i.e. where some part of the benefit remained at the level of the investor without being passed along to the funds).

Further support can be found in the *Bouygues* case where the ECJ held:

> '[For] the purposes of establishing the existence of State aid, the Commission must establish a sufficiently direct link between, on the one hand, the advantage given to the beneficiary and, on the other, a reduction of the State budget or a sufficiently concrete economic risk of burdens on that budget [...]. However, contrary to what the General Court found, *it is not necessary that such a reduction, or even such a risk, should correspond or be equivalent to that advantage*, or that the advantage has as its counterpoint such a reduction or such a risk, or that it is of the same nature as the commitment of State resources from which it derives.'[8]

Again, while it is necessary to show a link to the (direct or indirect) use of State resources it is to be pointed out that the financial advantage, the aid, does not need to be equal to the amount of resources foregone. This gives a nice twist to the ECJ's line of thought formulated in *PreussenElektra*:

> '[O]nly advantages granted directly or indirectly through State resources are to be considered aid within the meaning of Article [107(1) TFEU]. The distinction made in that provision between "aid granted by a Member State" and aid granted "through State resources" does not signify that all advantages granted by a State, whether financed through State resources or not, constitute aid but is intended merely to bring within that definition both advantages which are granted directly by the State and those granted by a public or private body designated or established by the State [...].'[9]

Combining *PreussenElektra* and *EDF/Bouygues* raises another interesting question. What if there is a leverage effect? By this I mean that an amount of €1,000 provided in tax benefits would result in an actual financial benefit to the undertaking involved of an amount of €1,001, €1,100 or €2,000 for that matter. Suppose that in the case of *FINECO* the success of the tax incentives offered to investors had exceeded expectations and that the actual increase in fees enjoyed by the investment funds had been double the amount of tax resources offered up by the government. What if we could still establish a clear link between the increase in fees and the giving up of (lesser) financial resources by the State? Could recovery of the benefit enjoyed then exceed the amount of resources given up?

The latter seems unlikely in light of current practice, but the *Bouygues* case leaves room for serious doubt. We should consider that amounts recovered go back to the State (including interest), so recovery of any additional benefit due to a leverage effect might not fit within the current picture. This would be different if the EU were to finally take a step that would lead to recovered amounts having to be transferred into the EU's budget at least in part. This may be a further deterrent for Member States to unlawfully grant

8 Joined Cases C-399/10P and C-401/10P, *Bouygues* [2013] ECR, not yet reported, paras. 109 and 110 (emphasis added).

9 Case C-379/98, *PreussenElektra* [2001] ECR I-2099, para. 58.

State aid, but with the many uncertainties in the definition of State aid and its compatibility that still remain, it is politically unfeasible at this time.

3. Do Directives Give Carte Blanche?[10]

In the sphere of indirect taxes, customs and excises, many of the actions of a Member State may follow directly from compliance with an EU Regulation or Directive. In order for State aid to exist, any use of State resources must be attributable to the Member State itself.[11] This raises a number of issues that may also affect other fields of law.

We already know from case law that where Member States must grant a tax exemption or a lower tax rate in order to comply with a Directive, such action is not considered attributable to that State. In *Deutsche Bahn* it concerned the implementation of a clear and precise obligation not to levy an excise duty on fuel used by commercial airlines.[12] In *Puffer*, allowing undertakings the right to deduct (i.e. reimbursement of) value added tax (VAT) paid was at issue, again in line with a Directive.[13]

For optional schemes that are included in Directives and available to all Member States, the issue seems to have been settled as well (non-aid). In *Schmelz* the ECJ held that exercising an option to exempt resident small companies with very limited turnover from VAT was not attributable to a Member State either, despite the fact that the residence criterion would normally be considered a restriction on the freedom of services.[14] For State aid purposes, the attribution issue would have a similar outcome.

Options available upon request raise the most issues. What it comes down to is this: some Directives allow Member States to apply to the Council for an authorisation to divert from, for instance, minimum excise duty rates prescribed in a Directive. This is of particular interest in cases where the Commission, upon request, puts a proposal before the Council and where the Council then decides to attach additional criteria to an authorisation that may lead to selectivity after all, such as regional restrictions (regional aid). Would the Council's involvement now heal the fact that it was the Member State that requested the exemption that turned into selective aid?

The ECJ was called upon to settle this in the *Alumina II* case, but the Court did not address the merits of the case due to procedural flaws. The case concerned an exemption of alumina producers from an excise tax on mineral oil used as fuel in the production of alumina. The ECJ ruled as follows:

> 'The General Court held that the advantages which the exemptions at issue might have conferred on their beneficiaries had been granted in accordance with the authorisation decisions, and consequently they were attributable not to the Member States but to the European Union and, accordingly, the Commission was not entitled, even in the exercise

10 See footnote 2 and R.H.C. Luja, 'The Attribution of State Aid to Member States in the Exercising of Options in Directives', *EStAL (European State Aid Law Quarterly)*, 2013, vol. 1, pp. 119–125.

11 See, for instance, Case C-482/99, *Stardust* [2002] ECR I-4397. para. 24.

12 Case T-351/02, *Deutsche Bahn* [2006] ECR II-1047, para. 102.

13 Case C-460/07, *Puffer* [2009] ECR I-3251, paras. 69–71.

14 Case C-97/09, *Schmelz* [2010] ECR I-10465, para.54.

> of its almost exclusive powers under Articles [107 and 108 TFEU], to classify those exemptions as State aid. [...] By holding that the exemptions at issue were attributable to the European Union, the General Court, rather than raising a plea based on an infringement of essential procedural requirements, [...] instead raised a plea going to the substantive legality of the contested decision, which falls within the scope of an infringement of the [TFEU].'[15]

As the General Court raised the attribution issue *ultra petita*, this part was set aside.[16] The ECJ, however, continued:

> '[A] Council decision authorising a Member State [...] to introduce an exemption of excise duties could not have the effect of preventing the Commission from exercising the powers conferred on it by the Treaty and, consequently, setting in motion the procedure laid down in Article [108 TFEU] in order to review whether that exemption constituted State aid and on the conclusion of that procedure, if appropriate, to adopt a decision such as the contested decision. [...] The fact that the authorisation decisions granted full exemptions from excise duties while setting detailed conditions of a geographical and temporal nature and that those conditions were strictly respected by the Member States had no effect on the division of powers between the Council and the Commission and therefore could not deprive the Commission of the right to exercise its powers. [...] [The] concept of State aid corresponds to an objective situation and cannot depend on the conduct or statements of the institutions [...]. Consequently, the fact that the authorisation decisions were adopted on a proposal from the Commission could not preclude those exemptions being classified as State aid, within the meaning of Article [107(1) TFEU], if the conditions governing the existence of State aid were met. That fact however had to be taken into consideration in relation to the obligation to recover the incompatible aid, in the light of the principles of protection of legitimate expectations and legal certainty [...].'[17]

This consideration, while not specifically aimed at the issue of attribution, does point out the relationship between the Council's decision to authorise and the concept of aid, but it leaves many questions unanswered. The case has been referred back to the General Court, even though it will not be able to address the attribution issue once again.[18] For now, we must assume that these authorisation decisions, often initiated by the Member State itself, do not put the authorised action beyond the reach of State aid scrutiny.

15 Case C-272/12P, *Commission v Ireland and others (Alumina II)* [2013] not yet reported, paras. 30 and 33.

16 See Joined Cases T-50/06 RENV, T-56/06 RENV, T-60/06 RENV, T-62/06 RENV and T-69/06 RENV, *Alumina II* [2012] not yet reported.

17 Case C-272/12P, footnote 15, paras. 49, 50 and 53.

18 See Cases T-50/06 RENV II, T-56/06 RENV II, T-60/06 RENV II, T-62/06 RENV II and T-69/06 RENV II, pending.

4. The GBER as a Procedural Nightmare[19]

The General Block Exemption Regulation (GBER) has recently been redrafted. In 2012 it was indicated that nearly 40% of all schemes that were considered approved under the GBER by the respective Member States had flaws in them in respect of compliance with GBER conditions.[20] With the State Aid Modernisation (SAM) project this number is likely to reduce, but this number still raises some serious concerns. The GBER as such is not really suitable for many tax incentives, as it essentially (and – from the perspective of managing State aid – rightly) requires *ex ante* control mechanisms to prevent overcompensation. This, by itself, already creates challenges in the tax field where the impact of tax benefits may depend on the amount of profit in a given year, especially in systems where the applicable tax rate progresses with an increase in profit. Without becoming too technical here, it is possible to neutralise such progressive rates, but not without raising the level of complexity of the tax system. This is also true for non-accumulation of aid, where for instance a tax benefit in a national corporate income tax might have to be capped due to a municipality giving a local cash subsidy. Again, doable but hardly manageable. In some circumstances we need to calculate the current value (the net present value) of future tax benefits a company will receive for the next couple of years; sometimes this requires the use of rough estimates based on a large number of assumptions.

These more general restrictions imposed by the GBER are sometimes overlooked in the design of tax schemes. Now suppose that you are a diligent businessman and you have the option to opt in to a nice tax scheme. However, you have doubts about the scheme potentially resulting in (unnotified) State aid. Being a businessman, you would probably like to opt in to the tax scheme but you would want the government (the tax authority) to first make sure that the scheme complies with, for instance, the GBER. If you are the first to opt in, a government may be open to such suggestion, but if you are the 121st a government is unlikely to notify a scheme that late if uncertainties were to arise. Now, what should you do? As a potential aid recipient you have no direct access to the Commission, unless you decide to complain as a competitor and decide not to opt in (yet).[21] Getting a domestic court to order the government to notify may be a possibility, but here we may have some issues concerning legal standing in court as the State aid regime is meant to protect competitors and not potential beneficiaries.

All in all, while the ECJ refers to being a diligent businessman as the standard to strive for in State aid cases, that same businessman may have a hard time getting around a reluctant national government in his pursuit of a nice but State-aid-proof tax incentive. Maybe it is time to give his position a bit more thought and to try and improve his timely access to national courts. This may not be considered part of State aid enforcement in the

19 See footnote 2 and R.H.C. Luja, 'Does Modernisation of State Aid Control Put Legal Certainty and Simplicity at Risk?', *EStAL*, 2012, vol. 4, pp. 765–766.

20 Speech by Commissioner Almunia, of 7 June 2012, SPEECH/12/424.

21 Member States may require an opt-in at the time of filing the tax assessment, in which case a diligent businessman might lose this option once and for all and become ineligible, if he decides to await the outcome of a State aid assessment.

traditional sense, but with an increase in block exemptions the (lack of) protection of beneficiaries is likely to become a more prominent issue.

5. *Ex Officio* References by National Judges[22]

5.1. *Tax Courts Invoking State Aid*

In discussions about national judges and State aid, the focus has often been on the protection of competitors and safeguarding their rights under Article 108(3) TFEU. Here I would like to focus on situations where no such competitors are directly involved. Let us start with an example.

Suppose that an EU Member State is, again, offering a nice tax scheme, for instance an investment incentive. Initially the tax authorities decline the taxpayer's claim to this tax incentive, as a result of which the amount of tax due in accordance with his final tax assessment is €1 million higher than expected. The taxpayer, having exhausted administrative proceedings, then appeals to the national judiciary.

The national judge now finds that the taxpayer is eligible for the tax incentive and, accordingly, the tax assessment should be lowered by €1 million. However, in the judge's own view the tax scheme would result in State aid that has not been notified (nor exempt from notification). The State aid issue has not been raised by either party.

Now what is this national judge supposed to do? On the one hand he might raise the State aid issue *ex officio* as it is a core element of EU law. On the other hand, such action might be considered by some to go *ultra petita*. This, however, we should put into perspective. If the national judge were to object to the tax scheme because of it amounting to unlawfully granted State aid, the result would be that the original tax assessment would stand. The taxpayer would not be worse off than before entering into the proceedings (so no *reformatio in pejus*).[23]

In the last 10 years we have seen a small but significant number of situations where national judges raised the State aid issue on their own. I will address three of them.

In *Paint Graphos* a taxpayer claimed entitlement to special tax treatment as a cooperative society. This was initially denied by the tax authorities, but the Italian Supreme Court (*Corte suprema di cassazione*) disagreed. Before ruling in favour of the taxpayer, however, it referred the case to the ECJ in order to determine whether the special tax scheme for cooperatives amounted to State aid. In the Supreme Court's view, as paraphrased by the ECJ,

22 See R.H.C. Luja, 'The Selectivity Test: The Concept of Sectoral Aid', *supra* n. 3, para. 7.4, R.H.C. Luja, '(Re)shaping Fiscal State Aid', *Intertax*, 2012, vol. 2, pp. 120–131, R.H.C. Luja, Annotation to *Paint Graphos, H&I ET (Highlights & Insights on European Taxation)*, 2011, vol. 11, pp. 106–108, and R.H.C. Luja, Annotation to *Frucona Košice, H&I ET*, 2013, vol. 4, pp. 122–123, and R.H.C. Luja, 'De rol van nationale rechters bij de handhaving van de standstillbepaling in fiscale zaken', *Tijdschrift voor Staatssteun* (upcoming).

23 Compare Joined Cases C-430/93 and C-431/93, *Heemskerk en Van Schaap* [2008] ECR I-8763, paras. 46–48.

> '[o]wing to the direct effect of Article [107(3) TFEU], if those benefits were found to be incompatible, the national authorities, including the judicial authorities, would be obliged to disapply [national law].'[24]

The outcome was quite interesting: the ECJ more or less ordered the Member State to introduce domestic safeguards to prevent taxpayers from choosing the special regime for tax planning purposes only.[25] But most importantly, the ECJ did accept the case for preliminary ruling despite arguments of inadmissibility as the matter could indeed be relevant for national proceedings.[26]

A similar approach has been taken by the Austrian Administrative Court (*Verwaltungsgerichtshof*) in a very recent case concerning a tax deduction of costs specifically related to foreign take-overs. In the case brought before it, only the freedom of establishment was brought into play by the parties concerned. Even though the establishment matter was referred to the ECJ as well, the request for a preliminary ruling started off with a request for guidance on the presence of State aid, again raised *ex officio*.[27]

The case of *P Oy* seems to have been an *ex officio* reference as well. The Finish Supreme Administrative Court (*Korkein hallinto-oikeus*) had to deal with an authorisation scheme that would allow companies to deduct previous losses from future profits (a so-called 'carry-forward' of losses). Such deduction would normally be blocked after a >50% change of ownership, but the tax authorities could derogate from this. Regardless of the technicalities, the national court was uncertain,

> 'in essence, whether the provisions of EU law on State aid, in particular the criterion of selectivity interpreted in the light of the degree of latitude enjoyed by the tax authorities in the present case, *preclude a decision authorising the deduction of losses of a company*, notwithstanding changes of ownership, so long as that measure has not been duly notified to the European Commission in accordance with Article 108(3) TFEU.'[28]

In response the ECJ only pointed out that the latter was not the case if the aid scheme at hand would qualify as existing aid, which seemed likely. The Court did not address the nature of the reference or the national court's role in this matter had it been new, non-notified aid.

So the question is whether other tax and administrative courts will follow this lead as well. From my perspective, national judges must be vigilant not to become instrumental in the granting of unlawful aid. We should keep in mind that the national court would not necessarily go beyond the ambit of the dispute at hand when (temporarily) refusing aid, as it would rather be maintaining the administrative decision under appeal. Much will depend on whether national law allows judges to raise legal issues on their own

24 Joined Cases C-78/08 and C-80/08, *Paint Graphos* [2011] ECR I-7611, para. 25.
25 Ibid, para. 74.
26 Ibid, para. 30–35.
27 VwGH 2013/115/0186 of 30 January 2014, registered at the ECJ under C-66/14 on 10 February 2014.
28 Case C-6/12, *P Oy* [2013], not yet reported, para. 11 (emphasis added).

motion; here national law may give more leeway to (lower) administrative courts than to civil courts or *cours de cassation*.[29] Even so, the standstill obligation of Article 108(3) TFEU is of such fundamental importance to safeguarding the Union's internal market that it should be considered part of the Union's *ordre public*.[30] As such most national courts will be in a position to invoke it to protect the public interest at large even when both parties carefully avoided bringing up this provision by themselves.

5.2. *National Tax Authorities Invoking State Aid in Court*

In the matter of tax authorities raising the issue of State aid in the national courts, we have also seen some innovative approaches here that may be of interest in non-fiscal administrative proceedings as well. I would like to focus on two examples of preliminary references.

The *Heiser* case was one of the first where national authorities invoked State aid themselves in order to get out of a domestic legal obligation to give a tax benefit. Austria had failed to comply with an EU Directive that would have put an end to the deduction of value added tax (VAT) to medical practitioners as of 1997. In particular, Austria failed to implement a rule that would have adjusted and disallowed previous tax deductions in part. The failure to implement the Directive properly could, of course, not be held against the taxpayer. The tax inspector still refused the restitution of VAT, however, as it would lead to (sectoral) State aid. That finding was upheld by the ECJ.[31]

In *Frucona Košice*, State aid was called upon in another innovative way.[32] A Slovakian tax inspector agreed to a creditor arrangement in an insolvency procedure that led to cancelling a large part of the tax debt of Frucona Košice. The local inspector did so against recommendations of the Ministry, which indicated that it was most likely that most if not all taxes could be recovered in the event of initiating bankruptcy. The tax authorities would be a privileged creditor in such proceedings. After signing the agreement, which was subsequently endorsed by the civil court, the tax inspector was relieved from duty. His successor, having no way out under domestic civil law, argued that he was not bound to abide by to the agreement as it would lead to granting unlawful State aid. The General Court agreed.

In turn, the ECJ held that if the Commission had not taken the expected duration of a full bankruptcy procedure into account in its analysis of the private creditor test, it made a manifest error of assessment. A private creditor may be weighing his options of going through a lengthy procedure with certain inherent risks versus the immediate repayment of part of the sum originally due. If the Commission had taken the duration

[29] See, for instance, Joined Cases C-430/93 and C-431/93, *Van Schijndel* [1995] ECR I-4705, paras. 20–22.

[30] Also see the Opinion of A-G Geelhoed in Case C-119/05, *Lucchini*, [2006] ECR I-6199, para. 62; T. Corthaut, *EU Ordre Public*, Phd Thesis KU Leuven, 2009, p. 261, available at https://lirias.kuleuven.be/bitstream/123456789/233756/1/TimCorthaut.pdf; P. Wattel, in B. Terra and P. Wattel, *European Tax Law*, 2nd edition, Kluwer, Deventer, 2012, pp. 130.

[31] Case C-172/03, *Heiser* [2005] ECR, I-1627. For a full overview of the facts and background of the domestic dispute I recommend reading A-G Tizzano's Opinion of 28 October 2004.

[32] Case T-11/07, *Frucona Košice* [2010] ECR II-5453.

into account, it failed to set out sufficient reasons in its decision. The case was referred back to the General Court to rule on other issues not previously addressed.[33]

All in all, even though these cases are few, they show that from an EU point of view, national authorities could, if needed, invoke their standstill obligations under Article 108(3) TFEU in order to avoid having to give a tax benefit that would be unlawfully granted otherwise.[34] But given the national hierarchical and legal implications, these cases have been scarce to date.

6. How Does an Analytical Taxation of Royalties Fit within the State Aid Framework?[35]

In the EU many Member States have been using 'synthetic' income tax systems and corporation tax systems. This means, in essence, that all sorts of incomes are taken together and that sum is then subjected to a particular tax rate (either at a fixed rate or at a rate that increases with the size of profit or taxable income, a so-called progressive rate). Next to these more traditional schemes, we also have 'analytical' tax systems where different categories of income may be taxed separately and at different rates. An example of these general categories of income, to the extent relevant in a State aid analysis, is normal business income, as well as dividends, royalties, interest, income from real estate and income from capital gains.

Member States may also choose to maintain a tax system that taxes profits from domestic activities (i.e. a territorial tax) or to tax profits received by a taxpayer for his worldwide activities (a tax on worldwide income). In essence, as direct taxes are not harmonised, it is up to Member States to design their own tax systems in the process of which they must of course abstain from violating EU law.

An ongoing investigation into Gibraltar's tax system raises a number of issues.[36] In 2011 Gibraltar introduced a new corporate income tax regime, in part because its previous regime was deemed to lead to unlawful State aid for its offshore industry.[37] It essentially introduced a territorial tax system, which also includes an exemption of dividends, interests and royalties received.[38] The Commission is again looking into

33 Case C-73/11P, *Frucona Košice* [2013] not yet reported. In the meantime the European Commission decided to revoke and replace its original decision. For that reason the pending proceedings were closed by Order T-11/07 RENV of 21 March 2014. Proceedings against the new decision are now pending at the General Court, registered under T-103/14 on 21 February 2014.

34 From a procedural perspective, a preliminary reference may settle the question of whether State aid is present relatively fast, without going through a two-step Commission investigation and possible further appeals. It may save some time to clarify things in situations where, if aid were present, there would be little chance of it being found compatible anyway.

35 See *supra* n. 2 and R.H.C. Luja, Annotation to *Gibraltar II* (opening decision), *H&I ET*, 2013, vol. 12, pp. 106–107.

36 See Commission decision to open a formal investigation (*Gibraltar II*) [2013] OJ C 348/184.

37 See Joined Cases C-106/09 P and C-107/09 P, *Gibraltar I* [2011] ECR I-11113.

38 Interest received as income from normal trade or business (trading income) would be taxable, income received from intra-group loans would not. This difference between active and passive income is also

whether this was construed to lead to a benefit for the offshore industry. Now the question is where this kind of reasoning will end.

For the purpose of this contribution I will focus on the exemption of royalties. Any company receiving royalties will benefit from such exemption. The mere fact that some companies will profit more than others does not make a regime like this State aid. I am not arguing here that an exemption like this is to be considered good tax policy and a sound budgetary approach, but these value judgements are of a more political nature and should be kept out of the discussion of whether or not there is State aid. (They may play a role in the next step of checking the compatibility of the exemption.)

To illustrate, in discussions on research and development with State aid experts, I often pose them the following question: 'An EU Member State allows for a tax deduction of R&D-related costs at 200% for any company. Is this State aid?'

Despite a massive amount of rules on R&D&I aid, included in guidelines, frameworks and the GBER, the answer to this is a plain and simple 'no'. Issues like maximum aid intensity, qualifying expenses, the stage of R&D (fundamental research, industrial research or experimental development) all remain irrelevant if we do not enter the realm of State aid first by meeting all requirements of Article 107(1) TFEU. Some companies will engage heavily in R&D and others will not or will to a lesser extent, but either way the fact that the increased deduction only relates to R&D does not make the measure above selective.[39]

Selectivity may arise, for instance, once we start to limit this deduction to certain sectors, certain types of R&D investments or when we require (too) substantial sums of investment in order to be eligible for a tax break. I cannot emphasise this enough, as the answer that I get to my question above in expert meetings is often disappointing.

You may have noticed that in the example above the benefit I chose was aimed at the fiscal treatment of R&D-related costs, while the *Gibraltar II* investigation focuses on the income derived from (successful) R&D. In the EU there is an ongoing dispute about whether Member States should be allowed to have a tax regime which exempts R&D income (i.e. royalties from patents, trademarks, etc.) in the first place, often sold as a stimulus for research, development and innovation. While in essence such exemption should not fall within the scope of State aid as long as it remains non-selective, we may wonder whether such approach to profit indeed stimulates actual R&D investment. Here these examples may be entering the sphere of (harmful) tax competition and leave the domain of State aid (provided that they were ever in it to begin with), which goes beyond the scope of this paper.

an issue that the Commission addressed in its opening decision. I will not address this here as part of this chapter; see *supra* n. 35.

39 Also see the 1998 Commission Notice on the application of State aid rules to measures relating to direct business taxation [1998] OJ C 384/3, para. 14: 'The fact that some firms or some sectors benefit more than others from some of these tax measures does not necessarily mean that they are caught by the competition rules governing State aid. [... Tax] incentives for environmental, R&D or training investment favour only the firms which undertake such investment, but again do not necessarily constitute State aid.' While self-evident, this consideration does not return in the draft version of the Notice on the notion of State aid, which the Commission circulated in January 2014.

7. Looking Forward: Taxation of Public Enterprises

While tax cases are an inherent part of the general State aid framework, some of the elements in them sometimes get ignored in mainstream European literature. In this contribution I have only addressed a few of those issues. Now what more can we expect in the non-tax sphere?

If I have to single out one issue, there should be some movement in the field of public enterprises and services of general economic interest (SGEIs). After recovering from the 2009 Lisbon Treaty negotiations, which initially seemed to become a little setback for free market principles, at least in wording, State aid law may have an even bigger role to play in future in respect of dealing with public enterprises.[40] The current practice of mainly leaving it up to national, regional and local authorities to define what SGEIs are will have to be revisited in order to come up with a more coherent approach on an EU level. We should be able to draw a more clearly distinct line between activities carried out either within or outside the domain of SGEIs, but in light of what happened in 2009 this seems quite wishful thinking.

For tax purposes, the position of public enterprises is cumbersome. Even if we operate from the presumption that a public enterprise should be subject to (corporate) income tax just as other enterprises, we are only half way there. From the perspective of creating a level playing field, subjecting public enterprises to tax does not guarantee that they strive to make a profit.

It will be of interest to see whether the developments we saw in 2006 and 2014 in respect of the R&D&I Guidelines/Framework will find their way in a more general approach towards profit making. While some public entities still operate on the presumption of having to cover costs only when offering their research services to third parties, the R&D&I framework only keeps this as a fallback position. Using normal market rates when rendering services is the gold standard. In the absence of a market price, there are two options: (i) a price covering integral costs plus a reasonable profit margin common to the sector concerned, or (ii) a price covering at least marginal costs, if the latter is the result of business-like (at arm's length) negotiations aimed at maximising economic benefit.[41]

This line of thought should be expanded to other goods and services sold or offered by public enterprises, outside of the domain of SGEIs. One caveat here: well-run (private) companies may decide to make specific offers below costs for genuine business purposes and as part of a sound business strategy (for instance, as an attractive offer for first-time clients or in order to secure enough work to keep permanent staff busy in case of a temporary setback as to cover part of current expenses). This option should remain available to public enterprises as well if we want to guarantee a level playing field, but it would be hard to reconcile with the prohibition of State aid in the traditional sense where

40 I refer to the introduction of the 'social market economy' in Article 3(3) TEU and Protocols 26 and 27 to the TEU and the TFEU.

41 Commission Communication C (2014) 3282 of 21 May 2014, Framework for State aid for research and development and innovation [2014] OJ C 198/1, para. 25.

we may not give selective advantages to market participants. One could argue that an offer below costs could be available to anyone under the given circumstances, but that would be a difficult path to go evidence-wise. Be that as it may, in my view public enterprises that offer or sell normal goods or services (other than SGEIs entrusted upon them) should generally use prices that include a market-like profit margin where possible in order not to provide a benefit to third-parties.

It should also be considered that governments that own or finance public enterprises may get into trouble with the market investor principle themselves if they would allow their enterprises not to make a profit structurally, again outside the domain of SGEIs. Market investors would normally expect a certain return on investment, or if loss making in the long run, even decide to bring certain investments to an end. All in all, public enterprises should essentially be taxed as regular enterprises in respect of their normal business activities. In order for this to have any useful result such enterprises should strive to make a profit first like other market participants. The latter may be out of reach of traditional tax law but arguably within reach of State aid scrutiny.

8. Concluding Remarks

Tax schemes and individual tax benefits need to comply with the traditional concept of State aid from the 1950s. This, as such, is doable. The problem mainly arises once State aid is found to exist, as the approval of tax schemes may be rather cumbersome given some (logical) restrictions in, for instance, the GBER. Examples of these are rules concerning the accumulation of aid (from different schemes or levels of government), overcompensation and the possible need for *ex ante* calculations of future tax benefits. We are now in a position where limitations on State aid threaten to make the tax system too complex and too uncertain, in particular (corporate) income tax.

While this may all benefit the internal market, the EU should keep in mind that other States and free trade zones may not have a similar regime in place that is as effective in stopping national governments from giving selective benefits to companies. Somewhere down the line, this will have an impact on the EU's competitiveness.

Judgments and decisions in fiscal aid cases may have a substantial impact in the non-fiscal aid domain; the reverse, of course, is also true. They are part of one and the same set of rules. Sometimes the complexity of tax cases may hide important developments that may be of relevance to a more general legal audience. In this contribution I have tried to single out only a few of them.

EX POST EVALUATION OF STATE AID

Caroline Buts and Marc Jegers*

1. Introduction

It is common practice for governments or politicians to support private industry. In order to prevent possible adverse effects of such aid measures, a general prohibition on State aid was already included in the founding Treaty of Rome. However, next to this prohibition, the original Treaty article also acknowledged that aid can be allowed in a limited number of cases. The Member State wishing to grant the aid notifies the measure to the European Commission, which then decides on its compatibility with the internal market. In addition to the articles in the treaties, and as a result of the Enabling Regulation,[1] the European Commission has exempted several aid measures from notification. Despite having a potentially high impact on the real economy, assessing whether State aid measures could be allowed or not was from the start mainly a legal matter.

However, over the past decade the role of economic analysis has grown. The State Aid Action Plan (SAAP) of 2005 can, with the introduction of the balancing test, certainly be considered to constitute a turning point in this respect. The goal of less and better targeted State aid necessitated a change in the approach taken so far. In this mind set, Friederiszick et al. (2007) propose an economic assessment methodology for future evaluations of State aid measures. Ever since, the role of economics in State aid control has become more prominent as well as more refined.

* Caroline Buts is an Assistant Professor at the Department of Applied Economics of the Free University of Brussels and a Post-Doctoral Research Fellow of the Research Foundation-Flanders (FWO). Marc Jegers is full Professor at the same department. Address for correspondence: Caroline Buts, Vrije Universiteit Brussel, Department of Applied Economics, Pleinlaan 2, BE-1050 Brussels, Belgium. E-mail address: caroline.buts@vub.ac.be.

1 Council Regulation No 733/2013 of 22 July 2013 amending Regulation (EC) No 994/98 on the application of Articles 92 and 93 of the Treaty establishing the European Community to certain categories of horizontal State aid OJ L204, 31 July 2013, p. 11.

Until now, the focus has been on *ex ante* control. Recently, another breakthrough was reached with the introduction of the revised General Block Exemption Regulation (GBER). The Commission, wishing to focus attention on the most distortive types of aid, exempts even more aid measures from the notification obligation. This revision of the GBER constitutes a considerable increase in responsibility for the Member States. This obviously needs to be balanced with appropriate control mechanisms, which are embodied in the GBER in the form of increased transparency and *ex post* evaluation. The latter in particular boosts the role of an economic approach, as large aid schemes will need to be evaluated. Discussions were held on the appropriate methodology to estimate the impact of an aid scheme. The challenge of evaluation surely lies in finding the appropriate counterfactual. As a result of these discussions, a common methodology for State aid evaluation has been proposed.[2]

The introduction of evaluation can truly be considered to constitute a milestone. It is of primary importance to have a 'closed' policy cycle, starting with a design phase of the State aid measures, followed by development (including *ex ante* evaluation), implementation and *ex post* evaluation. The result of this last step is to be taken into account for future policy making and thus contributes to organisational learning. We argue that, if well-developed, the *ex post* evaluation instrument could, and ideally should, also serve as the *ex ante* toolkit for screening proposed aid measures. This approach would rightly create a sound policy cycle.

The development of sound evaluation techniques is of primary importance and calls for the joint effort and attention of academics, practitioners and policy makers. Evaluation of State aid measures is thus the focus of this chapter, of which the remainder is organised as follows: first, the policy context is described in more detail and the role of economic analysis is explained. Next, we look at literature on the evaluation of aid measures and existing practices. Furthermore, we look into possibilities for multi-criteria analysis, a widely used tool to evaluate and compare public policies. A discussion and conclusion constitute the final part.

2. The Evolution of Economic Analysis and the Emergence of *Ex Post* Evaluation in State Aid Control

The role of economic analysis in State aid control has gained considerable importance over the past decade. Multiple reasons for this can be found. Maybe it did not attract the attention of sufficient researchers in the field of economics, as a system of State aid control is in fact rare and cannot be found in other major jurisdictions outside the EU, such as the US. Perhaps the economic and econometric models that should underpin State aid control are very complex since, to mention only one example, multiple effects need to be studied simultaneously. The effectiveness, efficiency and possible distortions of competition are measured in a different way and need to be taken into account. Is it because the primary objective of control was aiming to limit political decision making rather than assessing the effectiveness of aid measures? Most likely, a combination of the

2 For details, see section 4 below.

above-mentioned factors caused a relatively late emergence of economic analysis in the field of State aid, certainly compared to the evolution and role of economics in other fields of competition policy.

In 2005, the SAAP called for a change.[3] The primary goal of this plan was to evolve towards 'less and better targeted State aid'. The plan called for a strengthened role of economics. The basic framework put forward and explained further by Friederiszick et al. (2007) comprises a balancing test, where the positive effects of an aid measure need to be weighed against the negative ones. Only when the overall balance is positive can the aid be allowed. More specifically, attention needs to be given to whether the aid actually addresses a market failure or reaches an objective of common interest, whether the aid is well targeted and whether the distortion of competition is not too severe. The second element can be further divided into three aspects, i.e. the measure should be an appropriate one, should entail an incentive effect, and should be kept to the minimum necessary to achieve the objective.

Ever since, the role of economic analysis in the assessment of proposed aid measures as well as the academic interest in the economics of State aid has rapidly increased. However, while evaluations have been carried out *ex post* by several researchers, economic analysis in a policy context has focused on the *ex ante* control, that is, until now.[4]

Recently, the GBER underwent a thorough revision following several concerns such as the previous one being too narrow, too limited, too complex, creating black holes and lacking impact assessment. Consequently, new categories of aid that can benefit from the notification exemption were listed, thresholds and intensities were increased, procedures were simplified, transparency initiatives were taken and evaluation of large schemes was called for. This allows the Commission to focus on the most distortive aid measures, while also allowing Member States to potentially grant up to 90%[5] of all aid without notification. This increased responsibility put on Member States is balanced by an enhanced monitoring exercise, more transparency and evaluation. All three elements are essential in turning the revised GBER into a success story.

Article 1(2) of the GBER excludes large schemes and makes them subject to evaluation, changing the current scene from only *ex ante* to both before and after policy evaluation. This constitutes a highly desirable change as *ex post* evaluation is essential in every policy cycle as it allows one to study the real impact of a policy. The results of the evaluation should be taken into account in future policy making and in this way contribute to organisational learning. In addition, continuously improving policy results in more efficient resource allocation. Aid measures can be compared and best practices can be developed.

Already in 2011, the Court of Auditors recommended that the effect of State aid should be frequently assessed, *ex post* as well.[6] This becomes all the more relevant as

3 See also the contribution by D. Hildebrand in this book.

4 For more on the economic analysis of State aid, see for example Spector (2009).

5 European Commission, 'State Aid: The Commission adopts new General Block Exemption Regulation (GBER)', MEMO/14/369, 21 May 2014.

6 Court of Auditors, 2011, pp. 94–95.

increasing responsibility is now put on Member States by the broader GBER. Moreover, evaluation is not uncommon, as *ex post* assessments are performed with regard to, for example, Structural Funds.

The main purpose of the evaluation should be to verify whether the aid schemes reach their objectives and what their impact is on the market. As mentioned before, an ideal evaluation toolkit could also allow for *ex ante* screening. Guidance on the methodology is provided in a Commission staff working document and will be discussed further in section 4.

3. Literature Review

Academic interest in the economics of State aid has certainly increased over the years and covers very diverse aspects. This literature review will briefly discuss important work on the impact and effectiveness of aid measures. Also, within this specific strand of the literature, work has been quite diverse. It ranges from theoretical models to sophisticated empirical estimations, using a variety of methodologies. On the one hand, one can study the effectiveness or efficiency of aid measures and thus focus on their possible positive aspects. On the other hand, it can be interesting to look at potential negative effects such as competition distortion, excessive profits or wages, low productivity, and outdated industrial infrastructure. These differences, in combination with different time frames, geographic areas, objectives, and aid instruments unfortunately render comparisons of results mostly impossible.

The effect of State aid on competition has been theoretically modelled by Garcia and Neven (2005), Mollgaard (2005) and Jegers and Buts (2011). Garcia and Neven find that State aid leads to more distortion of competition when market concentration is high. The severity of the competition distortion also seems to be different depending on whether the aid impacts, for example, on marginal costs or rather on the quality of the product. Jegers and Buts (2011) analyse the severity of the competition distortion when State aid is provided in case of either perfect competition or oligopoly. Mollgaard (2005) models distortions of competition resulting from State aid, also when these are not visible in price levels, but are for example reflected by quality changes. Katsoulacos (2005) provides an overview of the different competition effects that State aid for R&D could trigger.

Empirically studying the true impact of State aid on competition is not straightforward. One has to choose between focusing on the evolution of individual market shares or concentration ratios and gather the necessary data accordingly. The main difficulty lies in isolating the State aid aspect from other influences as, obviously, State aid is not the only force at work when looking at firm performance.

Buts and Jegers (2012 and 2013a) take a broad perspective and econometrically study the influence of subsidies on market shares and concentration. It appears that beneficiary firms are able to increase their market shares. Moreover, worringly, industries where high amounts of State aid are granted tend to evolve to higher concentration levels, i.e. less intense competition.

London Economics (2004) studies rescue and restructuring aid by means of five case studies. Following the aid, they document an expansion of sales, contrary to what would be expected in a downsizing and restructuring process. However, they also document closure or takeover afterwards. Chindooroy (2007) and Glowicka (2008) also investigate the impact of State aid for rescue and restructuring. The former finds a 50% chance of survival. The latter indicates that bankruptcy is often merely delayed by the State aid instead of contributing to a well-designed restructuring process. Schweiger (2011) asserts that aid to firms in difficulty prevents an efficient allocation of resources. Whereas market shares are positively influenced by the aid, total factor productivity is not, pointing to a distortive effect.

Multiple assessments have also been carried out for 'good' types of aid. Aid seems to be especially popular in the field of R&D. The main debate is centred on a possible crowding out effect, i.e. the question of whether the firm would have carried out the R&D project even without the aid. This constitutes a very important topic as the objective of R&D aid is of course to create additional R&D. A literature review by David et al. (2000) concludes that about one third of the studies up until then indicate that aid replaces rather than complements private investment. Lach (2002) and Gelabert et al. (2009) state that such aid is in fact only effective when awarded to small firms (which could not have carried out the project without the aid).

Furthermore, aid specifically targeted at boosting employment has been studied. Results have been extremely diverse. Bergström (1998) finds no significant impact of this kind of aid measure. Buts and Jegers (2013b) study the influence of a wide array of subsidies on employment levels and document an increase in the employment level of beneficiary firms compared to a control group, lasting about two years. While there is evidence to be found of job creation at a reasonable cost, Tannenwald (2002) documents a cost up to $2.4 million per newly created job.

Ginevicius et al. (2008) and Ginevicius and Bruzgė (2013) use multi-criteria analysis to study the impact of structural funds spending in Lithuania. The former paper finds that aid for educational or research projects scores best. Both papers document that the aid intensity is more determining for its effect than the absolute amount. The latter paper specifies that the impact is the strongest when the intensity lies between 50% and 70%.

This brief literature overview clearly shows that there are wide differences with regard to research focus, methodology and results when studying the impact of aid schemes. This makes comparisons and a ranking of different aid measures impossible. This should be one of the main points of attention in the development of a proper *ex post* evaluation tool as comparing and ranking is of crucial importance in improving future policy, better allocation of resources, and ultimately welfare.

4. Existing Practices and Methodological Guidance

Ex post evaluation of State aid is developing quickly. The Commission published an issues paper, held a workshop to make an inventory of existing practices, published a methodological and guidance paper and has now made available the final staff working document. Several general points of attention are regularly brought forward, such as the need to include both positive and negative effects in the analysis. The need for a true policy cycle has been stressed, pointing to the importance of using the results for future policy. Further, evaluation cannot become a synonym for monitoring and reporting.

In April of 2013, an issues paper (European Commission, 2013a) was published by DG Competition and a workshop was organised, collecting information on existing practices from Member States. During the fall of the same year, a draft methodological guidance paper was released (European Commission, 2013b) and updated the next year (European Commission, 2014). An overview of the proposed evaluation process to be followed is presented in Figure 1.

Figure 1. Timeline of the evaluation process

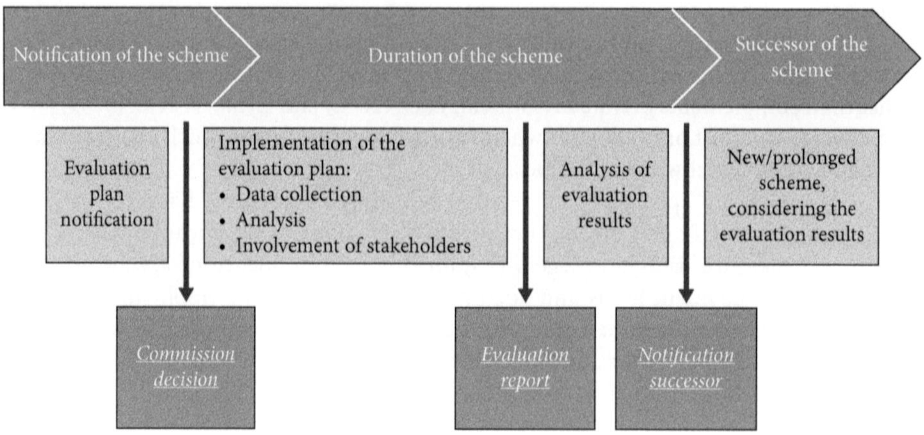

Source: adjusted from European Commission (2014), p. 12.

With regard to the methodology to be followed for evaluation, guidance has been provided in a draft methodological guidance paper and then in a Commission staff working document. These documents list and explain the minimum steps that are required in a good evaluation. These minimum steps are (European Commission, 2013b and European Commission, 2014):

(1) objective;
(2) evaluation questions;
(3) indicators;
(4) methodology;
(5) monitoring, data collection and availability;
(6) timeline;
(7) who conducts the evaluation; and
(8) publicity.

In order to evaluate the effectiveness of a scheme, it is necessary to spell out the objective of the aid measure from the beginning. In addition, the positive as well as the negative impact should be predicted. The direct as well as the indirect impact of the aid on the achievement of its objectives should be measured, as well as the possible distortions of competition. It is clear that different objectives call for a diverse set of indicators to be measured.

Next is the search for an appropriate methodology. The task is to assess the impact of the aid, meaning that one has to find the difference between the situation with the aid and what would have been the situation without the aid, the so-called counterfactual. One of the main difficulties can be found in isolating the effect of the aid, i.e. separating the aid impact from other possible influences such as the economic cycle.[7] It is for example not sufficient to study the development of investments in R&D following an aid scheme. It is also important to estimate what would have been this development without the aid in order to precisely isolate the aid effect. It could be that the firm already planned an increase in R&D spending for the development of a new product and that these plans were furthered as a result of the aid. In this case, only the increase in spending can be attributed to the government support. Not constructing a counterfactual would thus lead to an overestimation of the impact.

A more detailed description of possible methodologies is proposed in the annex of the Commission staff working document. One possibility is to identify a proper control group and subsequently test for significant differences between the aid beneficiaries and the control group. Testing for significant differences can be done by means of linear regression or matching techniques.[8] More or less sophisticated econometric methods can be used to estimate the effect most accurately. Several techniques are put forward, such as randomised experiments, quasi-experimental methods and structural estimation.[9] Commenting on this methodological draft, Oxera (2014) proposes the use of a dynamic panel, using a difference-in-difference approach, and points to the difficulties in the Commission's methodology if several indicators need to be assessed. Gaál and Boutin (2014) consult multiple stakeholders and conclude that a comparison with a counterfactual analysis is indeed the most logical choice as it is already used for evaluations of the European Regional Development Fund, the Cohesion Fund and the European Social Fund. This means that we could draw from experience and existing practices.

The reliability of an evaluation obviously also depends on the quality of the data used. In order to have all the relevant data, it is necessary to define data requirements as early as possible. In addition, a clear timeline of the aid in combination with an evaluation is proposed. An evaluation plan is developed together with the design of the aid measure and both are jointly notified to the Commission. Pre-notification contacts could also be useful in this regard. An evaluation report is issued after a specified time and the results

7 As discussed by Kemp (2014) amongst others.

8 See for example Angrist and Pischke (2008).

9 For more information see European Commission (2014).

are taken into consideration when deciding on a prolongation of the scheme or the design of a new measure.

The Commission calls for impartial evaluations, carried out by a body that is 'at least functionally independent' from the granting body. The evaluator should be described or selection criteria should be spelled out in the evaluation plan. Obviously, the earlier an evaluator is involved, the higher the chances are of a successful evaluation of the measure. Lastly, the evaluation plan, report and data should be made publicly available for transparency reasons and to allow interference of other stakeholders. This in a way replaces the part on peer review and quality control mentioned in the draft document.

Overall, a sound *ex post* evaluation framework should, first of all, be set up at the very beginning of the design of the aid measure. Next, it should also allow for mid-term evaluation permitting corrective action along the way and should respect possible time and resource constraints. The methodology should enable a joint evaluation of multiple effects. The outcome should be clear and results should preferably be comparable. From both the literature review and the existing practices, it is clear that comparisons are, at present, very difficult. The reasons can be found in different objectives of the aid measures, diverse methodologies, timeframes, geographic areas, etc. An ideal evaluation tool would obviously surmount these shortcomings and the substantially detailed methodological framework should for this reason best be proposed and ready to be used. Lastly, it is important that the evaluation be carried out by an independent organisation and that the process is sufficiently transparent.

5. Possibilities for Multi-Criteria Analysis

The Commission staff working document (2014) explains the most important steps of an *ex post* evaluation. In addition, it puts together an inventory of possible methodologies that can be used. However, no attention is given to multi-criteria analysis, a methodology often used in policy decisions with regard to large projects. The limitation to assess the impact of the aid on one indicator per test is a major drawback of the proposed methods as State aid needs to be evaluated on positive as well as negative aspects. This becomes possible when using multi-criteria analysis.

Multi-criteria analysis is frequently used when evaluating policy alternatives. The method is widely accepted and explained in handbooks, articles, and government manuals, for example, in Communities and Local Government (2009) and Zopounidis and Pardalos (2010). Figure 2 schematically presents the different steps.

Figure 2. Steps in the multi-criteria analysis

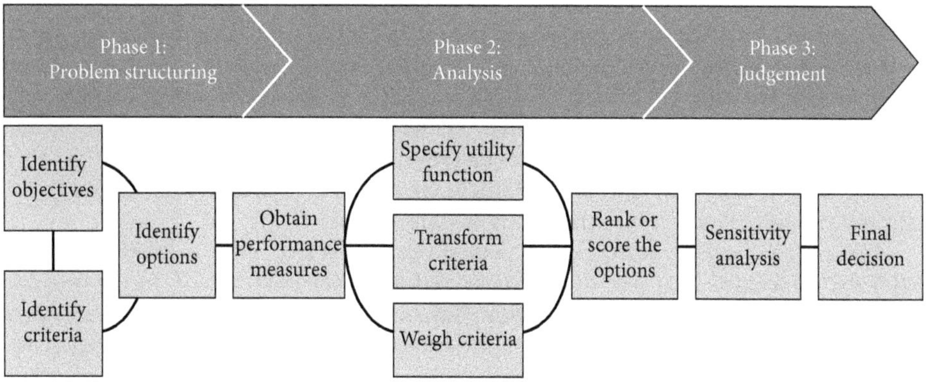

Source: adjusted from Hajkowicz (2008).

After having extensively studied the context, the objectives of the policy need to be well defined. In order to measure the performance of the policy, criteria (and possibly sub-criteria) are linked to these objectives.[10] Next, one decides how to score and rank the criteria. The process ensures room for quantitative as well as qualitative analysis, an indispensable characteristic when it comes to State aid policy evaluations as not all objectives or consequences can easily be expressed in a numerical value. In the case of State aid, the positive as well as the negative effects of the aid can thus jointly be taken into account at this stage. It is possible to attach different weights to the criteria if one or several of the criteria are considered to be more important than other. After having evaluated all the criteria, an overall score is computed, taking into account weights, should they be defined. Multiple policy options can here be evaluated by different methods, such as linear additive models, outranking methods or the analytical hierarchy process. The process of choosing between the diverse methods is well described by Guitouni and Martel (1998). The method thus enables a comparison between different State aid measures, but in principle also between a State aid and another policy alternative targeting the same objectives.

Where only one State aid is to be evaluated, it becomes important to design and provide a more standard evaluation tool which can be adjusted depending on the objective of the aid concerned. This standard tool also has the advantage that comparisons with other measures are facilitated afterwards. In addition, it provides more guidance and clarity to the Member States having to carry out the evaluation. Member States can then perform the evaluation mid-term or *ex post* by following the steps of multi-criteria analysis and the framework provided by the Commission. The output generates a general score and in addition sets out the partial scores on all criteria. These scores are to be examined and are subject to a sensitivity analysis. The goal of the sensitivity analysis is to check that small changes in scores or weights do not drastically alter the results.

10 For example, an aid designed under the objective regional development could be evaluated on a number of criteria, such as newly created jobs, regional unemployment level, overall investment level and/or GDP per capita.

This brings us to probably the main advantage of multi-criteria analysis in this context. Although emphasis is now put on *ex post* evaluation, once the framework is developed and learning from experience, it can, and ideally should, also be used for *ex ante* evaluation by the Commission itself. In this set-up, thresholds and vetoes can be developed for the different criteria. If the overall score is sufficient and not a single veto blocks the proposal, the aid measure can be allowed. If the overall score is inadequate or a veto comes up, the aid measure is considered to be incompatible. Applying the same methodology *ex ante* and *ex post* will allow for sound comparisons of the predicted effects with the real outcome, a truly 'closed' policy cycle.[11]

As mentioned in European Commission (2014), the last step in the evaluation process, publicity, is included to ensure transparency and to involve stakeholders in the process. Including stakeholders is indeed a valuable addition to each policy process. This option is also available in a structured way in the multi-criteria framework discussed, extending the multi-criteria analysis into a multi-actor multi-criteria analysis (MAMCA) as described in Macharis et al. (2004). This methodology is amongst others applied by Vashishta and Ramachandran (2006), studying power and energy management policies and by Dooms (2010) in the case of a policy decision on the expansion of the number of night flights.

Figure 3 presents the process of multi-criteria analysis extended with the inclusion of stakeholder objectives.

Figure 3. Including stakeholder analysis[12]

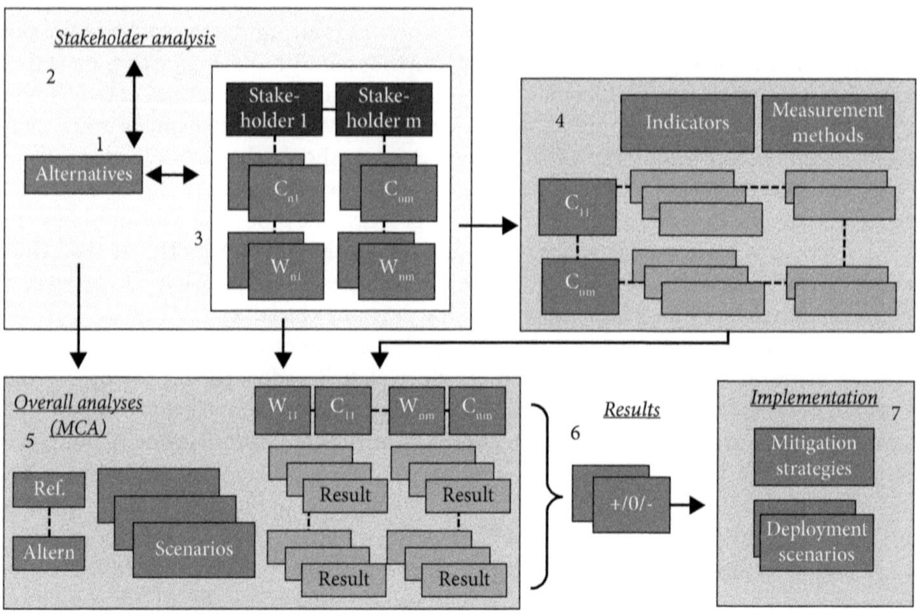

Source: adjusted from Macharis (2004).

11 At first sight, this could seem to be a costly process. However, the idea is that the savings obtained from improving future policy and making it more efficient largely outweigh the cost of evaluation.

12 'C' and 'W' stand for criteria and weight, respectively.

Stakeholders should ideally enter the process at an early stage. The inclusion of stakeholders is of great added value in the definition of the objectives. Based on stakeholder views and the ensuing objectives, evaluation criteria are defined. Possible weights that are given to the criteria can be deduced from the importance that the stakeholders attach to them.

Including stakeholders obviously brings extra complexity in the decision making process and will be time- and resource-consuming. In addition, also dynamic aspects of stakeholder inclusion cannot be ignored, as described by Dooms (2010). However, these complications should largely be outweighed by better insights, increased transparency and broader consensus on the policy outcome.

6. Conclusion

Governments and politicians regularly grant State aid to their domestic firms. However, the Treaty on the Functioning of the European Union sets out the limits for public spending. Only aid measures that are designed to cope with market failures can be considered compatible with the internal market. They aim to boost, amongst others, employment levels, research and development, or environmentally friendly investments. Essentially, aid can be allowed on the basis of efficiency as well as equity reasons. In addition, State aid proved to be indispensable while dealing with the recent financial crisis.

All Member States have to notify State aid measures (or State aid schemes) *ex ante* to the European Commission for approval (except when they fall under the *De Minimis* Regulation or are block exempted). Evaluations are thus made *ex ante* involving a balancing test, weighing the positive versus the negative effects. However, the entry into force of the revised GBER introduced several changes, one of them being *ex post* evaluation. This constitutes a very important step and should contribute to better policy making.

The correct methodology is crucial to ensuring reliable results and successful implementation of *ex post* evaluation as an integral part of the State aid policy cycle. Multiple options have been proposed by the Commission (2014). This chapter puts forward an alternative for the evaluation of State aid measures with a very broad application potential, namely multi-criteria analysis with the structured possibility of stakeholder participation. In this light, the Commission could propose a general framework as well as a specified one per aid objective, which is easy to use for the bodies that are entrusted with the evaluation. This brings the additional advantage of comparability over different types of measures and, if well designed, can, and ideally should, even lead to an *ex ante* tool for screening State aid proposals. This will in turn allow a comparison between predicted (positive as well as negative) effects and the real outcome.

The design of this framework is obviously a crucial step, where future research and experience should guide policy makers in the right direction.

References

J. Angrist and J. Pischke, 2008, *Mostly harmless econometrics: An empiricist's companion*, Princeton University Press.

F. Bergström, 1998, 'Do capital subsidies to firms increase employment?' in G. Eliason and N. Karlson (eds.), 2001, *The limits of government: on policy competence and economic growth*, New Brunswick, Transaction Publishers.

C. Buts and M. Jegers, 2012, 'A note on "State aid" and concentration: the case of Belgium', *European Competition Journal*, vol. 8, pp. 153–162.

C. Buts and M. Jegers, 2013(a), 'The effect of "State aid" on market shares: an empirical investigation in an EU Member State', *Journal of Industry, Competition and Trade*, vol. 13, pp. 89–100.

C. Buts and M. Jegers, 2013(b), 'Does State aid policy create jobs? The short and mid-term employment effects of subsidies', *European State Aid Law Quarterly*, vol. 12(4), pp. 651–658.

R. Chindooroy, P. Muller and G. Notaro, 2007, 'Company survival following rescue and restructuring State aid', *European Journal of Law and Economics*, vol. 24, pp. 165–187.

Commission Regulation (EU) No 651/2014 of 17 June 2014 declaring certain categories of aid compatible with the internal market in application of Articles 107 and 108 of the Treaty OJ L187.

Communities and Local Government, 2009, *Multi-criteria analysis: a manual*, London. Available online at http://eprints.lse.ac.uk/12761/1/Multi-criteria_Analysis.pdf (last consulted on 25 July 2014).

Court of Auditors, 2011, Do the Commission's procedures ensure effective management of State aid control?, Special Report No. 15. Available online at http://eca.europa.eu/portal/pls/portal/docs/1/10952771.PDF (last consulted on 19 March 2014).

P.A. David, B.H. Hall and A.A. Toole, 2000, 'Is public R&D spending a complement or substitute for private R&D? A review of econometric evidence', *Research Policy*, vol. 29, pp. 497–529.

M. Dooms, 2010, *Crafting the integrative value proposition for large scale transport infrastructure hubs. A stakeholder management approach*, Brussels, Academic and Scientific Publishers.

European Commission, 2005, State Aid Action Plan, less and better targeted State aid: a roadmap for State aid reform 2005 to 2009. Available online at http://eur-lex.europa.eu/legal-content/EN/ALL/;ELX_SESSIONID=2nYQTQ1TcvvLLQr1lq34GJGfwjRNv51tH6j5ycqh9fhp0X4BxJRv!-1120470413?uri=CELEX:52005DC0107 (last consulted on 24 July 2014).

European Commission, 2013(a), Evaluation in the field of State aid. Issues paper. Available online at http://ec.europa.eu/competition/state_aid/modernisation/evaluation_issues_paper_en.pdf (last consulted on 19 March 2014).

European Commission, 2013(b), Evaluation in the field of State aid. Draft methodological guidance paper. Available online at http://ec.europa.eu/competition/consultations/2013_state_aid_modernisation/draft_guidance_paper_en.pdf (last consulted on 19 March 2014).

European Commission, 2014, Commission Staff Working Document. Common methodology for State aid evaluation. Available online at http://ec.europa.eu/competition/state_aid/modernisation/state_aid_evaluation_methodology_en.pdf (last consulted on 24 July 2014).

H.W. Friederiszick, L.H. Röller and V. Verouden, 2006, 'European State aid control: an economic framework' in P. Buccirossi (ed.), 2008, *Handbook of antitrust economics*, Cambridge, MIT Press.

N. Gaál. and X. Boutin, 2014, 'Modernising State aid through better evaluations. Insights from recent discussions with stakeholders', *European State Aid Law Quarterly*, vol. 13(1), pp. 67–70.

J-A. Garcia and D. Neven, 2005, 'State aid and the distortion of competition, a benchmark model', HEI Working paper no. 06/2005. Available online at http://repec.graduateinstitute.ch/pdfs/Working_papers/HEIWP06-2005.pdf (last consulted on 24 July 2014).

L. Gelabert, A. Fosfuri and J.A. Tribo, 2009, 'Does the effect of public support for R&D depend on the degree of appropriability?', *The Journal of Industrial Economics*, vol. 57, pp. 736–767.

G. Ginevicius and S. Bruzge, 2013, 'Evaluation of the effect of state subsidies on business', *Business, Management and Education*, vol. 11, pp. 50–76.

G. Ginevicius, V. Podvezko and S. Bruzge, 2008, 'Evaluating the effect of state aid to business by multicriteria methods', *Journal of Business Economics and Management*, vol. 3, pp. 167–180.

E. Glowicka, 2008, *State aid and competition policy: the case of bailouts in the European Union*, Dissertation, Berlin, Humboldt-Universität.

A. Guitouni and J.M. Martel, 1998, 'Tentative guidelines to help choosing an appropriate MCDA method', *European Journal of Operational Research*, vol. 109(2), pp. 501–521.

S. Hajkowicz, 2008, 'Rethinking the economists evaluation toolkit in light of sustainability policy', *Sustainability: Science, Practice and Policy*, vol. 4(1), pp. 17–24.

M. Jegers and C. Buts, 2011, 'State aid and between country competition in an economic union: a microeconomic analysis' in M. Dumont and G. Grayp (eds.), 2011, *International business, not as usual*, Antwerp, Garant, pp. 81–94.

Y. Katsoulacos, 2005, 'State aid to R&D and competition: an economic assessment methodology'.

A. Kemp, 'Evaluating sector support using secondary data', OECD evaluation paper. Available online at www.oecd.org/dac/evaluation/dcdndep/37678896.pdf (last consulted 24 March 2014).

S. Lach, 2002, 'Do R&D subsidies stimulate or displace private R&D? Evidence from Israel', *The Journal of Industrial Economics*, vol. 50, pp. 369–390.

London Economics, 2004, 'Ex-post evaluation of the impact of rescue and restructuring aid on the international competitiveness of sector(s) affected by such aid'. Final report to the European Commission- Enterprise Directorate General. Available online at http://londoneconomics.co.uk/wp-content/uploads/2011/09/89-Ex-post-Evaluation-of-the-Impact-of-Rescue-and-Restructuring-Aid-on-the-International-Competitiveness-of-the-Sectors-Affected-by-Such-Aid.pdf (last consulted on 24 July 2014).

C. Macharis, A. Verbeke and K. de Brucker, 2004, 'The strategic evaluation of new technologies through multi-criteria analysis: the advisors case' in E.J. Bekiaris and Y.J. Nakanishi (eds.), *Economic Impacts of Intelligent Transportation Systems. Innovations and case studies*, Amsterdam, Elsevier, pp. 439–460.

P. Mollgaard, 2005, 'Competitive effects of State aid in oligopoly'. Available online at www.fep.up.pt/conferences/earie2005/cd_rom/Session%20VI/VI.H/Mollgaard.pdf (last consulted on 24 July, 2014).

Oxera, 2014, Oxera comments on draft European Commission guidance on how to conduct state aid evaluation. Available online at www.oxera.com/getattachment/Latest-Thinking/Publications/Reports/2014/Modernising-state-aid-through-better-evaluation/Modernising-state-aid-through-better-evaluation.pdf.aspx?ext=.pdf (last consulted 24 March 2014)

H. Schweiger, 2011, 'The impact of State aid for restructuring on the allocation of resources', European Bank for Reconstruction and Development, Working paper no. 127.
D. Spector, 2009, 'State aids: economic analysis and practice in the European Union' in X. Vives (ed.), *Competition policy in the EU. Fifty years on from the Treaty of Rome*, Oxford University Press, pp. 176–202.
R. Tannenwald, 2002, 'Are state and local revenue systems becoming obsolete?', *National Tax Journal*, vol. 55, pp. 467–489.
S. Vashishta and M. Ramachandran, 2006, 'Multicriteria evaluation of demand side management implementation strategies in the Indian power sector', *Energy*, vol. 31, pp. 2210–2225.
C. Zopounidis and P. Pardalos (eds.), 2010, *Handbook of multicriteria analysis*, Berlin, Springer.

THE EVOLVING TREATMENT OF SERVICES OF GENERAL ECONOMIC INTEREST UNDER EU LAW

Wouter Devroe and David Gabathuler*

1. Context

The importance of services of general interest (SGI), including services of general economic interest (SGEI) to the operation of many vital activities in the Member States has long been recognised in the EU and was given further legal support most notably through the adoption of specific provisions in the Amsterdam Treaty, the Lisbon Treaty and in the Charter of Fundamental Rights of the EU.

In 1997, the Amsterdam Treaty explicitly confirmed the role of SGEI in the Union with the introduction of a new article. Article 16 of the EC Treaty (now Article 14 of the Treaty on the Functioning of the EU (TFEU)) specifically highlighted, amongst other things, 'the place occupied by services of general economic interest in the shared values of the Union as well as their role in promoting territorial and social cohesion'. The Lisbon Treaty of 2007 added a Protocol (No. 26) stressing the importance of services of general interest, including SGEI, to the Union and emphasising, amongst other things, their essential role and their diversity as a result of different geographical, social or cultural situations. In addition, Article 36 of the Charter of Fundamental Rights of the Union also highlights the importance of 'access to SGEIs as provided for in national laws and practices, in accordance with the Treaties in order to promote the social and territorial cohesion of the Union'. Nonetheless, there is an inherent tension between these provisions that seek to preserve the public service traditions of the Member States and the competition rules, which remain the exclusive competence of the EU.[1]

* Wouter Devroe is Professor of Competition Law at Maastricht University, full Professor of Law and Chair of the Economic Law Department at KU Leuven, of Counsel with Allen & Overy and Assessor at the Belgian Competition Authority. David Gabathuler is a research member of the Economic Law Department at KU Leuven and also works in private practice in the field of EU law and competition law.

1 For a discussion of the national public service traditions and their contrast with EU law in the context of SGEI and the evolution of the case law on Article 106(2), see Schweitzer, Heike, 'Services of general economic interest: European law's impact on the role of markets and of member states', in *Market*

The far-reaching nature of the competition rules in the TFEU, including the State aid rules, means that competition provisions are potentially applicable to many SGEI since the granting of an SGEI could lead to the distortion competition, and in particular may constitute State aid. As is well known, the Treaty provides for an exception to the application of the competition rules to SGEI at Article 106(2) TFEU in so far as the application of such rules obstructs the performance, in law or in fact, of the particular tasks assigned to them.[2]

In its *Altmark* judgment[3] (and its earlier case law),[4] the Court of Justice of the EU sought to place limits on the application of the EU State aid rules to compensation granted for the provision of SGEI. However, the complexity of the SGEI concept and the difficulty in applying the Altmark criteria resulted in the Commission introducing a package of measures in 2005 to provide Member States with greater clarity and certainty on these issues. An expanded and updated package introduced in 2011 builds on the original 2005 package and consists of four measures that apply to the grant of compensation for the provision of SGEI, namely a Communication, a *de minimis* Regulation, an (exemption) Decision and a 'Framework'. The package also strengthens the reporting obligations on the Member States.

This chapter explains the key concept of an SGEI and some of the underlying elements in the light of EU case law and Commission practice and guidance, before discussing some of the critical components of the 2011 package. The chapter also explains the application of the EU Framework applicable to SGEI in (i) the energy sector and (ii) the environment and waste sector in order to give further insight into how the treatment of SGEI has developed under EU law.

Integration and Public Services and Public Services in the European Union, edited by M. Cremona, OUP (2011). For a more historical context to the development of EU law on SGEIs, see Prosser, Tony, 'Services of General Economic Interest, the Commission, and Reform' in *The Limits of Competition Law Markets and Public Services*, OUP (2005). For a more recent contextual discussion of SGEI, see 'Services of general economic interest and the Treaty of Lisbon: opening doors to a whole new approach or maintaining the "status quo"', *EL Rev.* 2011, 36(2), 226–242.

2 Article 106(2) provides that: 'Undertakings entrusted with the operation of services of general economic interest or having the character of a revenue-producing monopoly shall be subject to the rules contained in the Treaties, in particular to the rules on competition, in so far as the application of such rules does not obstruct the performance, in law or in fact, of the particular tasks assigned to them. The development of trade must not be affected to such an extent as would be contrary to the interests of the Union.'

3 Case C-280/00 *Altmark Trans GmbH and Regierungspraesidium Magdeburg v Nahverkehrsgesellschaft Altmark GmbH* [2003] ECR I-7747 (Altmark). See Santamato and Pesaresi, 'Compensation for services of general economic interest: some thoughts on the Altmark ruling', DG Competition, Competition Policy Newsletter, No. 1 – Spring 2004, p. 17; TILEC Discussion Paper, Sauter, W., 'The criterion of advantage in state aid: Altmark and services of general economic interest', April 2014 (ISSN 1572-40420); Lenaerts, K., 'Defining the concept of "services of general interest" in light of the "checks and balances" set out in the EU Treaties', (2012).

4 For example, Case C-53/00 *Ferring SA v Agence centrale des organismes de sécurité sociale (ACOSS)* [2001] ECR-I 9067. See Vedder and Holwerda, 'The European Courts' Jurisprudence After *Altmark*; Evolution or Devolution?' in *Financing Services of General Economic Interest: Reform and Modernization*, edited by Szyszczak and van de Gronden.

2. What is an SGEI?

There is no generally accepted definition of an SGEI under EU law. The Court of Justice has determined that SGEI exhibit special characteristics as compared with those of other economic activities.[5] In particular, the provision of the service in question must, by definition, assume a general or public interest.[6]

Due to the diverse public service landscape across the EU, Member States enjoy a wide margin of discretion in defining a given service as an SGEI. The Commission's jurisdiction – outside of harmonised sectors[7] – is limited to checking whether there is a manifest error in the definition of the service as an SGEI.[8]

Much is to be said for an approximation of the concepts of 'SGEI' and 'universal service'. This would lead us to define SGEI as services which society (this is a policy choice, not a legal issue) deem to be so essential that everyone needs to have access to them at a reasonable price and with a reasonable quality. 'Everyone' includes those citizens to whom the service cannot be provided at a profit, which prevents social exclusion.

However, the Court of Justice's case law and the Commission's guidance and practice deviate from this definition in certain regards, especially by now demanding that an SGEI can only be recognised when a market failure is established.

The following defining elements common to an SGEI can be identified under current Commission guidance and, to a certain extent, under current case law of the Court of Justice:

- provision of a service in the general interest;
- the existence of a market failure; and
- the universal and compulsory nature of the service.

2.1. Provision of a Service in the General Interest

The Commission's Communication on the application of the EU State aid rules to compensation granted for the provision of an SGEI (hereinafter, 'Communication') states that '[t]he concept of SGEI is an evolving notion that depends, among other things, on the needs of citizens, technological and market developments and social and political preferences in the Member State concerned'.[9] In its Guide to the application of the EU rules on state aid, public procurement and the internal market to SGEI (hereinafter, 'SGEI Guide'), the Commission highlights the definition of an SGEI given in a prior EU document (Quality Framework):[10]

5 Case C-179/90 *Merci convenzionali porto di Genova* [1991] ECR I-5889, para. 27.
6 Case T-289/03 *BUPA and others v Commission* [2008] ECR II-81, para. 178.
7 For example, telecoms, post and energy sectors.
8 Case T-17/02 *Fred Olsen v Commission* [2005] ECR II-2031; Case T-289/03 *BUPA*, paras 166–169.
9 The Commission Communication on the application of the EU State aid rules to compensation granted for the provision of SGEI, OJ C 8, 11.01.2012, p. 4.
10 Communication from the Commission 'A quality framework for services of general interest in Europe', 20 December 2011, COM(2011) 900 final.

> 'SGEIs are economic activities which deliver outcomes in the overall public good that would not be supplied (or would be supplied under different conditions in terms of objective quality, safety, affordability, equal treatment or universal access) by the market without public intervention. A PSO is imposed on the provider by way of an entrustment and on the basis of a general interest criterion which ensures that the service is provided under conditions allowing it to fulfil its mission.'[11]

> 'Generally speaking, the entrustment of a particular public service task implies the supply of services which, if it were considering its own commercial interests, an undertaking would not assume or would not assume to the same extent or under the same conditions'.[12]

EU law does not create any obligation to designate formally a task or a service as being of general economic interest, except when such an obligation is laid out in EU law.[13] It is therefore for the public authorities in the Member States to determine whether or not a service is in the general interest.

A very extensive range of activities has been categorised as SGEI, including public service obligations concerning electricity distribution, postal services, maritime transport, electricity generation for indigenous fuel sources, (basic) financial services, broadband, public service broadcasting, health care, social services (economic) and waste management.[14]

The broad discretion is not absolute and the Court of Justice has held that a Member State must state the reasons why it considers that the service in question, because of its specific nature, deserves to be characterised as an SGEI and to be distinguished from other economic activities. In the absence of such reasons, even a marginal review by the EU institutions with respect to the existence of a manifest error by the Member State in the context of its discretion would not be possible.[15] The broad margin of discretion enjoyed by the Member States is arguably evidenced by the small number of cases where manifest errors of assessment in the designation of SGEI have been identified.[16]

11 Reference to definition provided in the Commission's Quality Framework set out in the Guide to the application of the EU rules on state aid, public procurement and the internal market to SGEI of April 2013, p. 21.

12 Communication, para 47.

13 SGEI Guide, p. 22.

14 Commission Staff Working Document: 'The Application of EU State Aid Rules on SGEI since 2005 and the Outcome of the Public Consultation', Brussels, 23 March 2011, SEC(2011) 397.

15 Case C-179/90 *Merci convenzionali porto di Genova* [1991] ECR I-5889, para 27.

16 The SGEI Guide highlights, amongst other things, the following examples of manifest errors of assessment in the designation of SGEIs: (i) port operations are not necessarily SGEIs which exhibit special characteristics as compared with the general economic interest of other economic activities (Case C-179/90 *Merci convenzionali porto di Genova*, para 27); and (ii) disposal of animal corpses being only in the interest of the economic operators that benefit from it; these operators should bear the costs of disposing the waste they have caused ('polluter pays principle') (Commission decision concerning State aid No SA.25051 – Germany – Association for disposal of dead animal bodies, discussed in section 4.3. below).

2.2. *Existence of a Market Failure*

The Commission has explicitly provided in the Communication that there should be a market failure for a Member State to establish an SGEI. The Communication states that:

> '[I]t would not be appropriate to attach specific public service obligations to an activity which is already provided or can be provided satisfactorily and under conditions, such as price, objective quality characteristics, continuity and access to the service, consistent with the public interest, as defined by the State, by undertakings operating under normal market conditions.'[17]

The Communication also considers that if a service is already provided by the market, albeit under conditions that are considered unsatisfactory by the Member State concerned, for instance because the market cannot provide it with the level of quality or at a price that public authorities might consider as being in the public interest, such a service can still qualify as an SGEI.[18] If the market may be able to provide it in the future, the Member State can still qualify the activity as an SGEI, but the Member State must reduce the entrustment period accordingly and monitor the evolution of the market to determine that a further entrustment of a public service is needed.[19]

The need for a market failure in order to qualify an activity as an SGEI has so far only been confirmed in one judgment involving support for the roll-out of very high speed broadband networks in France (the *Hauts-de-Seine* judgment).[20] The General Court supported the Commission's position and stated that the existence of a market failure is a precondition for classifying an activity as an SGEI and, therefore, in finding that there was no State aid. It further added that the notion of a market failure is an objective concept the determination of which is based on an analysis of the market.[21] However, in its judgment the General Court rejected the private operators' arguments that state intervention was unjustified since they had failed to furnish credible evidence that the private sector could supply the service in the near future.[22]

If applied strictly, the market failure requirement could significantly limit the scope for Member States to introduce SGEI and may be subject to legal challenge in the future, especially given the discretion that Member States have enjoyed when determining which services to qualify as SGEI.

17 SGEI Communication, para. 48.

18 SGEI Guide, p. 26.

19 SGEI Guide, p.27.

20 Cases T-79/10 *Colt Télécommunications France v Commission*; T-258/10 *Orange v Commission*; and T-325/10 *Iliad and Others v Commission*, judgment 16 September 2013.

21 *Hauts-de-Seine* case, pp. 17–18.

22 Three years according to the Commission's broadband guidelines. Communication from the Commission – EU Guidelines for the application of State aid rules in relation to the rapid deployment of broadband networks, OJ C 25, 26.01.2013, p. 1.

2.3. Universal and Compulsory Nature of the Service

The case law of the Court of Justice also requires an activity to be of a universal and compulsory nature in order for it to be classified as an SGEI. In a notable case concerning a risk equalisation scheme in the Irish private health insurance market (the *BUPA* case),[23] the General Court specifically clarified the scope of the two requirements.

In the case, the General Court rejected the private health provider's argument that the SGEI must constitute a universal service in the strict sense and provided the following explanation on the requirement of universality:

> 'The fact that the SGEI obligations in question have only a limited territorial or material application or that the services concerned are enjoyed only by a relatively limited group of users does not necessarily call in question the universal nature of an SGEI mission within the meaning of Community law.'[24]

SGEI are services addressed to citizens or in the interest of society as a whole. The compensation for the SGEI must, therefore, be related to the cost of providing the service directly to the public. It does not seem possible for a SGEI to be for the benefit of a given undertaking.[25]

As regards the compulsory element, the General Court rejected a narrow interpretation and provided the following explanation of the requirement:

> '[T]he court observes that the compulsory nature of the service in question is an essential condition of the existence of an SGEI mission within the meaning of Community law. That compulsory nature must be understood as meaning that the operators entrusted with the SGEI mission by an act of an authority are, in principle, required to offer the service in question on the market in compliance with SGEI obligations which govern the supply of that service.'[26]

The court further explained that the compulsory element makes it possible to distinguish a service forming part of an SGEI mission from any other service provided on the market and, accordingly, from any other activity carried out in complete freedom.[27]

3. The Present: Altmark, SGEI Package and Member State Reporting

3.1. Background (Altmark)

Compensation granted by the state which can be categorised under EU law as an SGEI and which affects trade between Member States will not constitute State aid within the

23 Case T-289/03 *BUPA and others v Commission.*
24 Case T-289/03 *BUPA*, para. 187.
25 See SGEI Guide, p. 26.
26 Case T-289/03 *BUPA*, para. 188.
27 Case T-289/03 *BUPA*, para. 190.

meaning of Article 107 TFEU provided four cumulative conditions set out in the *Altmark* judgment are met,[28] namely:

> 'i. the recipient undertaking must have public service obligations (PSOs)[29] to discharge and the obligations must be clearly defined;
> ii. the parameters on the basis of which the compensation is calculated must be established in advance in an objective and transparent manner to avoid it conferring an economic advantage which may favour the recipient undertaking over competing undertakings;
> iii. the compensation cannot exceed what is necessary to cover all or part of the costs incurred in the discharge of PSOs, taking into account the relevant receipts and reasonable profit; and
> iv. where the undertaking which is to discharge the PSOs, in a specific case, is not chosen pursuant to a public procurement procedure [...] the level of compensation needed must be determined on the basis of an analysis of the costs which a typical undertaking, well run [...] would have incurred in discharging those obligations.'

The criteria are intended to determine whether the compensation simply offsets the net costs of carrying out such PSO, and as a consequence, the provider is not gaining any economic 'advantage' for the purposes of EU State aid rules.[30]

The Altmark criteria have been found to be difficult to interpret and apply, especially the benchmark requirement which applies in the absence of a public procurement procedure (fourth criterion).[31] The ruling, therefore, meant that a significant number of SGEI were potentially State aid which required *ex ante* notification to the Commission prior to implementation.

In order to clarify the application of the State aid rules to the financing of SGEI and in particular with regard to how to interpret the Altmark criteria, the Commission produced a package of measures in 2005 aimed at providing the Member States with greater legal certainty. The 2005 SGEI package (often referred to as the 'Monti-Kroes' Package) consisted of a Commission Decision[32] that block-exempted SGEI in certain sensitive sectors (e.g. hospitals and social housing), provided certain conditions were met, and a Framework for State aid in the form of public service compensation which set out the conditions under which compensation outside the scope of the Decision would

28 Case C-280/00 *Altmark*, paras. 87–93.

29 PSO and SGEI are treated as interchangeable concepts for the purposes of this article.

30 See Chapter 5 in this volume by Nicolaides, P., 'Compensation for the Net Extra Costs of Public Service Obligations' which examines recent case law of EU courts and the decisional practice of the European Commission on methods of public service compensation that are compatible with the internal market.

31 See Klasse, M., 'The Impact of Altmark: The European Commission Case Law Responses', in *Financing Services of General Economic Interest: Reform and Modernization*, edited by Szyszczak and van de Gronden.

32 Commission Decision of 28 November 2005 on the application of Article 86(2) of the EC Treaty to State aid in the form of public service compensation granted to certain undertakings entrusted with the operation of services of general economic interest, OJ L 312, 29.11.2005, p. 67.

be compatible with the State aid rules.[33] Furthermore, in 2006 the Commission issued an amended Transparency Directive imposing requirements of accounting separation on providers who receive compensation for the provision of SGEI and who also perform other activities.[34]

Following an extensive review,[35] the 2005 SGEI package was updated and strengthened in 2011 with the adoption of revised and new measures.[36] The 2011 SGEI Package (or 'Almunia Package', or 'second Altmark Package') is intended to provide Member States with a simpler, clearer and more flexible framework.[37] It consists of (i) a new Communication clarifying the conditions under which public service compensation is to be regarded as State aid,[38] (ii) a new *de minimis* Regulation specifically applicable to SGEI,[39] (iii) a revised Decision,[40] and (iv) a revised Framework.[41] Each of these instruments is discussed below.[42]

33 Community framework for State aid in the form of public service compensation, OJ C 297, 29.11.2005, p. 4.

34 Commission Directive 2006/111/EC of 16 November 2006 transparency of financial relations between Member States and public undertakings as well as on financial transparency within certain undertakings, OJ L 318, 17.11.2006, p. 17.

35 Commission staff working paper, 'The Application of EU State Aid rules on Services of General Economic Interest since 2005 and the Outcome of the Public Consultation', 23 March 2011, SEC(2011) 397, p. 16. Commission Communication, 'Reform of the EU State Aid Rules on Services of General Economic Interest', 23 March 2011, COM(2011) 146 final.

36 For further discussion about the new package, see (i) 'New State aid rules for services of general economic interest'; (ii) 'The SGEI Communication'; and (iii) The New State Aid Rules for Services of General Economic Interest (SGEI): the Commission Decision and Framework of 20 December 2011. Authors Pesaresi, Nicola et al, Competition Policy Newsletter (DG Competition), 2012–1. See also Syszczak 'Introduction' (Chapter 1) in *Financing Services of General Economic Interest: Reform and Modernization*, edited by Syszczak and van de Gronden.

37 Commission press release, IP/11/1571, 20.12.2011.

38 Communication from the Commission on the application of the European Union State aid rules to compensation granted for the provision of services of general economic interest, OJ C 8, 11.1.2012, p. 4.

39 Commission Regulation (EU) No 360/2012 of 25 April 2012 on the application of Articles 107 and 108 of the Treaty on the Functioning of the European Union to *de minimis* aid granted to undertakings providing services of general economic interest, OJ L 114, 26.04.2012, p. 8.

40 Commission Decision of 20 December 2011 on the application of Article 106(2) of the Treaty on the Functioning of the European Union to State aid in the form of public service compensation granted to certain undertakings entrusted with the operation of services of general economic interest, OJ L 7, 11.01.2012, p. 3.

41 Communication from the Commission – European Union framework for State aid in the form of public service compensation, OJ C 8, 11.01.2012, p. 15.

42 For further literature on the package, see Sinnaeve, Adinda, 'What's New in SGEI in 2012? – An Overview of the Commission's SGEI Package', *EStAL.* 2011 10(4) 347–367 and Sauter, W., 'The Altmark package mark II: new rules for state aid and the compensation of services of general economic interest', *ECRL* 2012, 33(7) 307–313; Szyszczak, E., 'Modernising state aid and the financing of SGEI', *JECL & Pract.* 2012, 3(4) 332–343. For a discussion of the legal and economic principles in the Commission's Framework and the need for the instrument to be applied with flexibility, see Geradin, D., 'Public Compensation for Services of General Economic Interest: An Analysis of the 2011 European Commission Framework' (30 March 2012) (SSRN 2031564).

3.2. *2011 SGEI Package*

3.2.1 'Altmark' Communication

The Communication is a new instrument that provides guidance on State aid concepts of most relevance to compensation granted for the provision of SGEI (e.g. concepts of undertakings and economic activity; State resources and effect on trade), and in particular provides guidance on how to interpret and apply the Altmark criteria.

3.2.1.1. Key State Aid Concepts

The State aid rules only apply to a transfer of resources by a public authority, public undertaking or part of the State administration to an 'undertaking'. The concept of an 'undertaking' has been defined through the case law of the European Courts as 'every entity engaged in an economic activity, regardless of the legal status of the entity and the way in which it is financed'.[43] The European Court has further stated that 'any activity consisting in offering goods and services on a given market is an economic activity'.[44]

The Court of Justice has generally taken a functional (case-by-case) approach to determining whether an entity is carrying out an economic activity – in particular by focusing on the economic or public nature of the activity. The following cases are illustrative of its approach:

- In the seminal *Höfner* case, the Court of Justice determined that the German Federal Employment Office was considered to be an undertaking. It specifically emphasised the following:

  > '[t]he fact that employment procurement activities are normally entrusted to public agencies cannot affect the economic nature of such activities. Employment procurement has not always been, and is not necessarily, carried out by public entities.'[45]

- The Court of Justice ruled that Eurocontrol (European Organisation for the Safety of Air Navigation) was not an undertaking engaged in economic activity even through it collected route charges. The tasks undertaken by Eurocontrol were aimed at contributing to the maintenance and improvement of air navigation safety – an activity in the public interest.[46]

43 Case C-41/90 *Klaus Höfner and Fritz Elsener v Macrotron GmbH* [1991] ECR I-1979, para. 21; Cases C-159 and 160/91 *Poucet and Pistre v Assurance Générales de France* [1993] ECR I-637, para. 17; Case 364/92 *SAT Fluggesellchaft mbH v Eurocontrol* [1994] ECR I-43, para. 18.

44 Case C-475/99 *Ambulanz Glöckner* [2001] ECR I-8089, para. 19.

45 Case C-41/90 *Klaus Höfner and Fritz Elsener v Macrotron GmbH* [1991] ECR I-1979, para. 22.

46 Case 364/92 *SAT Fluggesellchaft mbH v Eurocontrol* [1994] ECR I-43.

- It further held that Eurocontrol would not act as an undertaking even when conducting economic activities if those activities were connected with and inseparable from the exercise of its public powers.[47]
- It has held that 'data collection activity in relation to undertakings, on the basis of a statutory obligation on those undertakings to disclose data and power of enforcement related thereto, falls within the exercise of public powers'.[48]
- More recently, the Court of Justice has held that undertakings entrusted with supplying certification services in Italy – the receipt of an appropriate certificate being a necessary condition in order for interested persons to participate in public works contracts in accordance with national legislation – were activities of an economic character. It further highlighted that the undertakings issued certificates in return for remuneration and exclusively on the basis of actual market demand. Furthermore, they assumed the financial risks involved in the exercise of that activity.[49]

By contrast, activities which fall within the exercise of public powers are not of an economic nature justifying the application of the Treaty rules of competition.[50] This will be the case where a task 'forms part of the essential functions of the state and where the activity is connected by its nature, its aims and rules to which it is subject with the exercise of powers [...] which are typically those of a public authority'.[51]

The Communication provides general guidance on these concepts[52] and also provides additional explanation on their application to three sensitive areas (social security, health care and education). For example as regards social security, the Commission reaffirms the established position that social security schemes which are solidarity-based do not involve an economic activity and sets out a number of criteria to help determine that the solidarity-based element is met.[53]

The distinction between the concept of an economic activity and the exercise of public powers is crucial in helping to determine the application of the State aid rules to SGEI. It is, however, not necessarily a straightforward exercise to undertake in practice, especially as markets are increasingly liberalised and the provision of a service 'in-house' raises particular challenges. The Communication specifically highlights that a decision not to allow third parties to provide a certain service does not rule out the existence of an economic activity. It states the following in this regard:

> 'The decision of an authority not to allow third parties to provide a certain service (for example, because it wishes to provide the service in-house) does not rule out the existence of

47 Case C-113 *Selex Sistemi Integrati SpA v Commission*, judgment of 12 July 2012, [2009] ECR I-2207.

48 Case C-138/11 *Compass-Datenbank GmbH v Republik Österreich*, not yet published.

49 Case C-327/12 *Ministero dello Sviluppo economico v SOA Nazionale Costruttori*, not yet published.

50 Case C-138/11 *Compass-Datenbank*, para. 36.

51 Case C-343/95 *Diego Cali & Figli v Servizi ecologici porto di Genova* [1997] ECR I-1547, para. 23.

52 The Communication lists the following activities which are not of an economic nature: (a) the army or the police, (b) air navigation safety and control, (c) maritime traffic control and safety, (d) anti-pollution surveillance, and (e) the organisation, financing and enforcement of prison sentences. Communication, para 16.

53 Communication, paras. 18–19.

> an economic activity. In spite of such market closure, an economic activity can exist where other operators would be willing and able to provide the service in the market concerned. More generally, the fact that a particular service is provided in-house has no relevance for the economic nature of the activity.'[54]

The position in the Communication is in line with a Commission's State aid decision of 2011 and which is, amongst others,[55] cited in support. In the decision that relates to the financing of public transport operators for the provision of PSOs in Germany, the Commission finds that 'the fact that the companies may be qualified as in-house companies does not impede a possible effect on competition [of the financing system] since these companies act in a market together with other public and private companies.'[56]

In order to determine whether an activity is of an economic nature, it is, therefore, of direct relevance to identify the existence of a 'market' for the goods or services. This is particularly complex if it is necessary to consider 'hypothetical' competition which may have been excluded by the State through the grant of an exclusivity. The European Court's case law is not explicit on this point.

In the *Höfner* and *Ambulanz Glöckner* judgments,[57] the Court of Justice's definition is focused on 'any activity consisting in offering goods and services on a given market', whereas some of the statements by Advocates General seemingly indicate a willingness to take into account potential or even hypothetical competition.[58] The General Court has also stated in a case involving the activities of Eurocontrol that 'the fact that the services in question are not at the current time offered by private undertakings does not prevent their being described as an economic activity, since it is possible for them to be carried out by private entities.'[59]

There does not appear, however, to be any specific ruling by the Court of Justice on the question of whether it is necessary to take into account hypothetical competition and the Communication does not appear to sufficiently address the issue.[60] Furthermore, the Communication states that the Commission's assessment of whether a service can be

54 SGEI Communication, para 13.

55 Opinion of Advocate General Geelhoed in Case C-295/05 *Asociación Nacional de Empresas Forestales (Asemfo) v Transformación Agraria SA (Tragsa) and Administración del Estado* ECR I-2999, paras. 110–116.

56 Commission decision of 23 February 2011 on State aid C 58/06 (ex NN 98/05) implemented by Germany for Bahnen der Stadt Monheim (BSM) and Rheinische Bahngesellschaft (RBG) in the Verkehrsverbund Rhein-Ruhr, para. 208.

57 Case C-41/90 *Klaus Höfner*; Case C-475/99 *Ambulanz Glöckner*.

58 Advocate General Jacobs stated in *Ambulanz Glöckner* at para. 67 that 'the basic test is whether the entity in question is engaged in an activity which consists in offering goods and services on a given market and which could, *at least in principle*, be carried out by a private actor in order to make profits' (emphasis added). See also Opinion of Advocate General Tesauro in Case 364/92 SAT *Fluggesellchaft*.

59 Case T-155/04 *Selex Sistemi Integrati v Commission*, para 89.

60 Furthermore the Draft Commission Notice on the notion of State aid (2014) does not specifically address the issue and, in any event, appears unclear. See section 2 – Notion of undertaking and economic activity. The SGEI Guide does indicate that 'if the public funding of an economic activity performed by an in-house body within the meaning of the rules on public contracts meets the

provided by the market is limited to checking whether the Member State has made a manifest error.[61] However, there is some indication from commentators[62] that it is necessary to do so, but academic literature does not seem to specifically address this point extensively or in detail.

The Communication also provides guidance on the concept of 'State resources', which is a critical element in determining the application of Article 107(1). The Communication follows established Commission practice (an approach that has been upheld by the Court of Justice)[63] and adopts a broad notion of the concept. As regards SGEI, the Communication for example states that 'compensatory payments for the operation of SGEIs which are financed through parafiscal charges or compulsory contributions imposed by the State and managed and apportioned in accordance with the provisions of the legislation are compensatory payments made through State resources'.[64]

The Communication also provides guidance on the "*effect on trade*" concept. It explains that "such an effect generally presupposes the existence of a market open to competition".[65] As explained above, determining the existence of a market open to competition may not be straightforward. The Communication, nonetheless, emphasises that the State aid rules apply where "markets have been opened up to competition either by Union or national legislation or *de facto* by economic development".[66] The Communication also lists examples of purely local SGEI which will not trigger an effect on trade, e.g. swimming pools to be used predominantly by the local population, local hospitals aimed exclusively at the local population and local cultural events. These examples are extremely limited in scope and it can, therefore, be questioned whether they can provide a useful benchmark to assess more complex situations.

3.2.1.2. Altmark Criteria

In its *Altmark* judgment, the Court of Justice set out four specific criteria that had to be met for compensation granted for the provision of an SGEI to escape qualification as State aid, namely: (i) the entrustment of an SGEI, (ii) the advance formulation of parameters for calculating compensation, (iii) the avoidance of overcompensation and (iv) the selection of an SGEI provider on the basis of a public procurement or a benchmarking exercise. As already mentioned, the criteria are difficult to interpret and apply. The Communication that was issued in 2011 provides Member States with guidance on the application of each of these criteria.

conditions laid down in Article 107(1) of the TFEU and does not meet all the conditions set out in the *Altmark* judgment […], see Communication paras. 13 and 37)'. SGEI Guide, para. 44.

61 Communication, para. 48.

62 See Sauter, W. and Schepel, H., *State and Market in European Union Law. The public and private spheres of the internal market before the EU courts*, Cambridge, Studies in European Law and Policy, pp. 80–81.

63 See Case C-482/99 *France v Commission* [2002] ECR I-4397.

64 Communication, para. 36.

65 Communication, para. 37.

66 Communication, para. 37.

(i) *First criterion*: The Communication provides clarification on the concept of an SGEI, although it also highlights the wide margin of discretion afforded to the Member States in defining a given service as an SGEI and in granting compensation to the service provider. We refer to the discussion above on 'What is an SGEI?'. The Communication reaffirms the need for the PSO to be assigned to the provider by way act of entrustment. Due to wide divergences in the administrative and legal architecture of the Member States, the form of the act can vary between legislative, regulatory or contractual measure(s). The act must, however, contain a minimum set of information, including for example, the content and duration of the PSO (not necessarily each and every activity),[67] the undertaking and, where applicable, the territory concerned, and the nature of any exclusive or special rights assigned to the undertaking by the authority in question.[68] As discussed above, the Communication also provides that public service conditions should not be attached to an activity which is already provided or can be provided satisfactorily by undertakings operating under normal market conditions.
(ii) *Second criterion*:[69] The Communication emphasises that the parameters for calculating compensation must be established in advance in an objective and transparent manner, but it does not prescribe a specific formula that Member States must follow. The methodology for determining the costs to be compensated, must be determined and calculated at the outset where the Member State authority decides that it will compensate all cost items of the provider. However, only the costs directly associated with the provision of the SGEI can be taken into account (all revenue accruing to the undertaking from the provision of the SGEI must be deducted). In addition, the criteria for calculating the profit must also be established where the provider is offered a reasonable profit.
(iii) *Third criterion*: The Communication also specifies that the compensation must not exceed what is necessary to cover all or part of the costs in the discharge of the PSO, taking into account the relevant receipts and a reasonable profit.[70] A reasonable profit should be taken to mean the rate of return on capital that would be required by a typical company considering whether or not to provide the SGEI, i.e. using an Internal Rate of Return (IRR).[71] The Member States can also introduce incentive criteria relating in particular to the quality of service.
(iv) *Fourth criterion*: In order to avoid the application of Article 107(1) on the basis of the Altmark jurisprudence, the Court of Justice placed strict requirements on Member States when selecting the SGEI provider. The selection must be based on a public procurement or a benchmarking exercise, with the Commission expressing a clear

67 SGEI Guide, para. 55.
68 See Communication, para. 52 for a full list of the required information.
69 For examples of the Commission's practice in applying this criterion, see section on 'Pre-determined parameters of compensation and no over-compensation' in Chapter 5 of this volume by Nicolaides, P. on 'Compensation for the Net Extra Costs of Public Service Obligations'.
70 See Communication, para. 60.
71 See Communication, para. 61 and footnote (3).

preference in the Communication for public procurement which 'is often a mandatory requirement under existing Union rules'.[72]

The Communication states that an 'open' (procurement) procedure is acceptable, but indicates that this is also the case for a 'restricted' procedure unless interested operators are prevented to tender without valid reasons. By contrast, a competitive dialogue or a 'negotiated' procedure are only sufficient in exceptional cases.[73] The Communication further specifies that 'lowest price' and 'most economically advantageous tender' (if certain conditions are complied with) are award criteria satisfy the fourth Altmark criterion, but highlights circumstances when a procurement procedure cannot provide for the provision of the service on the least cost to the community.

The selection of the provider as a result of an efficiency benchmarking exercise with a typical undertaking, well run and adequately provided with the necessary means, is particularly complex and the Communication seeks to provide clarity on this topic. The Communication states that 'where generally accepted market remuneration exists for a given service that market remuneration provides the best benchmark for the compensation'.[74] The SGEI Guide, however, emphasises that such proof will depend on 'all the particularities of each individual situation'.[75] It is therefore a difficult test to satisfy. Where no such generally accepted market remuneration exists for a given service, the Communication states that the amount of compensation must be 'determined on the basis of an analysis of the costs of a typical undertaking, well run and adequately provided with material means so as to be able to meet the necessary public service requirements'.[76] The concept of a 'well-run undertaking' is to be based on objective criteria that are economically recognised as being representative of satisfactory management.[77] The Communication provides further guidance on how to correctly gauge that an undertaking qualifies as typical well run.[78]

Finally, the Communication specifies that it is without prejudice to the application of other provisions of Union law, in particular those relating to public procurement as well as Treaty requirements of transparency, equality of treatment, proportionality and mutual recognition.[79]

3.2.2. *De minimis* Regulation

The SGEI Package includes a new and separate *de minimis* Regulation specifically covering aid granted to undertakings providing SGEI that is likely to facilitate the

72 See Communication, para. 63.
73 See Communication, para. 66.
74 See Communication, para. 69.
75 See SGEI Guide, para. 71.
76 See Communication, para. 71.
77 See Communication, para. 71.
78 See Communication, paras. 72–77. The SGEI Guide also indicates that the Member States can use a pre-established reference cost provided that it can be justified. See SGEI Guide, para. 72.
79 Communication, para. 5.

compliance task of many authorities. The Regulation provides that the grant of compensation up to €500,000 over a three year period to an undertaking providing an SGEI will not constitute State aid. This is higher than the threshold in the general *de minimis* Regulation (€200,000).[80]

According to the Commission, this difference in approach can be supported by the fact that it can be assumed that the measures are at least in part compensating the undertaking for the extra costs incurred in providing a public service and that this is borne out by its own case law experience. This claim seems rather difficult to substantiate, but the sums involved are still relatively low and it can probably be justifiably argued that they are unlikely to affect trade between Member States and/or have an appreciable impact on competition in the vast majority of cases. The Regulation does not, in any event, apply to certain more sensitive sectors (e.g. fisheries, agricultural products and road freight transport).[81]

The Regulation also only applies to aid in respect of which it is possible to calculate precisely the gross grant equivalent of the aid *ex ante* without the need to undertake a risk assessment, i.e. transparent aid such as grants, interest rate subsidies and loans (where gross grant equivalent can be calculated on the basis of prevailing interest rates in the market). Non-transparent aid, e.g. capital injections and risk capital measures, should be notified to the Commission in accordance with Article 108(3) unless it meets the conditions of the (general?) *de minimis* Regulation.

The Regulation also includes rules dealing with the cumulation of aid and specifically prohibits cumulation where the aid intensity would exceed the figure specified in other State aid instruments or decisions.[82] In addition, the Regulation includes provisions dealing with the monitoring of *de minimis* aid falling within its terms.[83] It is also without prejudice to the requirements in EU law in the area of public procurement or of additional requirements fro the Treaty or sectoral legislation.[84] The Regulation will also be subject to a review five years after its entry into force.[85]

3.2.3. Commission Decision

The Decision 'exempts' certain categories of public service compensation granted to undertakings entrusted with the operation of SGEI from the application of the EU State aid rules. The aid is deemed compatible with the internal market and exempt from the *ex*

80 Commission Regulation (EC) No 1407/2013 of 18 December 2013 on the application of Articles 107 and 108 of the Treaty on the Functioning of the European Union to *de minimis* aid, OJ L 352, 24.12.2013, p.1.

81 Excluded sectors are aid to fishery and aquatic sectors, aid to primary production of agricultural products, aid to processing and marketing of agricultural products in specific instances, aid to export-related activities towards third countries or Member States, aid contingent on the use of domestic over imported goods, aid in the coal sector, aid to undertakings performing road freight transport for hire or reward and aid granted to undertakings in difficulty. See Commission Regulation (EU) No 360/2012, Article 1(2).

82 See Commission Regulation (EU) No 360/2012, Article 2(6).

83 See Commission Regulation (EU) No 360/2012, Article 3.

84 See Commission Regulation (EU) No 360/2012, Recital 21.

85 See Commission Regulation (EU) No 360/2012, Recital 23.

ante notification.[86] In particular, compensation not exceeding an annual amount of €15 million for the provision of SGEI is automatically exempted unless it relates to transport and transport infrastructure (covered by a *lex specialis*). There is, however, no aid limit for compensation relating to the provision of medical care by hospitals and the provision of services meeting specific forms of social needs.[87] The exemption for compensation granted for the provision of SGEI relating to air or maritime links to islands or the operation of airports and ports is dependent on the volume of passenger traffic.[88]

The Decision is prescriptive as to the terms on which compensation can be granted if such compensation is to be automatically exempted from the application of Article 107(1). The Decision emphasises that there must be no over-compensation and it must only cover the net cost incurred in discharging the PSO, including a reasonable profit. The reasonable profit is defined as the rate of return on capital that would be required by a typical undertaking considering whether or not to provide the service.[89] The Decision also explains the methodology for calculating the net cost, namely the difference between the costs and the revenues associated with the provision of the SGEI, or alternatively a methodology based on a net avoided cost methodology (discussed below in the section on the Framework Communication).

The Decision is only applicable to the operation of SGEI that have been formally entrusted to the undertakings concerned and which specifically make reference to the Decision in the entrustment act. The entrustment act for the operation of the SGEI must also not exceed ten years, unless significant investment is required which needs to be amortized over a longer period.

Finally, the Decision requires regular checks to be carried out on undertakings receiving compensation (exempt from notification) to ensure compliance with the terms of the Decision and, in addition, places transparency and reporting obligations on Member States.[90]

3.2.4. Framework Communication

The revised Framework explains the conditions under which public service compensation falling outside the scope of the 'exemption' Decision and thus potentially State aid within

86 If the conditions in the Decision are no longer met, the aid is to be notified in accordance with Article 108(3).

87 Health and long-term care, childcare, access to and reintegration into the labour market, social housing and the care and social inclusion of vulnerable groups. See Articlel(c) of Commission Decision of 20 December 2011.

88 As regards air or maritime links to islands – average annual traffic during the two preceding financial years of the assignment of the SGEI not exceeding 300,000 passengers. As regards airports and ports – average annual traffic during the two preceding financial years of the assignment of the SGEI not exceeding 200,000 passengers in the case of airports and 300,000 in the case of ports. See Articles 1(d) and (e) of Commission Decision of 20 December 2011, respectively.

89 A rate of return on capital does not exceed the relevant swap rate plus a premium of 100 basis points is regarded as reasonable. See Article 5(5)-(7) of Commission Decision of 20 December 2011 for further details on the methodology for determining a reasonable profit.

90 See Articles 6–10 of Commission Decision of 20 December 2011.

the meaning of Article 107(1) can nonetheless be regarded as compatible with the internal market pursuant to Article 106(2).[91] As compared to the 2005 version, the revised Framework is underpinned by more a more robust economic approach.[92] This is particularly evident from the strengthened framework for calculating the level of compensation to be granted for discharging PSOs as well as the requirement on Member States to introduce economic incentives for the efficient provision of SGEI.

The Framework states that the amount of compensation must not exceed what is necessary to cover the 'net cost' of discharging the PSO, including a reasonable profit.[93] The costs can be established on the basis of either expected costs and revenues, or the costs and revenues actually incurred, or a combination of the two.[94] The Framework proposes a new methodology for calculating the net cost of the SGEI, namely the 'net avoided cost methodology' which is defined as the difference between the net cost for the provider of operating with the public service obligation and the net cost or profit for the same provider of operating without that obligation.[95] The net avoided cost methodology is commonly applied in the telecommunications and postal sectors for determining the compensation due for the provision of the universal service obligation.[96] It should result in a more accurate calculation of the true cost of providing the PSO, although it is a complex analysis and can be difficult in practice to determine the level of costs that would have incurred without the PSO. The Framework therefore also permits the use of alternative methods for calculating the net cost to discharge the PSO, such as a methodology based on cost allocation. Other methodologies can only be relied upon where use of the net avoided cost approach is not feasible or appropriate.[97]

In terms of what constitutes a 'reasonable profit', the Framework follows the same approach used in the exemption decision, i.e. the rate of return on capital that would be required by a typical company considering whether or not to provide the SGEI for the whole duration of the entrustment act.[98] The Framework further provides for a specific safe harbour by stating that a rate of return on capital not exceeding the relevant swap rate plus a premium of 100 basis points is regarded as reasonable.[99] Other indicators than

91 Article 106(2) provides for an exception to the application of the Treaty provisions to SGEI in so far as the application of the competition rules in particular would obstruct the performance, in law or in fact, of the particular tasks assigned to them. The exception also only applies where the development of trade is not affected to such an extent as would be contrary to the interests of the Union.

92 For a discussion on the greater reliance of economic principles with respect to the application of the EU State aid rules, see Chapter 1 in this volume by Hildebrand, D. on 'Modernisation of State Aid Rules in the European Union – Application of economic Concepts and Principles'. See also Kavanagh, J., 'Financing Services of General Economic Interest: The European Commission's Economic Tests' in *Financing Services of General Economic Interest: Reform and Modernization*, edited by Szyszczak and van de Gronden.

93 See Framework para. 21.

94 See Framework para. 22.

95 See Framework, para. 25.

96 For example, see Study on the principles used to calculate the net costs of the postal USO, a report prepared for the European Commission, Frontier Economics, January 2013.

97 See Framework, para. 27.

98 See Framework, para. 33.

99 See Framework, para. 36.

the rate of return on capital can be used to determine what can constitute a reasonable profit (e.g. average return on equity, return on capital employed, return on assets or the return on sales), but must be duly justified.[100]

An important innovation in the revised Framework is an obligation on Member States to introduce incentives for the efficient provision of SGEI when devising the method of compensation, unless they can duly justify that it is not feasible or appropriate to do so. The introduction of efficiency incentives is intended to reduce the risk of providers benefitting from overcompensation, but may also lead in the medium or longer term to the granting of lesser amounts of aid.[101]

The Framework indicates that the Commission will generally apply a 'light touch' form of assessment when applying – for the purposes of Article 106(2) – the competition and distortion of trade tests. In particular, the Framework provides at para. 61 (section 2.11) that certain provisions in the Framework will not apply to aid which meets the conditions laid down in Article 2(1) of the Decision. This applies, amongst other things, to the granting of compensation not exceeding an annual amount of €15 million for the provision of SGEI. However, a more substantive assessment will be carried out in 'exceptional circumstances' where there are concerns that serious competition distortions could remain unaddressed. The Framework lists a number of instances where such distortions may arise, for example an entrustment duration that cannot be justified by objective criteria or an entrustment that bundles a series of tasks that are typically provided separately without any loss of efficiency and effectiveness.[102] If the aid may lead to competition distortions in the internal market, the Commission will examine whether they can be mitigated by requiring conditions or requesting commitments from the Member State.[103]

The Framework also includes, amongst other, strengthened provisions on transparency as well as obligations imposed on the Member State with respect to reporting and evaluation.[104] Furthermore, the Framework reinforces the importance of public procurement procedures by stating that aid will only be compatible with the internal market if entrustment is in compliance with EU public procurement rules, where applicable.[105]

3.3. *Reporting*

The 2005 SGEI package required Member States to report on their implementation of Decision for the period 2006–2008 and subsequently for the period 2009–2011. The outcome of the self-reporting was rather disappointing, with many Member State reports

100 See Framework, para 34.

101 For further discussion on the Commission's policy with the regard to the introduction of efficiency incentive requirements in the revised Framework, see 'The New State Aid Rules for Services of General Economic Interest (SGEI): the Commission Decision and Framework of 20 December 2011'. Authors Pesaresi, Nicola et al, Competition Policy Newsletter (DG Competition), 2012–1, p.16.

102 See Framework, paras. 54–59.

103 See Framework, para. 53.

104 See Framework, sections 2.10 (Transparency) and 3 (Reporting and Evaluation), respectively.

105 See Framework, para. 19.

lacking detail and providing only a basic and limited picture of the SGEI situation. There was also often a lack of consistency in the responses, apparently due to limited understanding in the Member States about the extent of their reporting obligations or possibly even a desire to not be overly transparent. In a few instances, Member States failed to provide any report to the Commission's services. Some Member States, such as Germany also specifically highlighted the difficulty of applying the Altmark criteria and requested additional guidance. In the table below we try to highlight the differences in reporting of a number of EU Member States.

Analysis of certain Member States' reports on the application of the SGEI Decision of 2005 during 2006-2008 and 2009-2011[106]

Country	Hospitals and social housing Art. 2(1)(b)	Air or maritime links to islands Art. 2(1)(c)	Airports and ports Art. 2(1)(d)	Compensation for general PSO (*inter alia* annual compensation < €30M) Art. 2(1)(a)	Other and/or comments
Czech Rep. 2006-2008	✓	×	✓ Airports	Only total figure provided, no specific split or indication by type of SGEI.	
Czech Rep. 2009-2011	✓	×	✓ Airports	Social services, public sports grounds or public facilities and undertakings providing economic development and regional stability No details provided	
Germany 2006-2008	✓	×	✓ (possibly 1 airport)		Only a few social activities considered to be economic in Germany as most carried out without profit. Example provided in report is family vacation holiday sites. Extensive discussion about the legislative and financial framework for (i) hospitals and (ii) social housing. Report also provides views on the Altmark Package and ways to improve it.

106 Commission Decision of 28 November 2005 on the application of Article 86(2) of the EC Treaty to State aid in the form of public service compensation granted to certain undertakings entrusted with the operation of services of general economic interest, OJ L 312, 29.11.2005, p. 67. The reports can be found on the DG Competition website – 'State aid', 'Public services and competition'.

Country	Hospitals and social housing Art. 2(1)(b)	Air or maritime links to islands Art. 2(1)(c)	Airports and ports Art. 2(1)(d)	Compensation for general PSO (*inter alia* annual compensation < €30M) Art. 2(1)(a)	Other and/or comments
Germany 2009–2011	✓	✓	×		Detailed report and extensive number of annexes, including adding earlier report of Germany from 2008 covering SGEI generally.
Ireland 2008	(?) Hospitals	×	✓ Airports	No indication of SGEI falling within the general category.	Notes explaining hospital sector and harbour sector. Payment to harbours specifically excluded as SGEI since considered as payment for work done. Note on hospitals indicates that certain activities are SGEI. Unclear though if truly economic services.
Ireland 2009–2011	n/a	n/a	n/a	n/a	Not submitted.
France 2006–2008	✓	✓	✓	SGEI reported under this category cover: (i) social action programmes (ii) employment, training and apprenticeships	Detailed report. Report states that many activities falling within the general category are dealt with by local authorities, especially those of a social nature.
France 2009–2011	✓	✓	✓	SGEI reported under this category cover: (i) social action programmes (ii) employment, training and apprenticeships	Detailed report – content is very similar to 2008 report.
Lithuania 2006–2008	n/a	n/a	n/a	n/a	One-page letter in Lithuanian that appears to indicate that Decision is not applicable.
Lithuania 2009–2011	n/a	n/a	n/a	n/a	One page letter in Lithuanian that appears to indicate that Decision is not applicable.
Slovak Rep. 2006–2008	✓	×	×		Lengthy report focused on health and some social services. It largely describes the legislative framework as well as the rules for operating in the sector, including state controls over compensation.

Country	Hospitals and social housing Art. 2(1)(b)	Air or maritime links to islands Art. 2(1)(c)	Airports and ports Art. 2(1)(d)	Compensation for general PSO (*inter alia* annual compensation < €30M) Art. 2(1)(a)	Other and/or comments
Slovak Rep. 2009–2011	✓ Health	×	×	Report also covers SGEI relating to public broadcasting	
UK 2006–2008	✓	✓	✓		The report indicates that SGEI are limited and identifies the following such services: (i) air links to islands (ii) maritime links to islands (iii) airports (iv) NHS professionals (special health authority) (v) social housing (not specified).
UK 2009–2011	✓	✓	✓		The report simply provides the figures for the amount of compensation. The figures presumably relate to the same activities that were covered in the report for the period 2006–2008.

The 2011 SGEI Package places a particular emphasis on the need for Member State reporting and has strengthened the reporting obligations, in particular by requiring Member States to report every two years and to cover specific elements. Similar reporting obligations are included in the Commission Decision and in the Framework Communication.

The Framework states that the reports must provide an overview of the application of the (Framework) Communication to the different sectors of service providers, including:[107]

(i) a description of the application of the principles set out in this Communication to the services falling within its scope, including in-house activities;
(ii) the total amount of aid granted to undertakings falling within the scope of this Communication with a breakdown by the economic sector of the beneficiaries;
(iii) an indication of whether, for a particular type of service, the application of the principles set out in this Communication has given rise to difficulties or complaints by third parties; and
(iv) any other information concerning the application of the principles set out in this Communication required by the Commission and to be specified in due time before the report is to be submitted.

The first Member State reports were due to be submitted by 30 June 2014.

107 See Framework, para 62.

4. Sectoral Application of the Rules on SGEI

4.1. *Introduction*

The application of the EU Framework applicable to SGEI in particular sectors gives further insight into how the treatment of SGEI has developed under EU law. Experiences in (i) the energy sector and (ii) the environment and waste sector provide useful examples of the ongoing evolution.

4.2. *Energy*

4.2.1. Legal Framework

The possibility for Member States to identify SGEI in the energy sector[108] is specifically addressed in the electricity and gas market directives of the third energy package (and previously the second energy package).[109] The directives foresee SGEI (specifically referred to as PSOs in the directives) relating to (i) security and (ii) environmental protection.

Article 3(2) of the Directive 2009/72/EC of 13 July 2009 concerning common rules for the internal market in electricity (Electricity Directive) provides the following explanation about the nature of the PSOs in the sector (identical wording in included in the Gas Market Directive):[110]

> 'Member States may impose on undertakings operating in the electricity sector, *in the general economic interest, public service obligations which may relate to security, including security of supply, regularity, quality and price of supplies and environmental protection, including energy efficiency, energy from renewable sources and climate protection*. Such obligations shall be clearly defined, transparent, non-discriminatory, verifiable and shall guarantee equality of access for electricity undertakings of the Community to national consumers'[111] (emphasis added).

Furthermore, the Electricity Directive requires Member States to ensure that all household consumers of electricity benefit from a universal service. The Electricity

[108] For a discussion of the external dimension of the EU energy policy in the area of services of general interest, see Delimatsis, P., 'The External Dimension of Services of General Interest in the Area of Energy', TILEC Discussion Paper No. 2013–025.

[109] Directive 2003/54/EC of 26 June 2003 concerning common rules for the internal market in electricity, OJ L 176, 15.07.2003, p. 37; Directive 2003/55/EC of 26 June 2003 concerning common rules for the internal market in natural gas, OJ L 176, 15.07.2003, p. 57.

[110] Article 3(2) of Directive 2009/73/EC of the European Parliament and of the Council of 13 July 2009 concerning common rules for the internal market in natural gas and repealing Directive 2003/55/EC, OJ L 211, 14.08.2009, p. 94.

[111] Directive 2009/72/EC of the European Parliament and of the Council of 13 July 2009 concerning common rules for the internal market in electricity and repealing Directive 2003/54/EC, OJ L 211, 14.08.2009, p. 55.

Directive and the Gas Market Directive also require Member States to protect final customers and in particular vulnerable customers.

The Court of Justice has emphasised in a case involving the interpretation of the same provision in the earlier Gas Market Directive that the wording laid down only minimal common rules and that the PSO requirements had to be capable of being interpreted, subject to the observance of EU law, on a national basis and taking into account national circumstances,[112] thereby underlining the need to take into account specificities at the Member State level.

4.2.2. Commission Practice

Commission scrutiny of SGEI in the energy sector as regards their compatibility with the State aid rules has generally been limited given the strategic importance of the sector. In its report on the Application of EU State aid rules on SGEI since 2005 and the Outcome of the public consultation (2011), the Commission stated that it had limited experience concerning State aid granted as compensation for the fulfilment of PSOs in the electricity and gas sector.

> 'The Commission has received no State aid notifications in recent years concerning public service compensations related to the electricity universal service, public service obligations for vulnerable customers or customers in remote areas, or suppliers of last resort. A possible explanation is that, where SGEI obligations are imposed on incumbent operators who have in any event maintained a strong position on their home market, the Member States concerned can decide that no separate financial compensation is needed. In such cases, incumbents may be able to maintain the financial equilibrium of their operations overall, even though the costs of certain public service obligations imposed on them may exceed the revenues that these generate.'[113]

The SGEI that the Commission has scrutinised *relate principally to PSOs aimed at ensuring security of supply*, in particular in respect of EU territories where there is a lack of interconnection capacity.

(i) *Ireland – PSO in respect of new electricity generation capacity for security of supply (decision of 16 December 2003)*[114]

The Commission determined that a PSO scheme providing new electricity generation capacity in order to ensure security of supply in Ireland did not constitute State aid since it met the four criteria set out by the Court of Justice in the

112 Case C-265/08 *Federutility and Others v Autorità per l'energia elettrica e il gas* [2010] ECR I-3377, para. 30.

113 Commission staff working paper, 'The Application of EU State Aid rules on Services of General Economic Interest since 2005 and the Outcome of the Public Consultation', 23 March 2011, SEC(2011) 397, p. 16.

114 State aid N475/2003.

Altmark judgment. In the decision, the Commission emphasised the need for Member States to put in place policies to control growth on the demand side as well developing interconnection capacity, before introducing supply side measures on the basis of PSOs. However, it noted that 'the specific geographical situation of some Member States would not allow [them] to meet security of supply shortfalls via the increase of interconnectors in an economically rational way'.[115]
Furthermore, in its decision, the Commission stated that meeting security of supply via the setting up of sufficient reserve capacity can be considered in itself a service of general economic interest to the extent that (a) a clear distinction is made between 'normal' capacity and 'reserve' capacity, (b) the reserve capacity is the additional capacity that would not be spontaneously provided by normal market forces, but is considered necessary in order to meet peaks of demand, (c) the need for reserve capacity is clearly and quantitatively demonstrated, (d) it does not exceed reasonable standards of capacity reserve, and (e) provisions have been made to manage demand and to enable the use of existing interconnectors to mitigate part of the capacity shortfall if possible.[116] The Irish government had also brought sufficient evidence that there was indeed a need for an urgent reserve capacity increase in the Irish network in order to ensure security of supply.[117]

(ii) *Germany – Municipal guarantee for loan for geothermal heat distribution network (decision of 10 May 2010)*[118]

The Commission also examined a guarantee that was designed to allow the publicly owned geothermal heat provider (GTU) in the city of Unterschleissheim to extend the geothermal heat supply network within the territory of the city. The German government argued that the municipality's obligation to ensure affordable and reliable district heat supply to its citizens was a basic service of general interest and that market forces might not be sufficient to provide heat supply through geothermal heat distribution in a satisfactory manner to all citizens of Unterschleissheim.
Notwithstanding the existence of other heat distribution systems that could be furnished by the market, the Commission agreed with the existence of a SGEI and concluded the following:

> 'Although heat distribution – alternative to geothermical heat distribution – could also be and is actually ensured by private companies (i.a. through electric heating or individual boilers), this does not preclude that the provision of geothermical heat distribution to parts of the population may therefore constitute a genuine SGEI, since, there is no evidence that market forces would be able to provide this kind of services at the conditions specified by the responsible bodies in Germany.'[119]

115 State aid N475/2003, decision, para. 34.
116 State aid N475/2003, decision, para. 35.
117 State aid N475/2003, decision, para. 38.
118 State aid SA.31261 (2011/N).
119 State aid SA.31261 (2011/N), decision, para. 29.

'It can be concluded from the above that the German authorities acted within their discretion when they declared heat supply a service of general economic interest and that they applied this discretion without a manifest error of assessment.'[120]

It is noteworthy, however, that the Commission's decision does not discuss the existence of a competing market driven system of heat distribution and its implications for the SGEI.

(iii) *Spain – PSO compensation linked to a preferential dispatch mechanism for indigenous coal power plants (decision of 29 October 2010)*[121]

The Commission carried out an in-depth analysis of a scheme that was intended to compensate owners of ten power plants running on indigenous coal (together with other fuels) for producing certain volumes of electricity out of indigenous coal. The Spanish government considered that the measures were necessary to address concerns relating to security of energy supply due to (a) the increase of electricity production from renewable energy sources (RES), (b) the fact that electricity production from RES is 'intermittent' and (c) the lack of adequate interconnection capacities between Spain and other EU countries.

The Commission found that there was the presence of a genuine SGEI, taking into account in particular the specific provisions in the second electricity Directive. Notably, the second Electricity Directive allowed Member States for security of supply reasons – provided certain conditions were met – to regard production obligations imposed on power plants using indigenous primary energy resources as public service obligations.

Following an in-depth investigation, the Commission did not find that the Spanish authorities had exceeded their margin of discretion when determining that the notified measure is a service of general economic interest. It highlighted, amongst other things, that market forces were not expected by themselves deliver the necessary additional capacities, interconnection capacity would continue to remain modest, renewable-based electricity production was intermittent, a full switch to imported coal could not be done rapidly for certain power plants and dependency on imported fossil gave rise to strategic risks.[122]

120 State aid SA.31261 (2011/N), decision, para. 30.

121 State aid No N178/2010. The Commission's decision was challenged before the General Court by a number of interested parties seeking annulment of the decision, and interim measures. The cases were withdrawn, but not before the President of the General Court had examined whether the provisional suspension of the Commission's decision ordered on 3 November 2010 should be maintained or whether, on the contrary, it should be lifted as soon as possible. Case T-484/10 R, T-486/10 R, T-490/10 R and T-520/10 R *Gas Natural Fenosa SDG, Iberdrola, Endesa & Endesa Generaçion and Comunidad Autonóma de Galicia v Commission*. See Court of Justice press release No 11/11, Luxembourg, 17 February 2011. For a discussion of the Commission's decision, the facts of the case and the issue of State aid to the coal industry in Spain, see Pérez Romero, Sonia, 'The Coal industry: Past or future energy production in Spain', *EStAL* 2011, 10(3) 565–574.

122 State aid No N178/2010, decision, section 3.1.

(iv) *Italy – Prolongation of scheme for compensation of instant interrupt ability services in Sardinia and Sicily (decision of 3 October 2012)*[123]

The Commission authorised the prolongation until 2015 of an Italian scheme which remunerates electricity companies for the provision of instant interruptibility services in Italy's largest islands, Sardinia and Sicily. Such services are typically provided by large electricity consumers, which accept cuts in their electricity supply without prior notice, to the transmission system operator (the TSO). The Commission found, in particular, that these services were still needed in order to ensure a high level of security and continuity of supply in Sardinia and Sicily. The service was also remunerated at market value; therefore the scheme did not constitute State aid. However, this finding was limited until the end of 2015 (three years). The initial 2010 decision specifically highlighted that the scheme specifically pursued objectives of general economic interest.

The Commission has been prepared to *open in-depth state aid investigations where it has had doubts the PSO schemes are necessary and well designed to perform SGEI aimed at ensuring security of supply.* In two specific instances, notifications were withdrawn by the Member States concerned following an in-depth investigation. In both cases, the schemes appeared to be predominantly to the benefit of the incumbent energy supplier.

(i) *Estonia – Aid for capacity payments for oil-shale fuelled electricity production (ET) (decision of 30 June 2011 – withdrawal)*[124]

The Commission opened an in-depth investigation into an Estonian project to grant state support of up to €1.5 billion spread over 20 years to the operators of two newly-constructed 300 MW power plants. The aid would have been paid for the mere availability of the plants, provided that they were mainly fuelled with oil-shale, a hydrocarbon widely available in Estonia. Estonia claimed that the aid was necessary to increase the security of energy supply. While the Commission acknowledged the importance of securing energy supplies, it had doubts that the proposed Estonian measure would be the least distortive means to achieve this objective. In particular, large-scale subsidies would have been allocated over a long period without a tender procedure.

(ii) *Malta – Environmental project for Delimara power station (decision of 6 February 2012 – withdrawal)*[125]

Under the plan notified to the Commission, Malta intended to support the modification of two boilers at the Delimara power station, which was owned and

123 State aid SA.35119 (2012/N) and NN24/2010.

124 SA.30531, Commission Press release: 'State aid: Commission opens in-depth investigation into grants for new oil-shale fuelled power plants in Estonia' (IP/11/349 – 23 March 2011). Decision to close investigation, OJ C 235, 11.08.2011, p. 8.

125 SA.29427, Commission Press release: 'State aid: Commission opens in-depth investigation into planned investment at Delimara Power Plant in Malta' (IP/10/1518 – 17 November 2010). Decision to close investigation, OJ C 278, 14.09.2012, p. 4.

operated by the State-owned electricity producer Enemalta. Malta argued, amongst other things, that the investment would extend the useful life of the boilers and serve to provide back-up capacity in case of supply disruptions. However, some of the investments seemed destined exclusively to reduce harmful dust emissions up to the requisite EU environmental level, and not to extend the life of the boilers. Moreover, the planned electricity interconnector with Sicily would have also considerably increased the future capacity of supply in Malta. Therefore, the Commission could not come to the conclusion that the planned investment subsidy was a compensation for the performance a service of general economic interest in line with EU rules.

4.3. *Environment and Waste*

The Commission has stated that it has had relatively limited exposure to SGEI in the environment and waste sectors and indicated in its report on the Application of EU State aid rules on SGEI since 2005 that:

> 'Member States have not notified to the Commission any plans to grant compensation for the provision of waste or water SGEI pursuant to Article 106(2) of the Treaty. This may owe something to the fact that the services provided are often local in nature, and so may fall within the thresholds in the SGEI Decision. However, where the local area concerned is a major city or broader agglomeration, the contracts concerned might typically be worth dozens of millions of Euros per year.'[126]

There is, however, an increasing body of case law that deals with SGEI in the waste sector, in particular. In the FFAD judgment, the Court of Justice stated that '[t]he management of particular waste may properly be considered to be capable of forming the subject of a service of general economic interest, particularly where the service is designed to deal with an environmental problem'.[127] The Commission has also approved compensation granted for the provision of an SGEI concerning hazardous waste disposal emphasising that 'there is an obvious public interest in appropriate treatment when hazardous waste is disposed of. There is as well a public and Community interest in ensuring the availability of sufficient domestic capacity for such disposal'.[128] In response to a Parliamentary question, Commissioner Almunia also indicated that 'the collection and sorting of bulky waste could in principle be an area that could be defined as a Service of General Economic Interest (SGEI)'.[129]

126 Commission staff working paper, SEC(2011) 397, pp. 17–18.

127 Case C-209/98, *Entreprenørforeningens Affalds/Miljøsektion (FFAD) v Københavns Kommune* [2000] ECR I-37777, para. 75.

128 C43/2003 CR43/03 – Aid in favour of AVR for treatment of 'C2' hazardous waste Commission decision of 22 June 2005, OJ L 84, 23.03.2006, p.84, para 79. See, however, Case C-126/01, *Ministère de l'Économie, des Finances et de l'Industrie v GEMO* [2003] ECR I-13769.

129 Question for written answer to the Commission (Rule 117), Françoise Castex (S&D), 21 November 2011 (E-010721/2011). Subject: Collection and sorting of bulky waste and services of general economic interest.

In the past, the Commission has also accepted the definition of the collection and subsequent destruction of carcasses and other animal waste that was unfit for consumption as an SGEI for the period 1999 to 2005 as an SGEI given the specific health context.[130] However, more recently the Commission determined that compensation paid by the German State to the Zweckverband Tierkörperbeseititgung (Association for Animal Carcass Disposal) in certain regions of Germany to ensure the safe disposal of specific forms of animal waste could not be classed as an SGEI since it was not fundamentally different from other economic activities. In addition, the introduction of specific EU rules, in particular provisions obliging the polluter to bear the cost of the disposal of the specific animal waste material, meant that there was no scope for the State to take on part of the cost on the grounds that the service was an SGEI. The Commission also determined that the obligation on the Zweckverband to maintain an epidemic reserve capacity could not be deemed to constitute an SGEI.[131] The Commission's decision was challenged by Germany and the association, but it was recently upheld by the General Court.[132]

In the area of nature conservation, the Commission has also accepted the existence of SGEI. It decided that the transfer of federal-owned natural heritage sites to the German regions and the German environment foundation as well as the funding of large-scale nature conservation projects could be classified as SGEI. It stated that:

> 'These tasks, which can be construed as services rendered to all citizens, clearly fall within the remit of the State acting as public authority, which however may find it appropriate to entrust them to other entities, for example for budgetary reasons. In that sense, the scheme differs from a classical environmental aid measure: in the latter case the activities which are beneficial for the environment cannot be carried out by the State, but can only be carried out by undertakings on a voluntary basis. Therefore, the Commission accepts that the conservation tasks at issue may constitute a service of general interest.'[133]

The notified schemes were nonetheless held to constitute State aid by the Commission, although they were declared to be compatible with the internal market. Germany challenged the Commission's findings before the General Court arguing that it was wrong to regard environmental organisations which did not pursue an economic aim

130 State aid C 3/09 (ex NN 41 A-B/03) implemented by Portugal for the collection, transportation, treatment and destruction of slaughterhouse waste (notified under document C(2011) 4888), Commission decision of 13 July 2011, OJ L 274, 19.10.2011, p. 15.

131 State aid SA.25051 (C 19/10) (ex NN 23/10) granted by Germany to the Zweckverband Tierkörperbeseitigung in Rhineland-Palatinate, Saarland, Rheingau-Taunus-Kreis and Landkreis Limburg-Weilburg (notified under document C(2012) 2557), Commission decision of 25 April 2012, paras 167 – 178.

132 Case T-295/12 *Germany v Commission*, judgment 16 July 2014, not yet published; Case T-309/12 *Zweckverband Tierkörperbeseitigung in Rheinland-Pfalz, im Saarland, im Rheingau-Taunus-Kreis und im Landkreis Limburg-Weilburg v European Commission*, judgment 16 July 2014, not yet published.

133 State aid NN8/2009 Transfer of natural protection areas to new owners and measures for bio diversity, Commission decision of 2 July 2009, para 58.

and the object of which was an activity in the general interest as 'undertakings' for the purposes of State aid rules.

The General Court ruled that through their secondary activities (e.g. sale of wood or rights for hunting and fishing), environmental organisations were offering products and services to the market.[134] It also stated that these activities have not and are not necessarily provided by public bodies. Furthermore, they were not legally obliged to provide these secondary activities, and by providing these activities, the environmental organisations were pursuing a distinct interest, which was separable from purely socially beneficial goal of environmental protection. The environmental organisations were carrying out economic activities even if the provision of the goods and services was being carried out without profit.[135]

In addition, the Commission was satisfied that a Dutch scheme concerning the acquisition of land for sustainable nature conservation management formed part of that wider purpose and justified the establishment of public service obligations.[136]

5. Conclusion

Of the five branches of EU competition law (restrictive practices, abuse of dominance, concentration control, State aid, SGEI and public undertakings) the last one remains the most opaque and the least developed by far. The updated 'Altmark Package' of 2011, which required Member States to report to the Commission by the end of June 2014, provides some clarity, but also raises new questions.

We have tried in this chapter to set out the currently applicable law and to apply it in some of the sectors where we expect particular problems, i.e. in energy, environment and waste management and to shed some light on the application of the rules to in-house services. Some fundamental questions remain, in particular:

- How can the very large discretion of Member States (motivated by 'subsidiarity', and appropriately so, or does subsidiarity serve as an excuse for lack of unity at the EU level?) be reconciled with the 'now', since the Lisbon Treaty, exclusive competence of the EU in EU competition matters.
- EU competition law is characterised by a large field of application, and subsequent exemption of practices (agreements, concerted practices, State aid, etc.). The *Altmark* judgment (and other judgments such as *Stardust Marine* or, outside State aid, *Wouters*)[137] is not consistent with that overall structure, as it limits the field of application by referring to grounds which one would normally expect to serve as exemption grounds at best. The Commission's Altmark Package can be seen as an effort to come to grips (to limit the effects of?) this inconsistency.

134 Case T-347/09 *Germany v Commission*, judgment 12 September 2013.
135 See paras. 39–43 of the judgment.
136 State aid SA.31243 (N308/2010) – Commission decision on a subsidy scheme for acquisition of land for nature conservation (Netherlands), 13 July 2011.
137 C-482/99 *France v Commission* [2002] ECR I-4397; *Wouters, Savelbergh and Price Waterhouse Belastingadviseurs BV v Algemene Raad van de Nederlandse Orde van Advocaten* [2002] ECR I-1577.

However laudable in principle the guidance in the updated Altmark Package may be, it also raises new questions, for example:

- To the extent that the Commission suggests that what is an economic activity can change from one Member State to another, this appears to implicitly but necessarily imply that economic activities are not activities which *can be offered* on a market according to market principles but activities which *are offered* on a market. The difference is of the essence. Under the first view, an activity which a Member State prefers to provide through a monopoly (e.g. waste management), fully in-house or not, is economic so that State aid rules, including the Altmark Package rules, can apply. Under the second view, EU competition law may simply not apply so that Member States do not have to worry about (reporting under) the Altmark Package.
- The Commission suggests, in the 'Format for reporting' under the updated Altmark Package, that Member States should report about in-house services. However, the notion of 'undertaking' requires not only an economic activity, but also an entity which is sufficiently independent. In the hierarchy of norms, this notion of 'undertaking' is safeguarded by the TFEU as interpreted by the Court of Justice, and therefore takes priority over Commission Decisions and Regulations (and *a fortiori* over Commission Communications). It is currently unclear for Member States which have engaged in forms of corporatisation – which comes in many variants of continued dependency on the State – whether or not these corporatised activities come under the scope of EU competition in general, and State aid rules in particular.

As to reporting under the Altmark Package, it is simply chaotic as appears from the comparison of Member State reporting in this chapter. Some Member States report much, others (almost) nothing; in some Member States regional and local authorities report and in others they do not; the range of activities covered is much more diverse than even subsidiarity can explain; and the format of reporting, even within one Member State, is extremely diverse, ranging from paragraphs to simple copies of legislation. Given the continued lack of clarity on, among other things, the economic nature of an activity and the degree of independence required for the reporting requirement to apply to in-house services, it can be expected (a) that reporting after the update of the Altmark Package will hardly be more consistent and (b) that Member States can hardly be blamed.

Generally, Member States should be fully aware of the consequences of reporting under the updated Altmark Package. As reporting requirements are inserted in the Decision (which in reality is a block exemption Regulation) and in the Framework Communication, Member States can, having made their report, no longer argue (a) that EU competition law does not apply to their case (e.g. no entity or no economic activity and therefore no undertaking, excluded sector, no cross-border impact) or (b) that the cumulative conditions for qualification as State aid are not fulfilled (e.g. no financial transfer, no artificial advantage, no selectivity, *de minimis* applicable, no State resources involved, no distortion of competition).

COMPENSATION FOR THE NET EXTRA COSTS OF PUBLIC SERVICE OBLIGATIONS

Phedon Nicolaides*

1. Introduction

The calculation of the compensation to be offered to providers of services of general economic interest (SGEI) is always a difficult and complex process. In order to be able to calculate the amount of compensation, it is first necessary to identify the relevant costs and revenues. These costs and revenues are those directly linked to the SGEI or the public service obligation (PSO).[1] This implies that before it is possible to count costs and revenues, it is essential to establish whether such costs and revenues are linked to a genuine SGEI or PSO.

The purpose of this chapter is to examine recent case law of EU courts and the decisional practice of the European Commission on methods of public service compensation (PSC) which are compatible with the internal market. The review of case law and Commission practice leads to the following findings.

First, in order to calculate the compensation properly, the public authority that imposes the PSO must start with the correct definition of the obligation itself. Correct definition leads to correct identification of eligible costs.

Second, despite the fact that the case law acknowledges that Member States are free to define SGEI, the services they classify as SGEI must be those which are not provided or satisfactorily provided by the market. Therefore, it is necessary to carry out a market survey or analysis to establish what the market fails to supply or offer at the required level of quality and affordable price.

Third, the providers of SGEI must be entrusted with specific tasks. This act of entrustment has economic and legal consequences that go beyond the signing of a contract between a public authority and one or more undertakings. In practice, it means

* Jan Tinbergen Professor of European Economics at the College of Europe, Bruges.

1 Following the judgment of the General Court in case T-289/03, *BUPA*, I consider that SGEI is interchangeable with PSO.

that SGEI providers are compelled to offer a well-defined service whose costs cannot be avoided and therefore they can be quantified later on for the purpose of calculating the amount of required compensation.

Fourth, the parameters of compensation must be determined in advance. Public authorities need to define the method or formula on the basis of which the compensation will eventually be calculated. In practice, this lays down another ceiling on the maximum amount of compensation that can be granted. It also precludes *ex post* allocation of costs and revenue between different services which may or may not fall within the SGEI scope.

Fifth, Member States need to ensure that the providers of SGEI are not over-compensated. In this respect, Member States are free to bundle together profitable with unprofitable segments of the market or related services, but in all cases they must be in a position to identify the costs and revenue which correspond to the defined SGEI or entrusted PSO.

The chapter starts first with three clarifications concerning the distinction between Altmark criteria and the criteria for compatibility of State aid granted in the form of PSC. Then it considers the relationship between SGEI and market failure and identifies the conditions that must be satisfied in order for PSC to be compatible with the internal market.

2. Clarifications: (i) Altmark vs. market economy investor principle, (ii) Altmark vs. compatible State aid, (iii) Altmark vs. Article 106(2) TFEU

Before proceeding to examine how the PSC may be calculated, it is instructive to make several important clarifications. As is well-known from the Altmark judgment,[2] PSC that satisfies the four criteria laid down by the Court of Justice does not constitute State aid in the meaning of Article 107(1) TFEU.

It is also possible that financial contribution by a public authority may not constitute State aid either if it conforms with the market economy investor principle (MEIP) or the synonymous market economy operator test (MEOT). In both cases, transfer of state resources falls outside the scope of Article 107(1).

Recently the Commission had occasion to explain the important difference between payments that satisfy the Altmark criteria and financial contributions that conform to the MEIP or MEOT.

In its Decision in case SA.32014 concerning PSC for the Sardinian ferry company Saremar, the Commission explained that:

> '[I]t is necessary to distinguish between application of the MEIP test and the fulfilment of the Altmark criteria. While both tests serve to assess the existence of an advantage for the beneficiary, they clearly refer to the different roles that public authorities can take when adopting financial measures in favour of a given undertaking. The MEIP applies when the public authorities act in their role of shareholders (i.e. in the first place with a view to obtain a profit from the operation), whilst Altmark is relevant when the public authorities pursue

2 Case C-280/00 *Altmark Trans.*

public interest objectives, which are not typical of a private operator (i.e. the perspective to make a profit is of secondary importance, if any).'[3]

The Commission also stressed that a measure could only be MEIP-compliant if it were based on sound viability perspectives for the beneficiary. No *ex ante* business plan had been prepared in the case of Saremar. Since the compensation could not be ascribed to the State acting as shareholder, it did not conform to the MEIP.

A second issue that needs to be clarified is the difference between compensation that complies with the Altmark criteria and compensation that is State aid but is compatible with the internal market. Obviously, the primary difference is the existence of State aid.

A close reading of the Commission Decision 2012/21[4] exempting PSC from notification and the Commission Communication on the EU Framework for notification of PSC[5] indicates that PSC is deemed to be compatible with the internal market when it satisfies the first three Altmark criteria: (i) definition of a genuine SGEI and entrustment through an act of a public authority, (ii) *ex ante* establishment of parameters of compensation and (iii) compensation many not exceed the net extra costs of PSO. It follows that the difference between Altmark-compatible compensation and compensation of compatible State aid is, in the case of the latter, the non-compliance with the fourth Altmark criterion: selection via a competitive procedure or that the chosen operator is efficient by industry standards.

One would have thought that the requirements for payments that do not constitute State aid would be more stringent than the requirements for payments that do constitute State aid. However, as shown later on, this belief is wrong because the Commission Decision and especially the Framework on PSC contain several additional requirements which are not mentioned in the Altmark judgment of the Court of Justice, as for example, the limitation of eligible costs to the net avoidable costs, the limitation of reasonable profit to the swap rate plus 1% and the imposition of efficiency requirements on SGEI providers.

A third question that often arises is the relationship between the Altmark criteria and the criteria in Article 106(2) TFEU. The General Court has confirmed that the first three Altmark criteria coincide with the criteria of exemption in Article 106(2). In the Brussels hospitals case, the General Court explained that 'the fourth Altmark criterion is not taken into account for assessing the compatibility of aid measures under Article 106(2)'.[6]

In a later judgment, the General Court elaborated that although the economic efficiency of the SGEI provider is a factor that must be taken into account in the fourth Altmark criterion, it has no 'pertinence' or relevance in the assessment of the compatibility of compensation on the basis of Article 106(2).[7] According to the General Court, the

3 Ibid, para. 168.
4 OJ L7, 11 January 2012.
5 OJ C8, 11 January 2012.
6 T-137/10, *CBI v European Commission*, para. 192.
7 T-275/11, *French Television 1 v European Commission*, para. 130.

exception in Article 106(2) allows Member States to choose the providers of SGEI. The requirement of proportionality of the aid aims to prevent SGEI providers from receiving funding that exceeds the net extra costs of the SGEI.

3. What Constitutes a Genuine SGEI?

The Court of Justice and the General Court have stipulated in several seminal cases that SGEIs are services that exhibit 'special characteristics' as compared with those of other economic activities.[8] However, although they have referred to such issues as universal provision of SGEI, they have not specified in an exhaustive manner what those special characteristics may be. It is up to Member States to define what they consider as SGEI and justify why they consider certain services as SGEI.

Even though we do not have a comprehensive definition, in several cases EU courts have defined essential elements that must be present in any SGEI. These elements are: (i) failure of the market to supply the desired service (at a satisfactory price, quality, terms, or geographic coverage),[9, 10] (ii) the service is provided to all those who are deemed to need the service (universality),[11] and (iii) the provider is compelled to supply the desired service.[12]

Very recently, in *Colt Telecom v European Commission*, the General Court explicitly stated that the existence of a market failure is a prerequisite for qualifying an activity as an SGEI.[13] The Court then went on to note that market failure is an 'objective concept' that depends on the factual situation in the market.[14]

In this particular case, the issue at hand was the imposition of PSO on broadband providers in the greater Paris area, which is one of the most networked places in Europe. The French authorities argued that areas of high coverage were adjacent to areas of low coverage and bundled together areas of different coverage. The General Court accepted that the coverage of profitable areas did not necessarily mean that the aid was excessive, since it was a source of income that could be used to finance coverage of the unprofitable areas and thus to reduce the amount of the aid.[15]

It is now obvious that the inability or unwillingness of the market to supply the desired service is critical in the classification of a service as an SGEI. The Commission Communication on compensation for SGEI is explicit on this point. Accordingly, it follows from Article 106(2) TFEU that 'undertakings entrusted with operation of SGEIs are undertakings entrusted with "a particular task". The entrustment of a "particular public service task" implies the supply of services which, if it were considering its own

8 See C-179/90, *Merci convenzionali porto di Genova*; C-242/95, *GT-Link*; C-266/96, *Corsica Ferries*; T-289/03, *BUPA*.
9 C-205/99, *Analir*.
10 T-79/10, *Colt Telecom v European Commission*.
11 T-289/03, *BUPA*.
12 Ibid.
13 T-79/10, *Colt Telecom v European Commission*, para. 154.
14 Ibid, para. 158.
15 Ibid, para. 186.

commercial interest, an undertaking would not assume or would not assume to the same extent or under the same conditions.'[16] Similarly the EU Framework explains that 'Member States cannot attach specific PSO to services that are already provided or can be provided satisfactorily and under conditions, such as price, objective quality characteristics, continuity and access to the service, consistent with the public interest, as defined by the State, by undertakings operating under normal market conditions.'[17]

Therefore, the first step in calculating any compensation is in determining whether the service in question is already supplied or can be supplied by the market at a satisfactory price, quality or other desired terms.

4. Under-Provision by the Market

Recent decisional practice of the Commission offers useful guidance on how to determine whether the market fails to supply the service in question.

In the *Saremar* case mentioned above the Commission accepted that although the operation of the routes between Sardinia and mainland Italy was not explicitly described as an SGEI, it could in principle be considered to be an SGEI because the entrustment acts referred to affordability of fares as a general pre-requisite of operation. But then in order to verify the existence of the PSOs entrusted to Saremar and whether it was necessary to compensate the latter for the supplementary costs incurred in meeting those obligations, the Commission examined:

(a) first, whether the service was inadequate, had its provision been left to the market forces alone in the light of the public service requirement concerning affordable fares, and
(b) second, whether the operator was indeed entrusted with public service obligations which were clearly defined.

We see in this case a perfect application of the two fundamental features of an SGEI: under-provision by the market and compulsion of market operators to offer the service.

The Commission found that at least during the summer months, demand was high enough and that the market could provide the required services. Moreover, the fares charged by Saremar were comparable and sometimes higher than those charged by other companies. During the winter season, the services were not disrupted and again the fares charged were not dissimilar to those charged by competitors. The Commission noted that the entrustment acts did not impose on other PSOs as regards the frequency, capacity, or regularity of the (mixed) services offered by Saremar. Therefore, the market did not appear to fail to supply the service.

With respect to whether Saremar was entrusted with clearly defined PSOs, the Commission noted that the precise routes to be operated were not chosen by the Sardinian authorities but rather left at the discretion of the operator. No specific obligation to

16 Ibid, para. 47.
17 SA.32015, *Saremar*, para. 13.

charge reduced fares on the designated routes was imposed on Saremar. Although a 15% discount applied to Sardinian residents, there was no specification of the precise level of fares to be charged by Saremar.

In the end the Commission found that:

> '[A] large discretion has been left to Saremar to adapt fares. Saremar retained the faculty to adjust fares so as to ensure economic viability of the activity and customer satisfaction. The Commission notes that SGEIs are by nature services which address market failures as the market does not autonomously provide them to the standard required by the public authority. Whilst the Commission considers that some flexibility with regard to prices may be left in some cases to public service providers, when the alleged public service obligation relates precisely to the necessity to offer affordable fares, the public authorities must define the maximum fares that the operator can apply or link that flexibility either to objective criteria, which allow to determine with a reasonable degree of certainty what fare level is to be considered as affordable, or to a prior authorisation procedure by the entrusting authority.'[18]

> 'In the present case, however, the provisions concerning applicable fares in the entrustment acts are not sufficiently precise so as to qualify as clearly defined PSOs ... Saremar's margin of manoeuvre was not linked to objective criteria or at least to criteria that were applied in an objective way.'[19]

On the basis of the above findings, the Commission inevitably concluded that the service provided by Saremar was no SGEI and that no PSO obligation was imposed on Saremar that could justify compensation.

A related case concerning transport between the island of Corsica and mainland France was subject of Commission Decision 2013/435.[20] It assessed aid granted by France to Société Nationale Maritime Corse-Méditerranée. The Commission examined whether the scope of the public service as defined by the public service delegation contract was necessary and proportionate to a 'real public service need', manifested by shortage of regular transport services in a situation of free competition. The Commission considered that the scope of the public service remit as defined by a public service contract had to be necessary and proportionate to a real public service need, as demonstrated by the 'lack of regular transport services under normal market conditions'.[21]

The Commission accepted that it would be legitimate, in circumstances where transport demand showed a marked seasonality, to include services for both peak and off-peak periods within the public service remit. On the basis of these considerations, the Commission made a distinction between 'basic' and 'additional' services. Additional

18 Ibid, para. 214.
19 Ibid, para. 215.
20 OJ L220, 18 August 2013.
21 Ibid, para. 136.

services were also offered by other market operators. The approach of the Commission was that additional services could be included in the public service remit if it could be determined that they were 'essential to the basic service, on the grounds of a set of technical and economic considerations.'[22] In certain circumstances, extending the scope of the public service may be justified in the presence of well-established complementary technical or economic efficiency considerations (synergies).

After thorough market analysis the Commission concluded that the operation of the additional services did not seem to be indispensable to the basic service. There was no technical complementarity between the basic service and the additional service.

The Commission stated 'that Member States may not impose specific public service obligations for services that are already provided or can be provided satisfactorily in conditions (price, objective quality features, continuity and access to the service) that are compatible with the public interest, as defined by the State, by companies operating under normal market conditions.'[23]

Although it rejected the claim that the additional services were not adequately provided by the market (in fact there was substitutability between the additional services and other services provided by market operators), the Commission accepted that the basic services could indeed be classified as SGEI because they ensured 'a minimum territorial continuity' between mainland France and Corsica. There was clearly under-provision by the market during the winter months of low tourism. The Commission considered 'that the shortage of private initiative on each line in relation to a clearly identified need for transport during the off-peak periods of the year alone is sufficient to justify the inclusion of the basic service within the scope of the public service for the whole year for all these lines.'[24]

More recently, the Commission, in Decision SA.34155 concerning compensation of school bus transport in Rhineland-Palatinate, Germany, accepted that the German authorities had identified a genuine SGEI by imposing a PSO on all bus and tram undertakings in the Land Rhineland-Palatinate. The PSO obliged them to offer reduced rates to students amounting to at least 15% of the standard rate for adults. In this case the market provided all the required services but not at an affordable price for students.

In conclusion, we see that SGEIs do not have to comprise services that are not provided at all by the market. In the Corsica case, the SGEI covered only basic services. In the Sardinia case, the SGEI could in principle cover services in a specific time period (winter) or at specific price level (affordable). In the Paris broadband case, the SGEI was a bundle of different geographic areas. Lastly, in the Rhineland-Palatinate case, the SGEI was the provision of the same service as that already offered by the market but at a 15% discount.

22 Ibid, para. 139.
23 Ibid, para. 166.
24 Ibid, para. 147.

5. Pre-Determined Parameters of Compensation and No Over-Compensation

In the *Saremar* case the Commission found that there was no explicit reference to any compensation to be granted to Saremar. Moreover, Saremar was given a margin of manoeuvre to adjust its fares precisely in order to break even. For these two reasons the Commission concluded that the parameters for the calculation of compensation were not established in advance in an objective and transparent manner. The Commission also rejected a compensation mechanism that was developed *ex post*.

Because Saremar was not entrusted with an obligation clearly defining the level of fares that were considered as affordable, it was impossible to define parameters of compensation. This is because the parameters for calculating the compensation for the discharge of PSOs concerning affordable fares must necessarily be linked to the level of fares considered affordable. Since that level was not clearly defined, the parameters for calculating the compensation could not be considered as established in advance in an objective and transparent manner.

Given that the Commission already concluded that the Sardinian authorities did not demonstrate the existence of a real public service need, it considered that Saremar was not entitled to receive any compensation.

The Italian authorities responded that the compensation was lower than the loss incurred by Saremar in serving the routes between Sardinia and the mainland and that it had been calculated according to the separate accounts for those routes. Therefore, compensation could not benefit any other activity of Saremar. The Commission rejected this argument on the grounds that in the absence of a clear definition of the obligations imposed on Saremar it was impossible to calculate the costs ensuing from those obligations.

In its Decision 2014/201 on compensation that was to be paid to the Italian bus company Simet for public transport services, the Commission also examined in detail whether 'parameters of compensation' has been objectively defined in advance and whether over-compensation could be avoided.[25] Simet was a private company providing scheduled passenger transport services by bus based on concessions granted by the Italian authorities. In addition to these services, which accounted for approximately two thirds of its revenue, Simet also provided other services, including international travel services, tourism services and bus hire with driver, which accounted for the remaining third of its revenue.

Simet, like other providers of inter-regional scheduled bus services in Italy, operated on the basis of licences (concessions) which were renewed annually at the request of the company. Those concessions gave the company the exclusive right to provide the relevant services. The fares proposed by the company itself were also reflected in the annual concession specifications defined by the Ministry for Infrastructure and Transport.

[25] OJ L114, 16 March 2014.

The Commission considered that no parameters were ever established in advance in an objective and transparent manner.[26] This meant that compensation calculations were necessarily based solely on *ex post* estimates of the net costs. In the absence of compensation parameters laid down in advance, any cost allocation would necessarily be conducted *ex post* on the basis of arbitrary assumptions.

Simet did not apply proper account separation. Consequently, it was impossible to demonstrate that compensation did not exceed the amount corresponding to the net financial effect of the public service obligation on the costs and revenues of Simet.

More importantly, the Commission did not accept the derived (*ex post*) costs which were based on the assumption that in each year all services provided by Simet had to bear costs which were in the same proportion as their revenues. An *ex post* calculation would 'necessarily result in full compensation of the costs incurred in the provision of the service'.

With respect to ensuring that there is no over-compensation, the Commission demonstrated how this should be done properly in its decision concerning the tariff reduction for transportation of students in the Land Rhineland-Palatinate. Germany imposed two ceilings on the maximum amount of compensation: (i) the amount could not exceed the difference between the normal ticket price for adults and the 15% lower price for students multiplied by the number of student passengers, and (ii) the amount could not exceed the net costs, if any, of transporting students.

This case demonstrates two important aspects of compensation. First, a PSO does not necessarily result in net losses for the undertakings on which the PSO is imposed. The mere fact that bus and tram operators in Land Rhineland-Palatinate had to price student tickets at a 15% discount did not mean that they actually suffered losses. It could only mean that their profits per ticket were reduced, but not to an extent that would make it financially impossible for them to operate the service in question. Second, irrespective of the specific method that each Member State uses to calculate the amount of compensation, it must be ensured at all times that the 3rd Altmark criterion and the corresponding requirements in the 2012 SGEI package (i.e. the Commission Decision and the EU Framework) are respected. Compensation may not exceed the extra net costs of the PSO.

6. Conclusions

The review of recent case law and decisional practice of the Commission on compensation for the next extra costs of public service obligations reveals that in order to calculate the compensation properly the public authority that imposes the PSO must start with the correct definition of the obligation itself. Correct definition leads to correct identification of eligible costs. The following tasks must be undertaken.

First, despite the discretion of Member States to define SGEI, the services they classify as SGEI must be those which are not provided or satisfactorily provided by the market. Therefore, it is necessary to carry out a market survey or analysis to establish what the market fails to supply or offer at the required level of quality and affordable price.

[26] Ibid, para. 93.

Second, the providers of SGEI must be entrusted with specific tasks. In practice this act of entrustment means that SGEI providers are compelled to offer a well-defined service whose costs cannot be avoided and therefore they can be quantified later on for the purpose of calculating the amount of required compensation.

Third, the parameters of compensation must be determined in advance. Public authorities need to define the method or formula on the basis of which the compensation will eventually be calculated. In practice, this puts another ceiling on the maximum amount of compensation that can be granted. It also precludes *ex post* allocation of costs and revenue between different services which may or may not fall within the SGEI scope, even if the allocation is done on the basis of widely acceptable accounting conventions.

Fourth, Member States need to ensure that the providers of SGEI are not over-compensated. In this respect, Member States are free to bundle together profitable with unprofitable segments of the market or related services, but in all cases they must be in a position to identify the costs and revenue which correspond to the defined SGEI or entrusted PSO.

TO PROCURE OR NOT TO PROCURE? THAT'S THE QUESTION!

Sarah Schoenmaekers*

When bodies established to meet needs in the general interest plan to purchase new goods, supplies or services, they have to consider whether or not they should apply a European public procurement procedure. This is often not an easy task.

First of all, it is not always straightforward for a particular entity to determine whether it falls within the scope of the European public procurement regulation. Directive 2014/24/EU on Public Procurement,[1] also called 'the General Procurement Directive', is only applicable to authorities and bodies that meet certain conditions.

Secondly, Directive 2014/24/EU is only applicable if certain thresholds are reached. In this regard public authorities may face difficulties when it comes to calculating their budget expenditures. Besides the fact that it may not be easy to determine in advance how much money a certain project will approximately cost, another challenge for contracting authorities is to determine whether certain separate purchases should be seen as part of one big project that is in its entirety equal to or above the threshold, or whether these separate expenses should be considered as separate purchases that each fall below the threshold.

In this contribution, these two issues will be discussed and scrutinised. By analysing some examples that have recently created a lively debate in the Netherlands (the status of Dutch housing cooperatives and health insurance companies under public procurement law) and by looking at the specific characteristics of purchases made by universities, the author hopes to shed some light on some of the difficulties that authorities or entities face when they plan to purchase goods, services or works. It should be noted that in this contribution, only Directive 2014/24/EU[2] will be referred

* Sarah Schoenmaekers is Assistant Professor of European Law at Maastricht University, Visiting Professor at Hasselt University, Post-Doctoral Researcher at the Open University and practising lawyer at Omnius-advocaten, Belgium.

1 Directive 2014/24/EU of the European Parliament and of the Council of 26 February 2014 on public procurement and repealing Directive 2004/18/EC, OJ L 94/65, 28 March 2014.

2 This Directive is part of the new procurement package that was published in March 2014 and which also includes Directive 2014/25/EU of the European Parliament and of the Council of 26 February 2014 on

to and that the solutions suggested or remarks made only represent the author's personal views.

1. The Notion of 'Contracting Authority'

On 28 March 2014, Directive 2014/24/EU on Public Procurement was published in the Official Journal. It repeals Directive 2004/18/EC and most of its provisions have to be transposed by the Member States by 18 April 2016. As opposed to its predecessor, Article 1(2) of the Directive gives a clear definition of procurement. It holds:

> 'Procurement within the meaning of this Directive is the acquisition by means of a public contract of works, supplies or services by one or more contracting authorities from economic operators chosen by those contracting authorities, whether or not the works, supplies or services are intended for a public purpose.'

Article 2 of Directive 2014/24/EU explains in detail what is meant by the term 'contracting authority'. The Article refers to the State, regional or local authorities, bodies governed by public law or associations formed by one or more of such authorities or one or more of such bodies governed by public law. In particular, the concept 'body governed by public law' has created many difficulties in the past since it has not always been easy to determine whether a particular organisation or institute fulfils all the conditions enumerated in the Directive. As indicated in Article 2(1)(4)[3], bodies governed by public law are bodies that have all of the following characteristics:

> '(a) they are established for the specific purpose of meeting needs in the general interest, not having an industrial or commercial character;
> (b) they have legal personality; and
> (c) they
> - are financed, for the most part, by the State, regional or local authorities, or by other bodies governed by public law; or
> - are subject to management supervision by those authorities or bodies; or
> - have an administrative, managerial or supervisory board, more than half of whose members are appointed by the State, regional or local authorities, or by other bodies governed by public law.'

Luckily the Court of Justice of the European Union has on many occasions shed some light on the exact scope of the concept 'bodies governed by public law'. In *Aigner*,[4] the

procurement by entities operating in the water, energy, transport and postal services sectors and repealing Directive 2004/17/EC, OJ L 94/243, 28 March 2014 and Directive 2014/23/EU of the European Parliament and of the Council of 26 February 2014 on the award of concession contracts, OJ L 94/1, 28 March 2014.

3 Article 1(9) of Directive 2004/18/EC had the exact same content.

4 Case C-393/06 *Ing. Aigner* [2008] ECR I-2339.

Court made clear that subsections (a), (b) and (c) are cumulative. In *Beentjes*,[5] the Court held that the term 'contracting authority' and thus also the concept 'bodies governed by public law' has to be interpreted in a *functional* manner and not in a *formal* manner. What is important is thus not how a certain authority or body is categorised within the State administration but how it functions within this administration. It follows that the definition of these concepts as used in the domestic legislation of the Member States is not relevant since both terms have been qualified as EU concepts.[6] Nevertheless, whether an entity has legal personality (subsection (b)), and whether it is thus capable of having legal rights and duties within a certain Member State, depends on national law.

To determine whether a body is established for the specific purpose of meeting needs in the general interest, not having an industrial or commercial character (subsection (a)), it is important to assess the circumstances which prevailed when that body was set up and the conditions in which it carries on its activity, taking account in particular of the fact that it does not aim primarily at making a profit, the fact that it does not bear the risks associated with the activity, and any public financing of the activity in question.[7] Needs in the general interest are those which the State chooses to provide itself or over which it wishes to retain a decisive influence for reasons associated with the general interest.[8] It follows that even companies governed by private law that were specifically set up by the state to meet needs in the public interest but which also engage in other profit-making activities can fall within the definition of 'bodies governed by public law', as long as they continue to attend to the needs which they are specifically required to meet.[9] Private bodies that take care of the removal of waste for example meet needs in the general interest. States are free to take care of this task themselves or to choose a provider over which they retain a decisive influence.

Subsection (c) reveals that there should always be a close dependency of bodies governed by public law on the State.[10] With regard to the financial aspect it should be noted that only payments which finance or support the activities of the body concerned without any specific consideration therefore may be described as 'public financing'.[11] Even if this is the case, the proportion of public finances received by an entity always needs to exceed 50%.[12] This financing may be indirect as well. This occurs for example if the State exercises a decisive influence with regard to the amount of contributions that have to be paid by taxpayers to public broadcasting bodies.[13]

5 Case C-31/87 *Gebroeders Beentjes BV v State of Netherlands* [1988] ECR I-4635. See also Case C-353/96 *Commission v Ireland (Teoranta)* [1998] ECR I-8580.

6 Case C-283/00 *Commission v Spain (SIEPSA)* [2003] ECR I-11697.

7 Case 18–07 *Arkkitehtuuritoimisto Riitta Korhonen Oy, Arkkitehtitoimisto Pentti Toivanen Oy, Rakennuttajatoimisto Vilho Tervomaa v Varkauden Taitotalo Oy* [2003] ECR I-5364; Case C-470/99 *Universale Bau* [2002] ECR I-11617.

8 Case C-360/96 *Gemeente Arnhem, Gemeente Rheden v BFI Holding BV* [1998] ECR I-06821.

9 See Case C-214/00 *Commission v Spain* [2003] ECR I-04667.

10 Case C-44/96 *Mannesmann Anlagenbau Austria and Others v Strohal Rotationsdruck* [1998] ECR I-73.

11 Case C-380/98 *R v HM Treasury ex parte University of Cambridge* [2000] ECR I-8035.

12 Ibid.

13 Case C-337/06 *Bayerische Rundfunk et al. v GEWA* [2007] ECR I-11173. See also Case C-526/11 *IVD GmbH & Co. KG v Ärztekammer Westfalen-Lippe* [2013] not yet published.

The State can also exercise a decisive influence when it exercises management supervision over bodies governed by public law. This influence should be substantial and should be exercised with regard to the conclusion of public contracts.[14] The supervision of compliance with management rules may in itself constitute a substantial amount of influence for the State, the regional of local authorities or other bodies governed by public law, as long as these rules are very detailed. If these authorities have in addition more far reaching powers, such as the power to wind up a body, there can be no question with regard to the decisiveness of the influence.

Finally, the 50% criterion is also applicable with regard to the last alternative of Article 2(1)(4)(c) of the Directive: if more than half of the board members of a certain body are appointed by the State, regional or local authorities or by other bodies governed by public law and conditions (a) and (b) are fulfilled as well, this body should be qualified as a body governed by public law.

Even though the Court has already given guidance on the interpretation of Article 2(1)(4) of the Directive on many occasions, it is not always easy to determine whether a certain entity falls within the definition of 'bodies governed by public law'. Interestingly, even in situations that are quite straightforward and have already been considered by the Court, entities contest the fact that they fall within the scope of the definition since this entails that they have to respect European public procurement legislation. In the Netherlands, a case decided by the Court of Breda (summary proceedings) and a legislative proposal on public housing have recently reopened the discussion on the status of Dutch health insurance companies and Dutch housing cooperatives under public procurement law and thus on the exact meaning and scope of the concept of 'bodies governed by public law'. These issues will now be discussed.

1.1. The Status of (Dutch) Health Insurance Companies

On 19 June 2014, the Court of Zeeland-West-Brabant delivered a judgement in summary proceedings on the status of CZ, a Dutch health insurer who had created a new purchase policy regarding the supply of colostomy materials to persons with a colostomy. According to this policy, CZ will select one health care provider for the supply of these materials from 1 January 2015 onwards until 31 December 2017 without applying any public procurement procedure. According to CZ, the absence of a public procurement procedure does not mean that the operator selected will not be chosen in a transparent, objective and non-discriminatory manner since CZ's policy is based on fair criteria. According to Holliser, a supplier of medical products, the policy of CZ violates the Dutch Public Procurement Act as well as the general principles of public procurement. It claimed that CZ had to follow a European public procurement procedure when selecting a supplier. In essence, the dispute concerned whether CZ should be qualified as a 'body governed by public law' as meant in Article 1.1 of the Dutch Public Procurement Act which is the implementation of Article 1(9) of Directive 2004/18/EC, as recently repealed by Article 2(1) of Directive 2014/24/EU.

14 Case C-373/00 *Adolf Truly v Bestattung Wien* [2003] ECR I-1931.

It was not the first time that a court had been confronted with the status of a health insurance fund under public procurement law. In *Oymanns*[15] the Court of Justice had already considered that the German statutory health insurance funds are corporations having legal personality that are established for the specific purpose of meeting needs in the general interest, not having an industrial or commercial character. Indeed, the task of the health insurance scheme is to maintain, restore or improve the state of health of the insured. In this regard they do not operate commercially and provide their services on a non-profit making basis. Since subsections (a) and (b) of Article 2(1)(4) of the Directive were fulfilled, the Court had to check the financing, management supervision and/or board membership of the fund. With regard to the financial aspect, the Court found that there was financing, for the most part, by the State since the activities of the statutory insurance funds are chiefly financed by contributions payable by members, which are imposed, calculated and collected according to rules of public law. In this regard it is important to note that the members' contributions are paid without any specific consideration in return and that the funds had only very limited discretion regarding the rates. Since the financial aspect had been fulfilled, the Court did not have to look at the management supervision or board membership of the funds since those criteria are alternative. It follows that the German statutory health insurance funds are bodies governed by public law that have to respect European public procurement legislation, at least if certain other conditions are also fulfilled.[16]

The facts in the Dutch case do not differ much from those in the *Oymanns* case. For this reason, the Dutch court had no difficulties in finding that CZ had legal personality and that it was financed for the most part by the State. Nevertheless, CZ held that the needs that it met in the general interest had a commercial character since health care insurers compete with each other for more clients and make profits. Accordingly, CZ should not be qualified as a contracting authority. The Dutch court was not convinced by this argument, however. It held that the fact that there is a certain level of competition on the market does not mean that health care providers operate under normal market conditions and risk suffering losses.[17] Indeed, all Dutch citizens are obliged by law to buy health insurance and the Dutch *Zorginstituut* is even allowed to buy insurance on behalf of uninsured persons. Furthermore, CZ faces only limited competition on the market, does not pursue any profits and does not face any risks. The Court therefore held that CZ is meeting needs in the general interest not having an industrial or commercial character and should thus be qualified as a body governed by public law. Consequently, CZ had to use a public procurement procedure for selecting the supplier of colostomy materials.

Even though this judgement may not come as a surprise at all, it was warmly welcomed health care providers who saw their chances of carrying out (at least part of) a contract grow extensively. Now that it has been clarified how the European Court and the Dutch Court of Breda apply the criteria mentioned in Article 2(1)(4) of the Directive to

15 Case C-300/07 *Hans & Christophorus Oymanns GbR, Orthopädie Schuhtechnik v AOK Rheinland/Hamburg* [2009] ECR I-4779.

16 In this regard it should be noted that the Directive is only applicable if certain thresholds are reached and if no exclusion grounds apply.

17 Case C-373/00 *Adolf Truley GmbH v Bestattung Wien GmbH* [2003] ECR I-01931.

determine whether a body should be qualified as a contracting authority, it will be explained why the question of whether housing cooperatives also fall within this definition is still a rather complex issue. This will now be discussed.

1.2. The Status of (Dutch) Housing Cooperatives

The Dutch government has always held that Dutch housing cooperatives should not be qualified as bodies governed by public law. In the Netherlands, the main task of housing cooperatives is to accommodate, preferentially, persons who face difficulties in finding suitable housing due to low income or other circumstances.[18] Over time, Dutch housing cooperatives have broadened their activities to encompass the development of communities and the erection of societal real estate such as community centres, sports centres, hospitals, etc. Based on Article 12a *Besluit beheer sociale-huursector* (BBSH),[19] housing cooperatives have to contribute to the quality of life in neighbourhoods and areas where their houses are located. Furthermore, to compete with developers on commercial markets, many cooperatives are pursuing increases in scale.[20] These changes – among others – have led the government to amend some provisions of the Housing Act in order to encourage housing cooperatives to focus again on their primary task. The current legislation will now be discussed and compared to the new situation under the revised Act. It should be noted that the final bill was sent to the Second Chamber on 20 June 2014. In the autumn of 2014, the competent parliamentary inquiry commission will deliver its final report with recommendations. These recommendations will have to be taken into account by the Second Chamber.

1.2.1. Current Regime

The first aspect that has to be considered is whether the Dutch housing cooperatives are established for the specific purpose of meeting needs in the general interest. In this regard it should be noted that erecting, administering and renting social houses or apartments are activities that do meet needs in the general interest. Under the current as well as under the prospective legislation, housing cooperatives have to provide for social accommodation. As held above, it is immaterial whether, in addition to its duty to meet needs in the general interest, an entity is free to carry out other profit-making activities, provided that it continues to attend to the needs which it is specifically required to meet.[21]

18 Article 70c (1) of the Dutch Housing Act of 29 August 1991, *Stb.* 1991, 439.

19 Besluit beheer sociale-huursector of 9 October 1992, *Stb.* 1992, 555.

20 Even though the amount of private landlords has increased in the Netherlands, the share of housing cooperatives is still around 75–80%. See Ministry of Interior and Kingdom Relations, *Ontwikkelingen in de huursector,* 201, available at http://webcache.googleusercontent.com/search?q=cache:LMS53sQMXMMJ: www.rijksoverheid.nl/documenten-en-publicaties/rapporten/2013/04/11/ontwikkelingen-in-de-huursector.html+&cd=1&hl=nl&ct=clnk&gl=be, last visited 12 August 2014.

21 Case C-393/06 *Aigner* [2008] ECR I-02339; Case C-44/96 *Mannesmann* [1998] ECR I-00073.

The second aspect that has to be analysed is whether housing cooperatives have legal personality. Since this is the case on the basis of Article 70 of the Housing Act and Article 19(1) of the new Housing Act *jo* Article 2:3 of the Dutch Civil Code, one can turn to the question of how Dutch housing cooperatives are financed and/or supervised and/or how their board members are appointed.

In order to determine correctly the percentage of public financing of a particular body, account must be taken of all of its income, including that which results from a commercial activity.[22] Even though specific subsidies for housing cooperatives were cancelled in the Netherlands in 1993, the Guarantee Fund for Social Housing (*Waarborgfonds Sociale Woningbouw*) provides a special guarantee which allows housing cooperatives to attract money at lower interest rates. Nevertheless, housing cooperatives obtain most of their financing from rental income and the development, erection and sale of real estate.[23] It follows that housing cooperatives are not financed more than 50% by the State.

With regard to membership of the board, reference should be made to Article 7(2)(a) *jo* Article 7(1)(d) BBSH which stipulates that neither the city councils nor the executive committees of the provinces are allowed to appoint persons to the boards. The central government has no say in this either. As will be pointed out below, this will not change after the legislative proposal is approved.[24] It follows that this aspect of Article 2(1)(4) is not also fulfilled.

The final issue that has to be checked is whether and to what extent housing cooperatives are subject to management supervision by the state. This issue has already been discussed in the *OPAC* case.[25] The case was about French low-rent housing corporations that could not, according to the French government, be considered to be contracting authorities within the meaning of the Directive even though they had legal personality and met needs in the general interest. The Court, however, held that they did fulfil the supervision criterion of the Directive for the following reasons:

1. Although the housing corporations are private companies, their activities are very narrowly circumscribed by Book IV of the French Construction and Housing Code (hereinafter: the Code);
2. The Code provides that the technical characteristics and cost prices are to be determined by administrative decision;
3. The Code indicates that the statutes of the housing corporations should contain clauses consistent with the standard clauses set out in the annex to the Code. These are very detailed as regards the objectives of those entities;

22 Case C-380/98 *University of Cambridge* [2000] ECR I-8035.

23 E. Wijnen, *Aanbesteden door Thuisvester 2.0 – Een onderzoek naar de aanbestedingsplicht van Thuisvester en de gevolgen voor haar beleid*, 2014, not yet published, and the references in this work to M.R. De Boer, 'Invloed van Europese regels en beleidsvoornemens op aanbesteding door woningcorporaties', *BR* 2006, p. 723; P.F.C. Heemskerk & B. Braat, 'Woningcorporaties zijn (niet) aanbestedingsplichtig', *BR* 2010, p. 786.

24 See Article 25 (2) *jo* Article 19(3) New Housing Act.

25 Case C-237/99 *Commission v France (OPAC)* [2001] ECR I-939.

4. Low-rent housing bodies are subject to supervision by the Ministers responsible for finance and construction and housing;
5. The Minister responsible for construction and housing is empowered to order that a housing corporation be wound up and can appoint a liquidator to suspend the managerial organs and a provisional administrator;
6. The Minister responsible for construction and housing may impose a specific course of management action on housing corporations either by requiring that they display a minimum level of dynamism or by placing limits on what is considered to be excessive activity; and
7. The interministerial task force is responsible for carrying out studies, audits or assessments in the field of social housing and can draw up proposals for the action to be taken following its inception reports. It also ensures that the persons concerned by its inspections implement the measures adopted by the Ministers.

It is clear that the provisions in the French Code reflect the close dependency of the French housing corporations on the State. Since the rules of management are very detailed, the mere supervision of compliance with them may in itself lead to significant influence being conferred on the public authorities.[26] As held by the Court, the fact that the Minister's power to wind up the corporation or to suspend the managerial organs can only be used in the event of serious irregularities or gross failure to act still implies permanent supervision, since this constitutes the only means of detecting gross mismanagement or failure to act. Mere verification of legality will not suffice. It follows that the French low-rent housing corporations are bodies governed by public law that have to fulfil their obligations under public procurement legislation.

The question then arises as to whether the Court's conclusion is also applicable to the Dutch situation. As held above, under the current Dutch legislation housing cooperatives are *not* considered to be bodies governed by public law. The reason for this is that Dutch corporations are organised differently from their French counterparts. With regard to the supervision aspect, the following indications can be found in the Dutch legislation:

1. Dutch housing cooperatives are supervised by the Minister of Housing, Communities and Integration (Article 70d Housing Act).
2. The housing cooperatives have to ask for permission to be active in the field of public housing to the Dutch Crown and to the Minister of Housing, Communities and Integration (Article 4 BBSH *jo* Article 70(1) Housing Act). The latter will ask the municipalities in which the cooperative will be active for advice (Article 5 BBSH). Permission can be refused if it seems not to be in the interest of public housing.
3. The statutes of the housing cooperatives have to contain the information mentioned in Article 7 BBSH.

26 See also point 67 of the Opinion of AG Mischo in Case C-237/99 *Commission v France (OPAC)* [2001] ECR I-939.

4. The Minister can withdraw permission to be active in the field of public housing if he considers that the housing cooperative is not exclusively[27] active in this field or has caused or may cause damage to the Dutch public housing policy (Article 70(2) Housing Act *jo* Articles 11(1), 11(2) and 44 BBSH).
5. The Minister has to approve every change in the cooperative's statutes (Article 9(1) BBSH).
6. The Minister has to approve certain mergers (Article 10a BBSH).
7. Housing cooperatives have to take the public housing policy of the municipalities in which they are active into account (Article 11f BBSH).
8. Housing cooperatives are in principle only allowed to sell their housing units to 'non-housing' cooperatives for a price of at least 90% of the private sale value (Article 11c(1) BBSH).
9. Housing cooperatives have to inform the Minister if they want to sell real estate or create a long lease, usufruct or certain other right *in rem* (Article 11d(1) BBSH).
10. There are specific rules regarding the determination of rental prices (Article 15a BBSH).
11. Housing cooperatives have to conduct a healthy (financial) policy and administration (Articles 21–25 BBSH).
12. Housing cooperatives have to inform the municipalities about their public housing activities on their territories on a yearly basis (Article 25a–g BBSH).
13. Housing cooperatives have to make annual financial reports and reports on their respective policies and send these to the respective municipalities (Article 26 BBSH).
14. Every year housing cooperatives have to send the Minister and the respective city councils and the board of the Central Fund for Public Housing a financial report and a report on their policy (Article 30 BBSH).
15. The reports mentioned above are evaluated by the Minister on a yearly basis (Article 33 BBSH). The Minister can require a housing cooperative to act in a certain way to remedy an illegal situation or oblige the cooperative to refrain from acting (Article 41(1) BBSH).
16. City councils and the Central Fund of Public Housing can ask the Minister to take a binding decision as mentioned in point 15. If this occurs, the Minister is obliged to decide upon such request (Article 39 BBSH).
17. If a housing cooperative causes serious damage to the Dutch public housing policy, the competent court can, upon request of the Minister, subject the cooperative to compulsory administration if no improvement is expected and no other measure is considered to be equally effective (Article 70e(1) Housing Act).

A close reading of all of these conditions reveals that once housing cooperatives have received permission to be active on the public housing market, they have to act in line with certain general rules and have to fulfil certain information obligations. Indeed, housing cooperatives can only be active in the field of public housing, they have to take

[27] In the *Novelle* to the new legislative proposal, it is stated that the cooperatives should be exclusively active in the field of public housing or should 'also' be active in the field of public housing.

into account the public housing policies of the municipalities and they have to draw up certain reports. It is important to note that these obligations are rather soft. The supervision mechanisms that are somewhat harder, such as the compulsory administration and the obligation to refrain from acting if a certain situation occurs, generally take place *after* the housing cooperatives have already operated in a certain way. It is not easy to determine whether these criteria can lead to the conclusion that there is a sufficient degree of management supervision by the state, as meant by Article 2(1)(4)(c) of the Directive. It should be remembered, however, that in *OPAC* the Court specifically held that it needs to be established whether the various controls to which the housing cooperatives are subject render them dependent on the public authorities in such a way that the latter are able to influence cooperatives' decisions in relation to public contracts. Taking this into account, it should be concluded that, as opposed to the French situation in which the Minister can impose a specific course of management action and in which the management rules of the housing cooperatives are codified in great detail, the Dutch rules are rather open and flexible.[28] For this reason, Dutch housing cooperatives have always been considered not to qualify as bodies governed by public law. They can take independent decisions with regard to public contracts.

1.2.2. Future Regime

After the introduction of the new rules on public housing, this conclusion can no longer be upheld, however. The *Herzieningswet toegelaten instellingen volkshuisvesting*[29] will change and add some new provisions to the Housing Act that will increase the supervision powers of the Minister and the municipalities considerably. The following are some *additional* supervisory powers:

1. The Minister can refuse permission to operate if the housing cooperatives do not have enough financial resources (Article 19(3) New Housing Act (NHA)).
2. A supervisory council, composed of natural persons that can act independently, will have to approve investments that are higher than €3 billion, changes in the statutes, the winding up of the cooperative, declarations of bankruptcy, important changes in the working conditions of the cooperatives' employees, the sale of real estate, etc. (Article 26 *jo* 30 NHA). With regard to the sale of real estate, the Minister has to give

28 See in this regard also Case C-373/00 *Adolf Truley* [2003] ECR I-1931 in which the Court held that a mere review does not satisfy the criterion of management supervision in the third indent of the second subparagraph of Article 1(b) of Directive 93/36/EC. That criterion is, however, satisfied where the public authorities supervise not only the annual accounts of the body concerned but also its conduct from the point of view of proper accounting, regularity, economy, efficiency and expediency and where those public authorities are authorised to inspect the business premises and facilities of that body and to report the results of those inspections to a regional authority which holds, through another company, all the shares in the body in question.

29 Wetvoorstel Herziening van de regels over toegelaten instelling en instelling van een Financiële Autoriteit woningcorporaties van 5 juli 2012, *Kamerstukken I* 2012/13, 32 769, A zoals gewijzigd door de novelle van 19 juni 2014, *Kamerstukken II* 2013/14, 33 966, nr. 2.

his approval as well (Article 27 NHA). The supervisory council has to supervise the board's policy and the daily business of the cooperative (Article 31(1) NHA). The board has to inform the supervisory council about its policy on an annual basis (Article 32(2) NHA).

3. Whenever the supervisory board decides to appoint members of the board, the cooperative has to ask the Minister for his advice on the suitability and trustworthiness of these members (Article 25(2) NHA).
4. If the board holds the opinion that the cooperative does not have enough financial resources, it has to report this immediately to the Minister (Article 29(1) NHA).
5. Housing cooperatives have to ask permission to operate in the municipality in which they want to be active as well as in the municipality in which they are established. These municipalities have to draw up a declaration of no objection. If a municipality has objected, the cooperative cannot be active on its territory (Article 41(1)–(2) NHA).
6. Housing cooperatives have to provide a yearly overview to the municipalities in which they are active on the activities that are planned in their territories and their contribution to the municipalities' public housing policies. The cooperatives have to contribute to the municipalities' public housing policy (Articles 42–44 NHA).
7. The cooperatives have to subject their plans that are not related to services of general economic interest to approval of the Minister (Article 44d NHA).
8. An independent institute that will be appointed by the Minister will conduct an investigation on site on the results of the cooperatives' activities from a public housing as well as a societal perspective at least once every four years (Article 53a NHA).
9. If certain conditions are fulfilled, the Minister can grant subsidies to cooperatives (Article 57 NHA).
10. The Dutch Court of Auditors is competent to check all documents and information available regarding housing cooperatives (Article 61a NHA).
11. If certain conditions are fulfilled, the Minister can impose an administrative fine or penalty on housing cooperatives (Article 105 jo 120b NHA).

This overview clarifies that public housing cooperatives will not only be subject to more stringent supervision by the Minister, but also by the municipalities in which they are active. They not only have to inform the Minister of their plans to sell real estate; they now even have to ask permission to do so. Furthermore, the Minister has to approve important investments and plans that are not related to the provision of services of general economic interest. An independent institute can conduct on-the-spot investigations. Not only can the Minister require housing cooperatives to act in a certain way to remedy an illegal situation, in the future he will even be able to impose administrative fines or penalties. It follows that the daily management of the cooperatives is definitely under closer supervision than before. The legislative changes increase the management supervision by the State and bring it to a level comparable to that in France. For this reason, it can be concluded that if the legislative proposal is approved, Dutch housing cooperatives will have to be qualified as bodies governed by public law and have to apply the public procurement directives, at least if the threshold is reached and all other conditions are fulfilled.[30]

2. Thresholds

In addition to the fact that it is not always easy for entities to determine whether they are bodies governed by public law, it can also be difficult to determine whether a certain threshold has been reached in order for the European public procurement directives to apply. Even though Article 4 of Directive 2014/24/EU is very clear on the threshold amounts that make the Directive applicable – €5,186,000 for public works contracts, €134,000 for public supply and service contracts awarded by central government authorities, and €207,000 for public supply and service contracts awarded by sub-central contracting authorities – it is not always clear how one has to calculate the estimated value of a contract. Consider for example aeroplane tickets that are bought/used by (the personnel of) a university within the scope of their professional activities. When these tickets are bought by a travel agency on behalf of the university, this constitutes a public service. In many cases, the personnel of the university buys these tickets without the involvement of a travel agency. This is perfectly legitimate since contracting authorities are not obliged to outsource activities if they can perform these in house.[31] In any case, it is very unlikely that the booking costs will exceed the threshold mentioned in the Directive.

The transportation aspect, on the other hand, is taken care of by airline companies. It is possible that the price of all tickets that are bought on a yearly basis does exceed the thresholds. It should be questioned, however, whether these purchases which are so different in terms of place of departure, place of destination, specific desires of the traveller, etc., should be purchased by making use of a framework agreement that exceeds the threshold of €207,000, or whether they can be individually separated, with the result that Directive 2014/24/EU is not applicable.

To the author's knowledge, the Court of Justice has not yet had to consider this issue. It follows that contracting authorities that regularly make purchases within the same category (e.g. transport) may be insecure about whether or not they have a procurement obligation when the products or services they buy are not entirely homogenous. In this regard it should be noted that contracting authorities, such as universities, may have good reasons not to procure these contracts. First of all, they often do not know well in

[30] It should be noted that even if a housing cooperative is not qualified as a body governed by public law as is the case under the current legislation, this cooperative may still be under an obligation to respect public procurement legislation. This is the case where the housing cooperative acts on behalf of a municipality that cannot personally carry out the procurement procedure since it is not the owner of the land or premises. In such cases, the municipality has to pass on the procurement obligation to the cooperative. Furthermore, since 28 June 2011, housing cooperatives have a procurement obligation with regard to the realisation of societal real estate on the basis of the Temporary Regulation regarding Services of General Economic Interest (*Tijdelijke Regeling Diensten van Algemeen Economich Belang Toegelaten Instellingen Volkshuisvesting*), *Stcrt.* 2010, 17515. See R.G. Wagelkamp, *Woningcorporaties en aanbesteding,* available at http://archive-nl.com/page/1576618/2013-03-10/http://vanvanriet.nl/publicaties/woningcorporaties-en-aanbesteding, last visited on 13 August 2014.

[31] Article 12 of Directive 2014/24/EU.

advance which specific transport services are needed. Professors and academic researchers may be invited on short notice to speak at a conference abroad and often do not know in advance which conferences they are going to attend. It follows that even if a framework agreement were concluded, the content and character of the subcontracts that will be made within the framework of this agreement will probably not be sufficiently clear to ensure an adequate level of competition on the basis of volume or quality that allows the selection of the best tender. Furthermore, the demands for every subcontract will be different. For example, many academic researchers are not of the same nationality as the country in which the university is located and may wish to depart from their home country when they go to a conference abroad. It is also possible that they may wish to fly back to their home country in order to take some holiday and visit their family.

Article 5(3) of Directive 2014/24/EU holds in this regard that the choice of method used to calculate the estimated value of a procurement shall not be made with the intention of excluding it from the scope of the Directive. A procurement shall not be subdivided with the effect of preventing it from falling within the scope of the Directive, unless justified by objective reasons. The author believes that when universities consider all these contracts as separate ones, they do not intend to avoid public procurement legislation. The use of a public procurement procedure would not be useful for them in order to select the best tender simply because they do not know what they need in advance. Even if the value of the threshold were to be reached and the contracting authority were considered to have made a subdivision with the effect of preventing the procurement from falling within the scope of the Directive, it can be argued that the heterogeneity of the services needed constitutes an objective reason for the Directive not to be applicable. In practice, it is unlikely that airline companies will apply for a tender due to this heterogeneity. It is more likely that travel agencies will be competing to be party to a framework agreement and will then award separate contracts to different airlines. It follows that, when calculating the estimated value of a procurement, contracting authorities first have to determine whether the expenses that will be incurred should be considered as part of one procurement or should be considered as several smaller units that may avoid the application of the Directive.

3. Conclusion

Respecting the European public procurement regimes is not always an easy task for (public) entities. Whether an entity should be qualified as a body governed by public law is not always easy to determine and has to be assessed on a case-by-case basis. Even though the definition is European, whether a certain type of entity is fulfilling the requirements of Article 2(1)(4) of Directive 2014/24/EU may differ per country and may change over time. It is very likely that in the Netherlands the status of public housing cooperatives will change in the near future. Contracting authorities may also face difficulties when deciding whether a procurement reaches the thresholds listed in the Directive. The Court of Justice has not yet had to give guidance on whether the total amount payable for all small, heterogeneous purchases that fall within the same category, such as the frequent purchase of airline tickets by universities, is relevant when applying Article 5(1) of the Directive or whether every purchase has to be considered individually.

2014 PROCUREMENT REFORMS AND BID RIGGING: MIXED BLESSINGS OR OUR HAPPILY EVER AFTER?

Stefan E. Weishaar*

1. Introduction

Bid rigging cartels are a frequently reported problem in public procurement contexts. Such bid rigging takes the form of coordination between firms which can adversely affect the outcome of any sale or purchasing process in which bids are submitted. Firms can for example agree upon their bidding behaviour in advance, or decide upon which company will be the lowest bidder. Alternatively, they may agree not to bid or to rotate their bids by number or value of contracts,[1] establish bid suppression schemes, complementary (or courtesy) bidding, or subcontracting schemes.[2]

Bid rigging cartels inflate prices of public tenders and mean that procuring entities are wasting scarce public funds. At times of tight budgets and significant public debt, concern about bid rigging conspiracies is increasing. Well-structured public procurement systems and competition law regimes are essential to foster economic prosperity and social welfare.

In the recent reform of the European public procurement laws the legislator has emphasised the relevance of bidders' competition[3] and included elements that are geared to prevent bid rigging conspiracies. This paper examines whether bringing procurement law and competition law closer is a 'happy marriage' for properly dealing with bid rigging

* Stefan E. Weishaar is Associate Professor of Law and Economics at the University of Groningen, The Netherlands.

1 European Commission – Directorate General for Competition, *Glossary of Terms used in EU Competition Policy: Antitrust and Control of Concentrations*, Brussels, July 2002, available at http://ec.europa.eu/competition/publications/glossary_en.pdf.

2 Attorney General – State of Connecticut, *Price fixing & bid rigging – it can happen in Connecticut. What are these violations and what to look for: an antitrust primer for procurement professionals*, 2009, available at www.ct.gov/ag/lib/ag/pricefixingbidriggingmc.pdf, p. 4.

3 Competition has been included in the procurement principles (Article 18) and the award criteria (Article 67(4)) of Directive 2014/24/EU of the European Parliament and of the Council of 26 February 2014 on public procurement and repealing Directive 2004/18/EC [2014] OJ L 94/65.

conspiracies. Evidently, the object and purpose of procurement law – as a field of administrative law – is different than competition law that is part of economic law.

Since the research question of whether bid rigging conspiracies are adequately addressed entails the examination of behavioural incentives of bidders, a law and economics approach is used. The next section of the paper (section 2) examines how the EU competition law is dealing with bid rigging and if there is a lack of deterrence, leaving thus incentives for bid rigging. Subsequently section 3 examines if the 2014 public procurement reforms (Directive 2014/24/EU) are likely to contribute to prevent bid rigging conspiracies. A conclusion will highlight the main findings.

2. Competition Law and Bid Rigging

This section examines if competition law is dealing effectively with bid rigging cartels.[4] After a short introduction of the law and economics insights on optimal enforcement, special attention will be paid to the relevant components of EU competition law, including fines, criminal sanctions, public and private enforcement.

Legal effectiveness necessitates an assessment of the incentives of bidders to adhere to the law. Following Nobel Prize laureate Garry Becker's work[5] it is believed that rational firms[6] are incentivised to restrict competition when the total expected costs (the sum of probability of detection multiplied with the sanction) are lower than the expected benefits of cartelisation.[7] Effective competition law provisions will deter violations if they increase costs to offenders sufficiently so as to make it unattractive to trespass. In Becker's model expected costs are based on the level of punishment and on the probability of detection. Increases in either punishment or detection would reduce expected returns from illegal behaviour. Comparing the cost effectiveness of both possibilities to reduce crime, punishments are more efficient since punishments, particularly if they take the form of fines, are considered to be less costly for society.

Examining the benefit side of cartels, there is literature suggesting that cartels allow undertakings to increase prices significantly. Estimates of cartel overcharges differ widely. Kroes (2009) for example estimates that overcharges range from 20% to 25% while Connor and Lande (2006) arrive at higher estimates ranging from 31% to 49%. Another study by Connor (2010) suggests that the median long-term cartel overcharge is estimated at 23.3%. These studies suggest that cartels cause a significant detriment to

4 This passage updates a similar treatment contained in Chapter 3 of S.E. Weishaar, *Cartels, Competition and Public Procurement, Law and Economics Approaches to Bid Rigging*, Edward Elgar, 2013.

5 G.S. Becker, 'Crime and punishment: an economic approach', *Journal of Political Economy*, 1968, vol. 76(2), pp. 169–217.

6 The interested reader can be referred to G.S. Becker, 'Irrational behaviour and economic theory', *Journal of Political Economy*, 1962, vol. 70(1), pp. 1–13, who shows that even economic subjects acting irrationally may chose outcomes similar to those rational actors would have selected.

7 If one would not only punish juridical institutions but also the decision makers directly, with sentences they can not easily be compensated for by the company, it might be assumed that incentive structures may be skewed in favour of refraining from illegal activity. One example is the threat of imprisonment as a form of legal liability of managers, rather than a monetary amount that could be reimbursed to them by the company.

society and that forming a cartel can be financially very attractive. The latter element does, however, depend on the probability of detection and the cost of punishments.

Considering the probability of detection, it bears mentioning that presenting statistics on detection of cartels is inherently difficult since unlike in other areas of law victims are often not aware that they have been damaged or are unable to establish that a cartel has been at work. It is estimated that the detection rate is relatively low, ranging between 10% and 30% (Connor, 2008).

To assess the effectiveness of competition law to deter bid rigging, it is important to assess not only the probability of getting caught, but also the fines and sanctions once convicted. Below administrative fines and criminal sanctions as included in EU legislation and applied by the Commission and the CJEU are examined. Subsequently public and private enforcement is treated.

2.1. *Fines*

The Court is imposing fines on bid rigging cartels that reflect the nature, gravity and duration of bid rigging infringements.[8] Fines are limited to a statutory maximum of 10% of the entire undertaking during the previous year.[9]

The basic fine for cartels is a maximum of 30% of the sales value of the cartelised goods in the relevant market during the period in which the cartel operated. Another 15% to 25% of the determined sales value is levied to deter price fixing or market-sharing agreements.[10] Moreover, the basic fine is increased by 100% in the case of repeat offences. Fines are also increased for cartel leaders, undertakings that have retaliated against breakers of the cartel agreement or for undertakings that obstructed investigations.[11]

To safeguard the deterrent effect of the fine, the Commission can increase the fine for undertakings with a large turnover so as to recoup undue profits earned from the cartel. The level of the fine is of course constrained by the statutory maximum[12] and must take the gravity and duration of the infringement into account[13] by an individual assessment.[14]

Whether fines offer sufficient deterrence to prevent bid riggings will depend on several issues: (i) the size of fines, (ii) profit margins and (iii) ability to pay. Firstly, fines of 10% of an undertaking's annual turnover appear to be quite sizable if a cartel only operated in a subset of an undertaking's markets. If the undertaking serves a single

8 Case T-23/99 *LR AF 1998 A/S, formerly Løgstør Rør A/S v Commission of the European Communities* [2002] ECR II-01705, paras. 225 ff.

9 See Article 23(2) Council Regulation (EC) 1/2003 of 16 December 2002 on the implementation of the rules on competition laid down in Articles 81 and 82 of the Treaty, OJ L 1, 4 January 2003, pp. 1–25.

10 Guidelines on the method of setting fines imposed pursuant to Article 23(2)(a) of Regulation No 1/2003 of 1 September 2006 [2006] OJ 210/2, recital (25).

11 Ibid, para. 28.

12 Article 23 of Council Regulation 1/2003.

13 Article 23(3) of Council Regulation 1/2003.

14 Joint Cases 100–103/80 *SA Musique Diffusion française and others v Commission of the European Communities* [1983] ECR 01825, para. 129.

market, however, a 10% fine may be too low to offer effective deterrence. Secondly, the ability of fines to offer deterrence also depends on the profit margin of a firm. If profit margins are high, fines are paid quickly. If profit margins are low, however, the fine may be equivalent to several years of a company's profits and thus constitute an effective deterrent.[15] Thirdly, fines will only offer a deterrence effect if they do not exceed the assets of the culprit (judgment proof problem). This problem is recognised by EU competition law by allowing adjustments of the fines.[16]

In assessing the actual level of fines, it bears mentioning that the benefits from cartels (presented above) seem to exceed the level of fines (at least for an undertaking operating on a single market). Even though the level of fines was increased under the 2006 guidelines, less than 9% of the cartels reached the 10% statutory maximum during the years 2007–2009.[17]

The adequacy of fines must of course be assessed on a case-by-case basis but in general the above seems to suggest that for undertakings with high profit margins, operating in one line of business and serving one market, there is likely to be under-deterrence since the statutory maximum might be reached.

2.2. *Criminal Sanctions*

In cases where monetary fines do not offer sufficient deterrence, criminal sanctions should be considered. Even after Lisbon, where the European Union has acquired some criminal powers, EU competition law is not enforced through criminal sanctions. Only in the area of fraud affecting the EU's financial interest are criminal sanctions available.[18] For all other bid rigging cases criminal sanctions will stem exclusively from Member State legislation.

It is not only fines and sanctions that contribute to deterrence, but also the potency of public and private enforcement. These are examined next.

2.3. *Public Enforcement*

European competition law is predominantly based on public enforcement. It is enforced by the European Commission with the assistance of the National Competition Authorities (NCAs) and national courts.[19] There is close cooperation between the

15 See A. Lever, 'Opinion: Whether, and if so how, the EC Commission's 2006 Guidelines on setting fines for infringement of Articles 81 and 82 of the EC Treaty are fairly subject to serious criticism', BDI – Federation of German Industries, Law and Public Procurement, *BDI Imprint* No. 406, 12 November 2007, available at www.bdi.eu/download_content/Publikation_BDI_Gutachten__Opinion__zu_EU_Bussgeldleitlinien.pdf.

16 Guidelines on the method of setting fines imposed pursuant to Article 23(2)(a) of Regulation No 1/2003 of 1 September 2006 [2006] OJ 210/2, recital (35).

17 J. Connor, 'Has the European Commission become more severe in punishing cartels? Effects of the 2006 Guidelines', *European Competition Law Review*, 2011, vol. 32(1), p. 31.

18 Council Act of 26 July 1995 drawing up the Convention on the protection of the European Communities' financial interests (95/C 316/03), pp. 0048–0057.

19 See Articles 4–6 Council Regulation 1/2003/EC.

NCAs[20] and the Commission but the relationship is hierarchical in nature when it comes to interpretation of the law.[21]

Regulation 1/2003 grants the Commission extensive investigatory powers.[22] To coerce compliance during the investigation the Commission can impose fines up to 1% of the total annual turnover for, *inter alia*, undertakings supplying incorrect or misleading information, for supplying incomplete records during inspections, for refusals to submit to an inspection, for giving incorrect or misleading answers, or for tampering with affixed seals.[23] In its investigation, the Commission is also supported by the NCA, which enhances the resources the Commission can draw upon for e.g. an on-site investigation of an undertaking.

Despite the support of the NCAs, over time the Commission has developed a backlog of cases. To reduce the investigative burden and to reduce its backlog, a settlement procedure[24] was introduced and first applied in 2010.[25] On the basis of this procedure, undertakings acknowledge their liability for the infringement, indicate the fine they are willing to pay, agree to a shorter investigative procedure and waive their right to access the Commission's file. In return they benefit from a 10% reduction of the fine. Moreover the statements of companies can be recorded orally so as to prevent private plaintiffs benefiting from the undertaking's statements.

Despite the Commission's ample enforcement powers, detecting bid rigging infringements is very difficult because victims are not normally aware that the bids have been rigged. Leniency policies[26] have been introduced to incentivise cartel members to cooperate with authorities in return for total immunity or a reduction of fines. Undertakings forcing others to join or to remain in the cartel are not eligible for a total waiver but they can still enjoy a reduction of fines.[27] Leniency policies have been very successful in detecting cartels,[28] and consequently contributed to the Commission's backlog of cases.[29] It bears mentioning, however, that tension can arise between incentives for cartel members to apply for leniency and private damage claims. The

20 Commission Notice on cooperation within the Network of Competition Authorities (2004/C 101/03), 27 April 2004.

21 See Article 16(1) and (2) Council Regulation 1/2003.

22 Chapter V Council Regulation 1/2003. On the relation between Member State and Commission enforcement powers see W. Wils 'EU antitrust enforcement powers and procedural rights and guarantees: the interplay between rights of the EU and the European Convention on Human Rights', *World Competition*, 2011, vol. 27(2), pp. 201–24.

23 For a complete list see Article 23(1) Council Regulation 1/2003.

24 Commission Regulation 622/2008 of 30 June 2008, amending Regulation 773/2004 [2008] OJ L 171/3, Article 10(a).

25 European Commission – IP/10/586 of 19 May 2010 'Antitrust: Commission fines DRAM producers €331 million for price cartel; reaches first settlement in a cartel case'.

26 Commission Notice on Immunity from fines and reduction of fines in cartel cases of 8 December 2006 [2006] OJ C 298/11.

27 Ibid, para. 13.

28 D. Chalmers, G. Favies and G. Monti, *European Union Law: Cases and Materials*, Cambridge University Press, 2010, p. 936.

29 A. Riley 'The modernization of EU anti-cartel enforcement: will the Commission grasp the opportunity?' *European Competition Law Review*, 2010, vol. 31(5), p. 194.

legislator has addressed this by protecting whistle blowers from EU civil liability by protecting their statements from discovery.[30] The draft Directive on Action for Damages (this Directive is currently awaiting approval at the Council)[31] ensures that neither leniency statements nor settlement submissions can be obtained from defendants or from third parties and that these documents cannot be used before the court if obtained through access of the file of a competition authority.[32]

Hence the above suggests that the European Commission enjoys substantive enforcement powers and can draw upon the support of NCAs. The leniency policies appear to be quite successful and the settlement procedures can help to speed up the enforcement process. Given that enforcement capacity is limited, there may be a focus on large offences while smaller infringements are not addressed. While this is desirable from an efficiency perspective, it may entail that smaller cases of bid rigging go unpunished. In these cases there is a role for private enforcement.

2.4. *Private Enforcement*

Until now, competition law enforcement has been predominantly a public affair. If, however, public enforcement is not able to offer sufficient deterrence in the form of administrative fines and criminal sanctions and if public enforcement of competition law is insufficient, there is a role for private enforcement to reduce incentives to engage in bid rigging. So far private enforcement of competition law in the EU has largely been a theoretical rather than an important practical reality. Its implementation is largely reliant upon Member State legislation.

On several occasions the Court has held that individuals can claim compensation for harm suffered in case they can prove a causal relationship between their harm and the violation of EU competition law rules.[33] The underlying motivation is of course that in the absence of private damage claims the effectiveness of EU competition law would be undermined[34] and that private enforcement contributes to the maintenance of effective

30 European Commission, *Commission Notice on Immunity from fines and reduction of fines in cartel cases*, 8 December 2006, [2006] OJ C 298/11, paras. 32 and 33.

31 See IP/14/455 of 17 April 2014, 'Antitrust: Commission welcomes Parliament vote to facilitate damages claims by victims of antitrust violations European Commission.'

32 See Amendments by the European Parliament to the Commission proposal Directive of the European Parliament and of the Council on certain rules governing actions for damages under national law for infringements of the competition law provisions of the Member States and of the European Union, available at www.europarl.europa.eu/sides/getDoc.do?pubRef=-//EP//NONSGML+AMD+A7-2014-0089+002-002+DOC+PDF+V0//EN, Articles 6(6) and 7(1).

33 Case C-453/99 *Courage and Crehan* [2001] ECR I-6297; Joined Cases C-295/04 to C-298/04 *Manfredi* [2006] ECR I-6619, para. 61; Case C-360/09 *Pfeiderer AG v Bundeskartellamt* [2011] ECR I-5161; Case C-199/11 *European Community v Otis NV and others* [2012] ECR I-0000, para. 43 and Case C-557/12 *Kone AG et al. v ÖBB-Infrastruktur AG* [2014] not yet published, para. 22.

34 Case C-453/99 *Courage and Crehan* [2001] ECR I-6297, para. 26; Joined Cases C-295/04 to C-298/04 *Manfredi* [2006] ECR I-6619, para. 60; Case C-199/11 *European Community v Otis NV and others* [2012] ECR I-0000, para. 41; Case C-536/11 *Donau Chemie and others* [2013] not yet published, para. 21; Case C-557/12 *Kone AG et al. v ÖBB-Infrastruktur AG* [2014] not yet published, para. 21.

competition that would be put at risk if individuals could not claim damages for losses resulting from anticompetitive behaviour.[35] In the absence of EU rules, it was for the Member States to ensure that the rights of individuals would be safeguarded.[36]

Already in 2005 the Commission's Green Paper[37] identified impediments to private enforcement of EC competition law which included (i) access to evidence, (ii) damages and procedural costs, (iii) the passing-on defence, (iv) collective redress, and (v) the interaction with public enforcement. In its 2008 White Paper the Commission made several suggestions for improvements including *inter alia* collective and opt-in redress, minimum standards of disclosure, binding effect of final decisions of national competition authorities for civil procedures, a clarification of the (rebuttable) fault standards and reductions of costs for damage actions.[38] Subsequently the Commission commissioned a study on quantifying antitrust damages[39] and held public consultations regarding the quantification of harm collective redress. Most recently the European Commission proposed a Directive on certain rules governing actions for damages under national law for infringements of the competition law provisions of the Member States and the European Union.[40] The draft Directive addresses *inter alia* the disclosure of evidence, and specifies the limits on disclosure of evidence from the file of completion authority and the limits on the use of evidence obtained through access to the files of competition authorities and time limits.

The legislator is clearly aware of the tension between private enforcement and the need for a well-functioning leniency policy. The Directive seeks to respect the disclosure provisions of whistle blowers under leniency policy and limits the liability of whistle blowers to injured parties that are direct or indirect purchases or providers. Only in exceptional circumstances in which the injured parties are unable to obtain redress from

35 Case C-453/99 *Courage and Crehan* [2001] ECR I-6297, para. 27; Joined Cases C-295/04 to C-298/04 *Manfredi* [2006] ECR I-6619, para. 91; Case C-360/99 *Pfeiderer AG v Bundeskartellamt* [2011] ECR I-5161, para. 29; Case C-199/11 *European Community v Otis NV and others* [2012] ECR I-0000, para. 42; Case C-536/11 *Donau Chemie and others* [2013] not yet published, para. 23; Case C-557/12 *Kone AG et al. v ÖBB-Infrastruktur AG* [2014] not yet published, para. 23.

36 Case C-453/99 *Courage and Crehan* [2001] ECR I-6297, para. 29; Joined Cases C-295/04 to C-298/04 *Manfredi* [2006] ECR I-6619, para. 62; Case C-360/99 *Pfeiderer AG v Bundeskartellamt* [2011] ECR I-5161, para. 24; Case C-536/11 *Donau Chemie and others* [2013] not yet published, para. 27; Case C-557/12 *Kone AG et al. v ÖBB-Infrastruktur AG* [2014] not yet published, para. 25.

37 Commission of the European Communities, *Green Paper on damages actions for breach of the EC antitrust rules*, 19 December 2005, COM(2005)672 final.

38 Commission of the European Communities, *White Paper on damages actions for breach of the EC antitrust rules*, 2 April 2008, COM(2008)165 final.

39 Oxera et al., *Quantifying Antitrust Damages: Towards Non-binding Guidance for Courts*, Luxembourg, Publications Office of the European Union, 2009, available at http://ec.europa.eu/competition/antitrust/actionsdamages/quantification_study.pdf.

40 Proposal for a Directive of the European Parliament and of the Council on certain rules governing actions for damages under national law for infringements of the competition law provisions of the Member States and of the European Union, COM(2013)404 final, 2013/0185(COD), Strasbourg, 11 June 2013. The Directive has been approved in first reading with amendments by the European Parliament on 17 April 2014 (see http://ec.europa.eu/prelex/detail_dossier_real.cfm?CL=en&DosId=202775#1215408) and is now awaiting approval by the Council.

other cartel members will a whistle blower be held liable.[41] The whistle blower is thus largely excluded from the joint and several liability provision of the Directive.

In light of recent case law this provision is very important because it limits the civil damages on whistle blowers. In *Kone* the Court recently held that cartel members are liable to pay punitive damages for price increases in public tenders where third parties unrelated to the cartel were able to submit higher tender prices (umbrella prices).[42] Tendering authorities can thus not only ask for damages related to a particular bid rigging cartel, but also recoup damages for less competitive market prices in tenders where a cartel was unsuccessful. Since this potentially reduces the burden of proof of causality between the actual operation of a cartel at a particular tender and the damage on the part of the tendering authority, prospects for private enforcement seem to be much improved and potentially capable of mitigating the under deterrence problem in private competition law enforcement.

It can therefore be concluded that EU competition law rules are designed reasonably well to contain bid rigging cartels if public enforcement is doing well. There are, however, some areas where under-deterrence has been found. Given that the gravity of fines perceived by the undertaking depends on the its profit margins, undertakings with higher profit margins should be investigated more frequently to prevent under-deterrence. In those cases where the statutory fines reach their maximum, either higher fines or criminal sanctions would be needed to ensure deterrence. If this is not feasible, private enforcement would be needed, but this is still a remote possibility due to high burden of proof requirements and the non-disclosure of information used in a leniency procedure. The recent *Kone* case may bring a rising number of private bid rigging cases relating to umbrella prices but it is still too early to tell. Therefore there is still the need for public procurement law to take a preventive approach to bid rigging since incentives to cartelise still remain under EU competition law.

3. Public Procurement and Bid Rigging

The previous section recognised the potency of the European competition law regime and concluded that in certain circumstances residual incentives for collusion in public tenders remain. Since the adequacy of the former procurement law (Directive 2004/18/EC) to prevent bid rigging conspiracies has been discussed elsewhere,[43] in this contribution only the changes under the new procurement legislation are considered. The scope of analysis is limited to Directive 2014/24/EU.

In the new Directive, competition enjoys a more prominent role. It is not only the inclusion of the principle of competition in Article 18 of Directive 2014/24/EU that is viewed to be positively influencing the respect for undistorted competition in practice,[44]

41 Ibid, Article 11(2).

42 Case C-557/12 *Kone AG et al. v ÖBB-Infrastruktur AG* [2014] not yet published.

43 S.E. Weishaar, *Cartels, Competition and Public Procurement, Law and Economics Approaches to Bid Rigging*, Edward Elgar, 2013.

44 See for example A. Sánchez Graells, 'Prevention and deterrence of bid rigging: a look from the new EU Directive on Public Procurement', forthcoming in G. Racca and C. Yukins (eds.), *Integrity and Efficiency in Sustainable Public Contracts*, Brussels, Bruylant, 2014, Working Paper Series.

but also that a number of pro-competitive steps have been taken that can help to undermine bid rigging conspiracies.

In line with earlier Procurement law reforms, also in 2014 the Commission sought to (i) lower bidding costs and to (ii) facilitate the participation of small and medium-sized companies in the procurement tenders. But it also emphasised the possibilities to (iii) exclude bidders from participating in a tender and also gave a more central role to (iv) the 'most economically advantageous tenders' that are believed to make it more difficult for cartel members to operate a cartel. Each is taken in turn.

3.1. *Lowering Bidders' Costs*

The Commission has sought to lower bidder costs by reducing the administrative burden on participating in public tenders. The underlying idea is that if costs of participating in tenders are lower, this should give rise to more competition, rendering the establishment and operation of a bid rigging cartel more difficult. Several measures affecting bidder costs are presented below.

The introduction of the European Single Procurement Document[45] for example allows bidders to take part in a tender without obliging them to present all required documents proving that they meet the tender criteria. A declaration made by bidders replaces such certificates relating to *inter alia* grounds of exclusion (Article 57) and selection criteria (Article 58). Only the bidder winning the tender will actually have to furnish the relevant documents, thus avoiding all other bidders the costs of attaining these documents.

Similarly, the online information system E-Certis[46] will provide an up-to-date list of certificates and other forms of documentary evidence that tendering authorities shall primarily rely upon. This online repository will reduce the information costs for bidders and thereby help facilitate their participation in a cross-border tender.

While the above are to be evaluated positively from a point of view of trying to counter bid rigging conspiracies, there are, however, a few developments which are reducing costs of tenders that could potentially have adverse effects on competition. The dynamic purchasing system can be applied where products that meet the requirements of tendering authorities are generally available on the market. In a completely electronic process the tendering authorities will invite all members of dynamic purchasing system that are listed for a particular type of product to submit a tender.[47] Because tenders in the dynamic purchasing system are pre-admitted, participation in a tender is not a costly affair. The problem might arise, however, if the dynamic purchasing system would be applied in a similar fashion as the Japanese 'business evaluation system'. This system attributes a certain point score to all construction companies. Based on the complexity of the project procuring entities determine a minimum point score that

45 Article 59 of Directive 2014/24/EU of the European Parliament and of the Council of 26 February 2014 on public procurement and repealing Directive 2004/18/EC [2014] OJ L 94/65.

46 Article 61 of Directive 2014/24/EU.

47 Article 34(6) Directive 2014/24/EU.

serves as a minimum entry requirement[48] to determine which firms are eligible to participate in a tender. The required benchmark for the tender as well as the business evaluation scores are publicly known. This effectively limits the number of potential competitors without any sizable information cost and thus facilitates collusion. In the dynamic purchasing system all listed undertakings under a specific product category are of course eligible to take part in the bidding, but it would still facilitate collusion if the identity of the listed companies was not kept secret.

Moreover, participating in tenders is made more attractive by reducing the time periods of tender procedures. The downside of shortened tender procedures might arise if due to shorter time periods fewer bidders would actually take part. Yet given that the time period is generally at least 30 days, the negative effects of this might be in practice limited.

Similarly, for restricted procedures and the competitive procedure with negotiation, sub-central contracting authorities such as local or regional authorities are able to follow a simplified prior information notice procedure in which they can avoid a fully fledged EU procurement publication procedure that is published on the tender's buyer profile and notified to the Publications Office of the European Union.[49] The administrative burden is alleviated by freeing the tendering authorities from the duty to announce a further call for competition. Interested companies can notify their interest and will be kept informed about the actual tender. Albeit this procedure is reducing the administrative costs of the tendering authorities it might lead to a reduction of transparency if the notified schedule is not specific enough or altered. This could lead to situations where bidders are not duly informed about bidding opportunities.

It therefore appears that the first three measures are making a useful contribution to preventing bid rigging conspiracies while the last three elements require more careful implementation so as to avoid a negative impact.

3.2. *Small and Medium-Sized Enterprises*

The new Directive strives to facilitate SME participation in cross-border procurements. This is achieved by restricting the turnover requirement to a maximum of twice the contract value size, except in duly justified cases.[50]

Moreover, the Directive provides the possibility for tendering authorities to subdivide a contract into smaller lots.[51] If the authority decides not to subdivide the contract, it must give an indication of the main reasons for its decision. The implicit incentive seems thus to be that lots will be subdivided, which should allow small firms to compete for contracts as well. On the hand this possibility allows for more competition because more SMEs are likely to be able to participate while it still allows large companies to take

48 In addition to this business evaluation score, procuring entities use selective criteria for the selection of participating companies.

49 See Article 48 Directive of 2014/24/EU.

50 See Article 58(3) of Directive 2014/24/EU.

51 See Article 46(1) of Directive 2014/24/EU.

advantage of their economies of scale.[52] On the other hand, however, it may facilitate cartelisation as more lots enable cartel members to better share the market. While on average it might indeed be true that a larger number of lots will be able to allow more SMEs to participate in the bidding process and may thus have a pro-competitive effect, it may also work as a double-edged sword that invites careful consideration before applying this provision. Anticompetitive effects take the form of facilitating the division of cartel proceeds but also facilitate collusion in the form of market sharing.[53] If a strong complementariness between lots is expected, package biddings can incentivise competition for well-designed packages,[54] while a sub-optimal division of lots may scare away risk-averse bidders. While creating the possibility under EU law is indeed very desirable and a notable improvement, it is a tool that must be carefully applied.

Similarly tendering authorities may limit the number of lots that may be awarded to one bidder.[55] Here too, an explanation requirement ensures that this provision is not used in a competitively restricting manner. This provision may prevent market concentration, but at the same time it may influence the bidding behaviour of cartel members as it reduces the number of competitors. Such provisions should therefore only be used in situations where the market is highly concentrated.

3.3. *Deterrence*

The legislator also expressly included competition law violations into the grounds for being excluded from taking part in tenders. Exclusion of undertakings on grounds of bid rigging violations were already possible under the previous Directive[56] but the express mentioning in the new Directive may help to strengthen the deterrent effect. The new rules provide that at any time during the tendering procedure tendering authorities may exclude or may be required by Member States to exclude bid riggers from taking part in procurements.[57] The violation of competition law can have taken place before or during the tendering procedure so as to also allow for sanctions in those circumstances where a violation of competition law is only discovered after the tendering procedure.[58] It is noticeable that the violation of competition law leading to exclusion from the tendering procedure does not need to be final in the sense of a

52 N. Dimitri, R. Pacini, M. Pagnozzi and G. Spagnolo, 'Multi-contract tendering procedures and package bidding in procurement' in N. Dimitri, G. Piga and G. Spagnolo (eds.), *Handbook of Procurement*, Cambridge University Press, 2006, p. 215.

53 For an example see V. Grimm, F. Riedel and E. Wolfstette, Low *price equilibrium in multi-unit auctions: the GSM Spectrum Auction in Germany*, Institut für Wirtschaftstheorie I, Humboldt Universität zu Berlin, 2001, 1–14.

54 N. Dimitri, R. Pacini, M. Pagnozzi and G. Spagnolo, 'Multi-contract tendering procedures and package bidding in procurement' in N. Dimitri, G. Piga and G. Spagnolo (eds.), *Handbook of Procurement*, Cambridge University Press, 2006, p. 201.

55 See Article 46(2) of Directive 2014/24/EU.

56 See A. Sánches Graells, *Public Procurement and the EU Competition Rules*, Hart Publishing, 2011, pp. 253–255.

57 Article 57(5) of Directive 2014/24/EU.

58 Article 57(5) of Directive 2014/24/EU.

conviction: a 'sufficiently plausible indication' that bidders entered into agreements aimed at distorting competition is sufficient.[59] The implementing conditions of when and how to make use of this exclusionary ground will be filled in by Member States' legislation.[60] Unless specified differently in a final judgment, the maximum duration of being barred from taking part in tenders on the grounds of a competition law violation is three years.[61]

Article 57(5) of Directive 2014/24/EU enables tendering authorities to put undertakings on a 'black list' and exclude them from taking part in tenders. They are thus able to increase the costs for undertakings that have committed bid rigging offences. In order to have an effective 'black list' system throughout the EU, unified rules and recognition of decisions taken in other Member States would be helpful. As criticised by Sanchez Graells,[62] a uniform system of black listing would enhance the deterrent effect of this provision. At the very least, a European reporting system would be necessary to inform tendering authorities within a Member State and throughout the Union that an undertaking has been black listed. This would enable other tendering authorities to take such decisions into account and exclude this as well, or at least take particular precautions when examining the submitted tender documents.

3.4. Most Economically Advantageous Tenders

One important feature of the new public procurement rules is that it overcomes the dichotomy of the 'most economically advantageous tender' (MEAT) and lowest price by replacing it by MEAT as the overarching award criterion.[63] Procurements on the basis of MEAT are selected on the basis of the price or cost, using a cost-effectiveness approach (e.g. lifecycle costing) but may include a price-quality ratio as an award criterion.[64] This allows procurement entities to take environmental considerations, social aspects and innovation into account.

The emphasis on MEAT is also important from a bid rigging perspective. By creating more complex award criteria, it becomes more difficult for cartel members to predict who will be awarded the tender. This makes cartel formation and distribution of proceeds more difficult because it requires cartel members to design more complex agreements and renders the payoff of the cartel more uncertain. That it becomes more difficult for cartel members to rig bids does, however, not mean that the procurement entities do

59 Article 57(4)(d) of Directive 2014/24/EU. To reduce the error costs Article 57(6) provides for self-cleaning actions in which an alleged infringement can be rebutted and evidence may be presented.

60 Article 57(7) of Directive 2014/24/EU.

61 Ibid.

62 A. Sánchez Graells, 'Prevention and deterrence of bid rigging: a look from the new EU Directive on Public Procurement', forthcoming in G. Racca and C. Yukins (eds.), *Integrity and Efficiency in Sustainable Public Contracts*, Brussels, Bruylant, 2014, Working Paper Series, p. 19.

63 See P. Boradalo Faustino, 'Award criteria in the new EU Directive on public procurement', *Public Procurement Law Review*, 2014, vol. 3, pp. 124–133.

64 See Article 67(1) of Directive 2014/24/EU.

enjoy an excessive amount of discretion to favour a particular supplier: Article 67(4) requires that effective competition is not impaired and that bidders are able to effectively assess how well they meet the award criteria.

The above can therefore be summarised as follows. There are a number of positive developments in the new public procurement law that help to mitigate bid rigging conspiracies. In all four areas discussed there are noticeable improvements. The most promising change stems from the MEAT and deterrence. In the area of deterrence, additional work is required to make it more effective. Lowering bidder costs is generally to be evaluated positively, but in case of the dynamic purchasing system, shorter tendering periods, and alleviating the tender process for sub-central contracting authorities, the effect on competition will depend on the implementation details and the actual application. The same is true for measures supporting SMEs. Overall there are thus important improvements in the public procurement framework that could help to mitigate the risk of bid rigging conspiracies.

4. Conclusion

The above treatment has shown that there is under-deterrence for bid rigging conspiracies under EU competition law. Recent case law in the area of private enforcement may help to mitigate this by inviting more private claims that may offer additional deterrence to engage in bid rigging. Public procurement law does thus have a role to play in addressing residual incentives for undertakings to participate in bid rigging conspiracies. The recent public procurement law reform provides for better capabilities to foster competition and to deter bid rigging. In this sense the recent reform thus constitutes a 'happy marriage' between the two fields of law to mitigate bid rigging conspiracies. Clearly the current relation between competition and public procurement law is not overcoming all incentives for undertakings to engage in bid rigging and thus leaves room for further improvements. It is thus not a 'happily ever after' but at the very least a happy beginning.

CONCESSIONS AND PUBLIC PROCUREMENT

Steven Van Garsse*

1. Introduction[1]

Concession contracts, and in particular public services and works concessions, have attracted growing attention in the last few years. This is in some respects due to the search for creative and innovative solutions to complex infrastructural problems, a lack of budgetary resources to finance some of the projects, and, as a consequence, the need for private financing. Examples of concessions can be found in the construction and operation of swimming pools, the construction and operation of motorways and tunnels, the operation of certain databases, of certain transportation routes, etc.

There has been no, or at least only very minimal, regulation of works and services concessions at the national and European levels. But, in recent decades, the European legislator has made several attempts to bring concessions (more) within the scope of the regulations on public contracts.[2] As we already know, the European Union does provide an extensive set of regulations on public procurement of works, services and supply contracts.

In 2011, the European Commission proposed a directive specifically for the award of concessions for works and services. The aim was to create a system for these contracts that, compared with the public contracts regulations, would be 'light' and 'flexible'.

This approach paid off. On 15 January 2014, the Directive was approved at its first reading, after a long and difficult passage through the European Parliament. The

* Steven Van Garsse works for the PPP Knowledge Centre, Government of Flanders, and is Professor at the Antwerp Management School and lecturer at the Law Faculty, research group on Government and Law, University of Antwerp.

1 This text is based on a lecture given during the seminar 'State Aid and Public Procurement in the European Union', Jean Monnet Module, Maastricht 27 May 2014. It is also partially based on a text published in *Jaarboek Overheidsopdrachten 2013–2014*, C. De Koninck, et al. (eds.), Brussels, EBP, 2014.

2 S. Van Garsse, *De concessie in het raam van de publiek-private samenwerking (The concession in the context of the public private partnership)*, Bruges, die Keure, 2007, pp. 618–630; C. Bovis, *EC Public Procurement Case Law and Regulation*, Oxford University Press, 2006, p. 337.

Directive was published in the Official Journal of 28 March 2014 and came into effect on 17 April 2014.[3] The Member States now have 24 months in which to transpose the Directive. Transposition of the Directive into Belgian law ensures the reinstatement of concession-specific legislation after a gap of more than 100 years. In other countries, such as France, the Directive implies an update and amendment of the existing framework.[4]

In this chapter, we analyse several aspects of the directive by way of an introduction. In particular, we look at the concept of the concession and at the scope of the new Directive. This is very important if we are to distinguish the concession from the public contract. We also comment briefly on the legal regime. The chapter concludes with several closing considerations.

2. The Concept of the Public Works and Services Concession is a Loaded One

Concession contracts for works and services have a long and established history in many of the countries of the European Union.[5] In Belgium, for example, we can refer back to the 'tollgate concessions' of the 19th century. In that period, there were some fairly extensive rules in place to regulate these concessions, which covered large infrastructural projects and were, in fact, the precursors to the public works concession.[6] In the 20th century, concessions were largely a way of managing public services.[7] Concessions do, therefore, relate directly to the way in which the government organises itself. This interpretation has carried weight in the debate about how concessions are to be regulated. For example, earlier attempts to regulate services concessions failed partly due to these reasons.[8]

The preparatory work for the recently passed Concessions Directive also reveals clear traces of this issue. This is why it expressly states in the Concessions Directive:

In Article 1(4):

> 'Agreements, decisions or other legal instruments that organise the transfer of powers and responsibilities for the performance of public tasks between contracting authorities or contracting entities or groupings of contracting authorities or contracting entities, and which do not provide for remuneration to be given for contractual performance, are considered to be

3 Directive 2014/23/EU of the European Parliament and of the Council of 26 February 2014 on the award of concession contracts OJ L 94, 28 March 2014, pp. 1–64.

4 Cf. the so called Loi Sapin of 29 January 1993 (no. 93–122).

5 X. Bezançon, *2000 ans d'histoire du partenariat public-privé*, Paris, Presses de l'école nationale des Ponts et Chaussées, 2004, p. 284.

6 S. Van Garsse, *De concessie in het raam van de publiek-private samenwerking (The concession in the context of the public private partnership)*, Bruges, die Keure, 2007, p. 390.

7 J.F. Auby and O. Raymundie, *Le service public. Droit national et droit communautaire. Régime juridique et catégories. Modes de gestion*, Paris, Le Moniteur, 2003, pp. 63–65 and 408.

8 Case C-324/98 *Telaustria Verlags GmbH and Telefonadress GmbH v Post & Telekom Austria AG* [2000] ECR I-10745, para. 50.

a matter of internal organisation of the Member State concerned and, as such, are not affected in any way by this Directive.'

And in Article 2:

'Principle of free administration by public authorities

1. This Directive recognises the principle of free administration by national, regional and local authorities in conformity with national and Union law. Those authorities are free to decide how best to manage the execution of works or the provision of services, to ensure in particular a high level of quality, safety and affordability, equal treatment and the promotion of universal access and of user rights in public services.
   Those authorities may choose to perform their public interest tasks with their own resources, or in cooperation with other authorities or to confer them upon economic operators.'

In recital (5) of the Directive we read, in the same sense:

'This Directive recognises and reaffirms the right of Member States and public authorities to decide the means of administration they judge to be most appropriate for performing works and providing services. In particular, this Directive should not in any way affect the freedom of Member States and public authorities to perform works or provide services directly to the public or to outsource such provision by delegating it to third parties. Member States or public authorities should remain free to define and specify the characteristics of the services to be provided, including any conditions regarding the quality or price of the services, in accordance with Union law, in order to pursue their public policy objectives.'

This perspective instantly clarifies the point that (public service) concessions cannot be equated with or even placed on the same footing as public contracts. Some authors, especially those from common law Member States, had nonetheless argued for this by saying that it would have been better to include concessions in the public contracts directives.[9] This point of view is hardly surprising, given that in a legal system of this kind, the public service concept will not be (as deeply) embedded.[10] In the end, the

9 For example M. Burnett, 'A New EU Directive on Concessions – the Right Approach for PPP', *EPPPL*, 2008, vol. 4, p. 193. Also S. Arrowsmith, *The Law of Public and Utilities Procurement*, London, Sweet & Maxwell, 2005, p. 330.

10 In fact public law in a legal system of that kind differs fundamentally from public law in continental systems based on civil law. It is even said that those countries have a long tradition of administrative non-law. See J. Bell, 'Mechanisms for Cross Fertilisation of Administrative Law in Europe' in K. Baetsen and T. Tridimas (eds.), *New Directions in European Public Law*, Oxford, Hart Publishing, 1998, p. 150. In the continental European tradition, the concept of public service has an important role and is even used to justify state interventions (central planning, excluding competition, setting up state-owned companies, etc.) See H. Schweizer, 'Services of General Economic Interest: European Law's Impact on the Role of Markets and Member States' in M. Cremona (ed.), *Market integration and Public Services in the European Union*, Oxford, Oxford University Press, 2011, p. 16; J.F. Auby and O. Raymundie, *Le service public*, Paris, Le Moniteur, 2003, p. 17.

European legislator decided not to take this approach. With the Concessions Directive, it is very clearly acknowledged that the two legal instruments differ considerably. This is also reflected in the recitals, albeit in a subtle way. We read, for example, in recital (2), '[t]he rules of the legislative framework applicable to the award of concessions should be clear and simple. They should duly reflect the specificity of concessions as compared to public contracts and should not create an excessive amount of bureaucracy.'

3. Concessions versus Public Contracts

The fact that there is a conceptual difference between concessions and public contracts does not preclude the existence of significant similarities between them or the fact that there is even a certain relatedness between these two legal concepts. The similarities come clearly to the fore when we compare the definition of the concession with that of the public contract.

So then, concessions and public contracts have quite a lot in common. Their relatedness is also evident from the issue surrounding their definition. A contract is either a public contract or a works or services concession. It cannot qualify as both at one and the same time. The nature of the contract can of course change if there is a shift in some of the risks. Whereas public contracts tend to relate to the purely material execution of certain works, or supply of certain products or services, concessions relate to the commercial organisation of a given service provision or the setup and exploitation of a certain work at the risk and expense of the concessionaire.[11] But take away that transfer of risk to the concessionaire and the Union legislator is of the opinion that this is no longer a concession, but a public contract. The contract is scaled down then, as it were, from a method of organisation to a purely material implementation tool, in which the economic operator bears little in the way of responsibility.

We summarise below the main characteristics of works and services concessions.

The European law on public procurement has traditionally assumed that a concession contract for services/works exists (from the viewpoint of European public procurement law) if there is talk of a (written) contract for a pecuniary interest, through which the concessionaire is given the right to exploit the service/work, or this right is conferred at a price.[12] Another requirement is that the operational risk, or at least a significant portion of that risk, is transferred to the concessionaire.[13] The latter specification is part of the jurisprudence of the Court of Justice. It will be seen below that the new Directive retains this approach in its entirety. What is more, reference to a few other points has been found in the current interpretations, as we shall see.

Thus, the preamble of the new Concessions Directive stresses that concessions are contracts for pecuniary interest in which one or more contracting authorities or

11 Case C-272/91 *Commission v Italy* [1994] ECR I-01409.

12 See, among others, Article 1(4) of Directive 2004/18/EC. But there is no explicit mention there of operational risk.

13 See Conclusion by AG P. Cruz Villalón of in Case C-348/10 *Norma-A SIA en Dekom SIA v Latgales plānošanas regions* [2011] ECR I-10983, para. 50.

contracting entities entrust the execution of works or the provision and management of services to one or more economic operators. The purpose of these contracts is, so it is said, to procure works or services by means of a concession, the consideration for which consists in either the right to exploit the works or service, or in that right together with payment. The Directive itself describes a works concession as 'a contract for pecuniary interest concluded in writing by means of which one or more contracting authorities or contracting entities entrust the execution of works to one or more economic operators the consideration for which consists either solely in the right to exploit the works that are the subject of the contract or in that right together with payment' and a services concession as 'a contract for pecuniary interest concluded in writing by means of which one or more contracting authorities or contracting entities entrust the provision and the management of services other than the execution of works referred to in point (a) to one or more economic operators, the consideration of which consists either solely in the right to exploit the services that are the subject of the contract or in that right together with payment.'[14]

The award of a concession for works or for services, involves, as further clarified in Article 5 of the Directive, a transfer to the concessionaire of the operational risk (read: exploitation risk) that is inherent in the exploitation of the works or services and contains the demand or supply risk, or both.

It follows from the above that, according to the Concessions Directive, there are three constituent components. To start with, it must be – as is the case with public contracts – a written contract for pecuniary interest. Secondly, it must be – as is the case with public contracts – a contract for the execution of works or the provision of services. Finally, there must be a transfer of the operational risk. These three elements are discussed below.

4. Written Contract for Pecuniary Interest

To qualify as a concession contract, a contract must be in writing and must also be for pecuniary interest. As described explicitly in recital (14) of the preamble, concession contracts are therefore separate from licences or authorisations, where the Member State or an authority of that State sets the conditions for the performance of an economic activity, including a condition by which a certain operation is carried out, which normally would be granted at the request of an economic operator and not on the initiative of the contracting authority or the contracting entity and by which the economic operator is free to withdraw from the execution of the works or the provision of the service. Other than in the case of these operations by a Member State, concession contracts provide mutually binding obligations, where the execution of these works or services is subject to specific, legally compelling requirements set by the contracting authority or contracting entity.

The 'for pecuniary interest' element also reveals the *quid pro quo* character of the contract. The authority thus acquires certain benefits. It is stated explicitly in recital (11)

14 See Article 5(1)(a) and (b) Concessions Directive.

of the preamble, for example, that such a contract may involve a transfer of ownership to the contracting authorities or contracting entities, although it is immediately stated that this is not necessarily the case. The contracting authorities or contracting entities do, in any case, obtain, so the preamble says, 'the benefits of the works or services in question'. The latter is phrased rather unfortunately, albeit unintentionally. This is because the benefits will not very often serve the government directly, but rather the citizens. The benefit to the government is largely – indirectly – in that it no longer needs to carry out the works or provide the service that it considered necessary at the time. In turn, the concessionaire obtains the right to exploit the works or service, or the right together with payment.

The written element, finally, is explained in Article 5(6) of the Concessions Directive. It is any expression consisting of words or figures which can be read, reproduced and subsequently communicated, including information that is transmitted and stored by electronic means.

The three requirements above are hardly surprising at first glance. It will suffice to look at the communication on concession contracts in European law.[15] We read, for example, that operations for which a government authority merely grants authorisation or a licence in relation to an economic activity (for example acts related to pharmacies or taxis), even if these operations are termed as concession in some countries, cannot be considered as concession contracts for services of the type referred to in the aforementioned communication.[16] Those acts cannot be considered as acts whereby a public authority entrusts to a third party the total or partial management of services for which that authority would normally be responsible and for which the third party assumes the risk. The same communication also makes it immediately clear that unilateral operations by which the authority outsources services to a third party, which will then carry the operational risk and to which that third party consents, can in fact be considered as concession contracts of the type referred to in the aforementioned communication.[17] This approach is hardly surprising. The name that the parties give the legal act, or that the national law requires, is not decisive when community law is applied. Moreover, it is to be expected that the aforementioned category of operation will be (re)qualified as a service concession to make it relevant to the Concessions Directive. As is the case with public contracts, it is only to be expected that a functional approach will be used and that the explanation will be such that the 'useful effect of the directive is assured'.[18]

The notion that concessions are contracts for pecuniary interest did not go unchallenged initially.[19] The reflex in the other direction should come as no surprise; it

15 Interpretative communication of the Commission on concession contracts in community law, *Pb* C/121, 29 April 2000.

16 Ibid.

17 Ibid.

18 Case C-399/98 *Ordine degli Architetti delle Province di Milano e Lodi and Others v Comune di Milano* [2001] ECR I-5435, paras. 52 and 85.

19 S. Arrowsmith, *The Law of Public and Utilities Procurement*, London, Sweet & Maxwell, 2005, p. 322 and references in footnote 86.

is best seen as a conceptual explanation of the fact that service concessions were not regulated by the public procurement regulations, despite the fact that they give a very broad definition of the public service contract.[20] The approach is not worthy of support and is difficult to maintain. This is because the concept of 'for pecuniary interest' covers not only a consideration, consisting in the payment of a price, but can also cover the granting of exploitation rights. As the jurisprudence would later clarify, both contracts are for pecuniary interest, but the essential difference lies in the form of the consideration in concessions ('that is the granting of an exploitation right that may or may not come with a payment').[21]

5. Execution of Works or Provision of Services

The execution of works or provision of services is a central tenet of the concession contract. This is illustrated and explained in different ways in the preamble to the Concessions Directive. It has already been explained above, for example, that it involves the execution of works or services subject to specific requirements defined by the contracting authority or the contracting entity, which are legally enforceable. The Directive further clarifies what should be understood by the concept 'execution of works'. This concept covers the execution, or both the design and execution, of works related to one of the activities referred to in Annex I or of a work (the outcome of building or civil engineering works taken as a whole, which is sufficient in itself to fulfil an economic or technical function), or the realisation, by whatever means, of a work corresponding to the requirements specified by the contracting authority or contracting entity exercising a decisive influence on the type or design of the work.[22] A work is described as the outcome of building or civil engineering works taken as a whole, which is sufficient in itself to fulfil an economic or technical function.[23]

The preamble to the Concessions Directive goes on to clarify in recital (12) that the mere financing, in particular through grants, of an activity, which is frequently linked to the obligation to reimburse the amounts received where they are not used for the purposes intended, does not fall under the scope of the Directive. This is logical. In this case, performance is not imposed by the authority in question and so will not be enforceable.

The preamble specifies that arrangements where all operators fulfilling certain conditions are entitled to perform a given task, without any selectivity, such as customer choice and service voucher systems, should not qualify as concessions, even those based on legal agreements between the public authority and the economic operators. These arrangements are, so it says, typically based on a decision by a public authority defining the transparent and non-discriminatory conditions on the continuous access of economic operators to the provision of specific services, such as social services, allowing customers

20 Ibid.

21 Case C-348/10 *Norma-A SIA en Dekom SIA v Latgales plānošanas regions* [2011] ECR I-10983.

22 Article 5(7) of the Concessions Directive.

23 Article 5(8) of the Concessions Directive.

to choose between such operators.[24] The example of service vouchers would seem an unfortunate choice. This is because there is nothing to prevent a system like this from being set up under a genuine concession contract. It seems that the legislator sought above all to differentiate concessions from authorisations and accreditations under which a given activity is regulated, while at the same time any company could, in theory, carry out the activity, at least if it satisfied the conditions and (as a consequence) was accredited by the authority or authorised to provide the services in question. The Directive concerns acts whereby a public authority procures and entrusts to a selected third party the total or partial management of services or works for which that authority would normally be responsible and for which the third party assumes the risk.

The preamble goes on to say in recital (15) that works and services concessions should be separated from contracts in which natural resources are exploited. Some contracts that have as their object the right of an economic operator to exploit certain public domains or resources under private or public law, such as land or any public property, in particular in the maritime, inland ports or airports sector, whereby the State or contracting authority or contracting entity establishes only general conditions for their use without procuring specific works or services, should not, we read, qualify as concessions in the sense of the Directive. This is normally the case, it explains, with public domain or land lease contracts (i.e. property rental), which generally contain terms concerning entry into possession by the leaseholder (i.e. tenant), the use to which the property is to be put (i.e. rented property), the obligations of the lessor and lessee (i.e. tenant and landlord) regarding the maintenance of the leased premises (i.e. rented property), the duration of the lease and the giving up of possession (i.e. rented property) to the lessor (landlord), the lease price (i.e. rent) and the incidental charges to be paid by the lessee (i.e. tenant). The Directive's history shows that there was some concern that all kinds of 'public domain concessions', such as port concessions, would fall within the scope of the Directive.[25] The aforementioned passages clarify that this was not the intention. And yet caution is advised. There is always the risk, when all kind of obligations and charges (more particularly in the area of works and services) are imposed in a public domain concession, that the contract could re-qualify as a works or services concession.[26]

We read in recital (16) of the preamble that agreements that grant rights of way covering the utilisation of public immovable property for the provision or operation of fixed lines or networks intended to provide a service to the public should also not be considered as concessions in the sense of the Directive, insofar as those agreements

24 Recital (13) of the Concessions Directive.

25 See Press Release ESPO: ESPO News 17.32 December 2011, 'Ports Covered by New Concessions Directive but Impact Still Unclear'. In the end, the situation was to some extent clarified by including a passage in the preamble. See also the report of 1 February 2013 by observer P. Juvin on the proposal for a directive from the European Parliament and the Council on the award of concession contracts (COM(2011)0897 – C7-0004/2012 – 2011/0437(COD)), and in particular amendment no. 11.

26 With regard to this issue, see: S. Van Garsse, *De concessie in het raam van de publiek-private samenwerking (The concession in the context of the public private partnership)*, Bruges, die Keure, 2007, pp. 355 and following.

neither impose an obligation of supply nor involve any acquisition of services by a contracting authority or contracting entity to itself or to end users.

These elements of the Directive do not add much, in effect, to the normal interpretation of the works or services concession. Note that some language versions of the Directive no longer mention public works, a term that was used in previous public procurement contract directives. But no importance should be attached to this. The term public works had already been used in the previous Directive, and so has no special usage in other language versions of these Directives.

6. Operating Risk

Where the element 'operating risk' (i.e. exploitation risk) is concerned, the preamble to the Concessions Directive is very explicit. This feature of the concession, together with the concept of the public contract, has led to a great deal of legal insecurity and many judgements by the Court of Justice of the European Union,[27] which is why some clarification was needed.

The main feature of a concession, i.e. the right to exploit the works or services, as we read in the preamble, always implies a transfer to the concessionaire of an operating risk of economic nature involving the possibility that it will not recover the investments made and the costs incurred in operating the works or services awarded under normal operating conditions. The European legislator explains the approach as follows:

> 'The application of specific rules governing the award of concessions would not be justified if the contracting authority or contracting entity relieved the economic operator of any potential loss, by guaranteeing a minimal revenue, equal or higher to the investments made and the costs that the economic operator has to incur in relation with the performance of the contract. At the same time it should be made clear that certain arrangements which are exclusively remunerated by a contracting authority or a contracting entity should qualify as concessions where the recoupment of the investments and costs incurred by the operator for executing the work or providing the service depends on the actual demand for or the supply of the service or asset.'[28]

In Article 5(1) *in fine* of the Directive, this is regulated as follows: 'The award of a works or services concession shall involve the transfer to the concessionaire of an operating risk in exploiting those works or services encompassing demand or supply risk or both.' The preamble explains the two concepts in recital (20). Demand risk means the risk relating to the actual demand for the works or services which are the subject matter of the concession. Supply risk means the risk relating to the supply of the works or services which are the subject matter of the concession, in particular the risk that the provision of services does not match the demand. However, the term supply risk gives little clarity. For

27 See, among others, CoJ EU 10 November 2011, C-348/10; CoJ EU 10 March 2011, C-274/09; CoJ EU 10 September 2009, C206/08.

28 Recital (18) of the Concessions Directive.

example, how exactly does it differ from the term demand risk? And what concessions did the legislator have in mind? It is worth noting that this term replaces the term 'availability risk' in previous text versions of the draft Directive. This term, which occurs frequently in all kinds of PPP contracts (especially the so-called DBFM contracts),[29] was clear, but in the end was not retained. This is because the approach would have meant that DBFM contracts, which are seen in many Member States as public procurement contracts and are awarded under public procurement procedures, would have been considered as concession contracts from that point on.[30] It is a case of waiting to see how narrowly or how broadly the term is interpreted by the Court of Justice. It is also a case of waiting to see whether the Court judges that the two risks are counterparts, meaning that the term supply risk should be given no significant bearing.[31] One possible approach might be that concessions should always involve a genuine market risk. In PPP contracts, where availability is the basis, the contracting authority is generally the sole purchaser, meaning that there is no real talk of a market. The concessionaire will indeed have to assume all kinds of risks, relating to price trends, etc., but these risks are also a feature – albeit usually to a lesser extent – of the traditional public procurement contract (see *infra*).

The concessionaire is deemed, according to Article 5(1) *in fine*, to assume the operating risk where, under normal operating conditions, it is not guaranteed to recoup the investments made or the costs incurred in operating the works or the services which are the subject matter of the concession. The part of the risk transferred to the concessionaire shall involve real exposure to the vagaries of the market, such that any potential estimated loss incurred by the concessionaire shall not be merely nominal or negligible. An operating risk should stem from factors that are outside the control of the parties. Risks such as those linked to bad management, contractual defaults by the economic operator or to instances of *force majeure* are not decisive for the purpose of classification as a concession, since those risks are inherent in every contract, whether it be a public procurement contract or a concession. This approach is anything but new. On several occasions, the Court of Justice has already ruled that:

> '[I]t should be noted that the economic operating risk associated with the service should be understood as the risk of exposure to the vagaries of the market (in this sense see the *Eurawasser* judgement, quoted above, points 66 and 67), which takes shape in the danger of competition from other participants in the market, the danger of imbalance between demand and supply of the services, the risk of insolvency of those who will pay for the services provided, the risk that the operating costs are not fully covered by the revenues and the risk of liability for damage due to an inadequate service provision (see in this sense the judgement of

29 Design Build Finance Maintain.

30 Nonetheless, there is something to be said for this approach. In DBFM contracts, especially those considered 'off balance' by Eurostat, a great many, and in the latter category the majority, of the risks are transferred to the private contractor. Here, of course, the contract also assumes all kinds of business risks (such as risks arising from bad management, financial risks arising from pre-financing, construction risks, etc.) and it is up to that contractor to take appropriate measures, within the bounds of his/her contract, to manage these risks.

31 See, for example, the judgement cited below.

> 27 October 2005, *Contse et al.*, C-234/03, Jurispr. page I-9315, point 22, and *Hans & Christophorus Oymanns* judgement, quoted above, point 74). 38 On the other hand, risks such as those linked to bad management or errors of judgement by the market participant are not decisive for the purpose of qualifying a contract as a public services contract or a service concession contract, given that these risks are inherent in any contract, irrespective of whether they are a public services contract or a service concession contract.'[32]

What is new is that it is specified that, with a view to assessing the operating risk in a consistent and uniform manner, account can be taken of the net present value of all the concessionaire's investments, costs and revenue.[33] With this, the legislator clarifies how the risks can be assessed. This is an explicit address of previous complaints from the legal doctrine.[34]

Both the text of the Directive and that of the preamble say, finally, that for qualification, it is not unacceptable that a part of the risk remain with the contracting authority or the contracting entity. There can even still be talk of a concession in such a case. The fact that the risk is limited from the outset should not preclude the qualification of the contract as a concession, so we read in the preamble. This can be the case, for instance, in *sectors with regulated tariffs* or where the operating risk is limited *by means of contractual arrangements* providing for partial compensation, including compensation in the event of early termination of the concession for reasons attributable to the contracting authority or contracting entity or for reasons of *force majeure*.

With the first part of this clarification in the preamble, the legislator returns to the jurisprudence of the Court of Justice. The Court of Justice ruled earlier that it is not unusual that for some sectors of activity, namely sectors linked to public utility activities, such as water supply and waste water drainage, regulations apply that can involve a restriction of the economic risks.[35] This is, or so the Court has ruled, not in itself problematic. But it will always be necessary for the contracting authority to transfer its operating risk, in full or at least to a considerable extent, to the concessionaire. For that matter, the preamble explains, in line with this, that where sector-specific regulation eliminates the risk by providing for a guarantee to the concessionaire on breaking even on investments and costs incurred for operating the contract, such a contract should not qualify as a concession within the meaning of the Directive. This approach too is anything but new. The same idea could be found earlier in the European Commission's interpretative communication on concession contracts in community law in relation to contractual regulations. Notwithstanding regulations for exceptional conditions (more on this below), the concessionaire cannot be assured, *a priori*, a fixed return and/or the certainty that his/her costs will always be covered.

The passages in the second part of this clarification in the preamble, which relate to 'contractual arrangements', explain that concessions do not lose their character if the contract contains clauses 'providing for partial compensation, including compensation in

32 Case C-274/09 *Privater Rettungsdienst und Krankentransport Stadler v Zweckverband für Rettungsdienst und Feuerwehralarmierung Passau* [2011] ECR I-01335.

33 See recital (20) of the Concessions Directive.

34 S. Van Garsse, *De concessie in het raam van de publiek-private samenwerking (The concession in the context of the public private partnership)*, Bruges, die Keure, 2007, p. 568.

35 Ibid.

the event of early termination of the concession for reasons attributable to the contracting authority or contracting entity or for reasons of *force majeure*'. It seems unfortunate to us that the text says arrangements providing for 'partial' compensation. This is because, in practice, in a case of *force majeure* and certainly in the case of termination by the principal, it is often the case that the contractor receives full compensation. Here, too, we are of the opinion that it is still defensible to say that in this case it is more about the part of the risk that has remained with the contracting authority or the contracting entity. In other words, in concessions, the risks are not only shared (which to a certain point is clearly perfectly acceptable), but divided. Risks related to special circumstances (e.g. circumstances that could be described as unforeseeable) are often retained by the contracting authority. The concept of the concession as defined in the Directive appears to us not to preclude *a priori* something akin to this. On the contrary, the legislator's stipulation that there can be no guarantee 'in normal market conditions' that costs or investments can be recovered, allows for the interpretation, in our opinion, that there is nothing to prevent concessions from containing clauses that would lead, in exceptional conditions, to compensation or a redress of the economic balance.

7. The Legal Regime in the New Concessions Directive

There is much that can be written about the new legal regime of concessions, particularly when compared to public procurement contracts. But it is beyond the scope of the present chapter to delve into this too deeply. We will confine ourselves to the few points below.

Public contracts are, as we know, extremely detailed and at times very rigidly regulated. The implementation of the public contracts regulations has given rise in many Member States to real codices of legislation on public contracts. The Concessions Directive takes another approach. Although inspiration was clearly sought, for some of its provisions, in the public procurement contract directives (copy and paste at times), the regulation of concessions can still be seen as 'light', all things considered. But roughly the same themes are covered.

Among other things, the Concessions Directive regulates the financial scope of the Directive (for concessions the threshold is €5,186,000) and gives provisions on how the estimate is to be made.

The Directive also contains a long list of exclusions. Various exclusions have been taken from the public procurement directives. It is not always easy to see their relevance. In other cases, it seems that exclusions have been added to reach a compromise on the text. Concessions for water supply and distribution, for example, have been excluded, remarkably enough. As in the public contract regulations, a 'light' regime was introduced for social and specific services.

The Concessions Directive contains, unlike the public contract regulations, specific provisions on the duration of concessions.[36]

The Concessions Directive contains, as do the public procurement contract directives, various procedural guarantees, which are often more flexibly regulated or regulated on

[36] Article 18 Concessions Directive.

the basis of principles. These are rules on: publication, communication, minimal time limits, qualitative selection and exclusion and award criteria, tender procedures, and judicial protection.

Finally, the Directive contains rules on substantial modification.[37] This regulation is identical to that in the public procurement directives. This might come as a surprise because the two types of contracts (regular contracts and concessions) do, however, differ significantly and we would expect more flexible regulations for concessions, as the ultimate contracts of duration.

8. Closing Considerations

The new Concessions Directive is no Copernican revolution. But the legislator has attempted to clarify the concept and has worked towards a light and flexible legal regime.

Analysis of the constituent parts of the concept of the works and services concession in the Directive shows that the European legislator has, to a considerable extent, sought alliance with the jurisprudence of the Court of Justice and the legal practice of the European Commission. This is perhaps quite understandable because, in the end, it was necessary to reach a consensus with a great many parties over the concept of the works and services concession.

The legal regime is noticeably more flexible than the public procurement directives. And this is, of course, quite understandable too. Services concessions were until very recently unregulated and works concessions were regulated only to a limited extent in secondary European law. The new Directive takes an important step forward. The most useful aspect is that it is based on (the clarification of) principles of primary law.

Does it solve all our future problems? Of course not. The Directive contains various concepts (such as the supply risk) that are not entirely clear. No doubt questions will arise when the new legal regime is applied. It is a matter of waiting to see how the European Commission and the Court of Justice will deal with these questions.

37 Article 43 Concessions Directive.

EU GREEN PUBLIC PROCUREMENT POLICY
MODERNISATION PACKAGE, ECO-LABELLING AND FRAMING MEASURES

Hanna Schebesta*

1. Introduction

On 20 December 2011, the European Commission tabled the so-called public procurement modernisation package, adopted by the Council on 11 February 2014.[1] The modernisation package consists of a revision of the classical and sector directives, as well as a new concessions directive, which all have to be transposed by the Member States until by April 2016. This contribution surveys the changes that the new classical Directive 2014/24/EU introduces with respect to green public procurement. It discusses in particular the issue of eco-labelling, taking into account the *Dutch Eco-Labels* case law, and the body of green procurement framing measures that complement the modernisation package.

1.1. Environmental Considerations in EU Public Procurement

Public procurement markets make up an important part of the EU's gross domestic product (commonly estimated at 17%). The fact that *governments* are buying makes procurement markets different from a market based on private transactions. The public buyer is expected to also pursue public goals, using public procurement as an instrument of public policy making. The rationales underlying public procurement regulation are based on a variety of concerns, combining (1) anti-corruption/transparency, (2) efficiency (the best value for money), (3) policy instruments such as social and environmental

* Hanna Schebesta is a Lecturer at the Law and Governance Group of Wageningen University and Research Centre (the Netherlands); Academic Assistant to the Alias project at the European University Institute (Florence, Italy).

1 Proposal for a Directive of the European Parliament and of the Council on public procurement, 20 December 2011, COM(2011)896 final. The modernisation package consists of Directive 2014/24/EU replacing Directive 2004/18/EC; Directive 2014/25/EU replacing Directive 2004/17/EC; and a new Directive on concessions, Directive 2014/23/EU.

considerations, (4) competition concerns and (5) building an internal market for government procurement in the EU context.[2]

At the EU level, these rationales translate into dispersed policy-making across different portfolios in the Commission, sometimes in tension with one another. The EU internal market building effort was the initial policy driver for procurement rulemaking and procurement legislation was shaped by the fact that the Internal Market Directorate General was responsible. Politically speaking, an impetus for developing a *green* procurement policy framework developed relatively late. It was enshrined in the political agenda with the EU Sustainable Development Strategy[3] (2001–2011) and the 6th Environmental Action Programme for 2002–2012[4] that identified green procurement as important, as did the Lisbon strategy and Europe 2020 within an economic context.

The main initial developments on green procurement therefore took place in another institution, namely the Court of Justice of the EU (CJEU). It developed an important legal subtext to the EU procurement directives in force at the time. This case law sheds an interesting light on the stance of the Commission. At the time, the Commission's submissions in these legal proceedings were driven by a rather uncompromised dedication to the internal market logic, and a strict interpretation of the procurement legislative framework that allowed no deviation for environmental considerations.[5]

1.2. *Early Case Law Driving the Development of a Green Procurement Policy*

Public procurement procedures under the Directives were to use either price or the most economically advantageous tender (MEAT) as award criteria. It was questionable how far social criteria could be reconciled with this economic approach. Did the economically most advantageous tender criterion leave room for considerations of wider policymaking nature, so-called secondary considerations?

In *Nord-Pas de Calais*,[6] the CJEU gave an affirmative answer to this question, holding that the MEAT procedure could include a long-term unemployment criterion as *award criterion*. Based on this judgment it was generally presumed that the reasoning would also apply to green criteria. The argument was soon tested in front of the Court in the *Concordia Bus*[7] case. The Commission had argued that environmental criteria were only acceptable where they conferred a direct economic advantage. The Court disagreed, holding that criteria did not have to confer advantages of a strictly economic nature. However, they had to be linked to the 'subject matter of the contract'. Accordingly, bus transport services could be awarded using award criteria that valued buses not to exceed

2 H. Schebesta, *Towards an EU Law of Damages? Damages claims for violations of EU public procurement law before national and European judges*, (2013) PhD thesis, European University Institute.

3 DOC 10917/06.

4 Decision No 1600/2002/EC.

5 P. Kunzlik, 'From suspect practice to market-based instrument: policy alignment and the evolution of EU law's approach to "green" public procurement', *Public Procurement Law Review*, 2013, vol. 3, pp. 97–115.

6 Case C-225/98, *Nord-Pas de Calais* [2000] ECR I-7445.

7 Case C-513/99, *Concordia Bus Finland v Helsingin Kaupunki* [2002] ECR I-7213.

noise and pollution emission limits. Such criteria were linked to the subject matter, as long as they were clearly defined (i.e. there was no unlimited choice for the contracting authority), had been duly published and were not discriminatory. In *EVN Wienstrom*,[8] the CJEU further held that an award criterion for the supply of electricity favouring renewable energy sources is in principle permissible. Again, the Commission had taken a largely restrictive approach on this, for example stating that technical specifications relating to the production processes and methods were not allowed unless they affected the product at consumption stage. The Court finally cast this interpretation away. The case, however, also imposed some limits on 'green' procurement. First of all, a green criterion was not allowed if the accuracy of the information in the tenders could not be verified. Secondly, an award criterion that allocated most points to the tenderer providing the most overall renewable energy to their customers (in excess of the volumes expected in the context of the procurement) was not permitted. Award criteria could be weighed only in respect of the subject matter of the contract, and not for the overall policy of an economic operator's production.

Following *Nord-Pas de Calais*, the Commission issued an interpretative communication on social considerations in public procurement in 2001.[9] In 2004, finally going back on its initially reluctant stance, the Commission issued the important *Buying Green!* Commission handbook,[10] followed in 2008 by the Commission communication on *Public Procurement for a Better Environment*.[11] The 2008 Commission communication defines public procurement as 'a process whereby public authorities seek to procure goods, services and works with a reduced environmental impact throughout their life cycle when compared to goods, services and works with the same primary function that would otherwise be procured'.

Green procurement is an exemplary illustration for the dialogue between the CJEU case law and the Commission legislative efforts. The Commission first entered the debate with soft law instruments.[12] Only much later, namely with the current public procurement modernisation package, did environmental concerns become one of the main issues

8 Case C-448/01, *EVN AG and Wienstrom GmbH v Austria* [2003] ECR I-4527.

9 Interpretative Communication of the Commission on the Community law applicable to public procurement and the possibilities for integrating social considerations into public procurement, Brussels, 15 October 2001, COM(2001)566 final.

10 European Commission, *Buying Green!: A Handbook on Environmental Public Procurement* (2004), which was published again in a fully revised version in 2011. Both editions are available at http://ec.europa.eu/environment/gpp/buying_handbook_en.htm.

11 European Commission Communication *Public Procurement for a Better Environment*, COM(2008)400, published on 16 July 2008 and which was accompanied by a staff working document and must be seen in the wider policy context of the Communication from the Commission to the European Parliament, the Council, the European Economic and Social Committee and the Committee of the Regions on the Sustainable Consumption and Production and Sustainable Industrial Policy Action Plan, COM(2008)0397 final.

12 Interpretative Communication of the Commission on the Community law applicable to public procurement and the possibilities for integrating social considerations into public procurement, Brussels, 15 October 2001, COM(2001)566 final. On 18 June 2003, the European Commission also adopted a Communication on 'Integrated Product Policy: Building on Environmental Life-Cycle Thinking', COM(2003)302 final. In 2009 the Commission issued a Communication entitled

addressed in legislative terms.[13] The general procurement Directive 2014/24/EU follows the mandate of Article 11 TFEU that states that environmental protection requirements are to be integrated into the definition and implementation of the Union policies and activities.[14] In the following, we examine the main changes to green public procurement for the general Directive introduced by the modernisation package.

2. Green Public Procurement and Directive 2014/24/EU

Even after the adoption of the procurement modernisation package, green procurement remains a rather technical effort. From the beginning, green procurement was tied to a nuanced understanding of the different requirements that contracting authorities may set in a procedure, the four different kinds of criteria being: (1) technical specifications, (2) selection criteria (i.e. exclusion and suitability criteria), (3) award criteria, and (4) contract performance clauses. Since they are often conflated, this contribution looks at the changes introduced by the modernisation package for green public procurement (GPP) through the lens of these criteria.

2.1. Technical Specifications (Article 42, Annex VII)

Technical specifications lay down the characteristics required of a works, service or supply. These relate to qualities of the product itself, not to qualities of the tenderer. They are now governed by Article 42, and a definition of technical specifications is included in point 1 of Annex VII of the Directive. Technical specifications are the 'totality of the technical prescriptions' of the purchase a contracting authority intends to make through the procurement procedure.

With the modernisation package, these characteristics may now also refer to specific processes or production methods 'even where such factors do not form part of their material substance, provided that they are linked to the subject-matter of the contract and proportionate to its value and its objectives.'[15] Technical specifications should be formulated (a) in terms of performance or functional requirements, including environmental characteristics or (b) by reference to technical specifications and national, EU and other standards accompanied by the words 'or equivalent'. Modernisation has codified that also production processes (which are not reflected in the quality of the product itself) can be considered, and that they can also be considered *for other stages in their life cycle.*

'Contributing to Sustainable Development: The role of Fair Trade and nongovernmental trade-related sustainability assurance schemes' (COM(2009)215 final).

13 'The proposed Directive is based on an enabling approach providing contracting authorities with the instruments needed to contribute to the achievement of the Europe 2020 strategic goals by using their purchasing power to procure goods and services that foster innovation, respect the environment and combat climate change while improving employment, public health and social conditions', proposal COM(2011)0895 final, p. 9.

14 Directive 2014/24/EU, recital (91).

15 Directive 2014/24/EU, Article 42(1).

2.2. *Qualitative Selection Criteria (Articles 57–64)*

By contrast, qualitative selection criteria target the potential counterparts of a contract, the entity that the contracting authority wants to contract with in its personal capacity.

Selection criteria are regulated by the Directive, which distinguishes between obligatory and possible exclusionary grounds (Article 57), plus suitability criteria in the narrow sense (Article 58). Obligatory exclusion grounds are a conviction for involvement in organised crime, corruption, fraud, terrorism, money laundering and child labour, as well as fraud in relation to tax and social security contributions. Contracting authorities *may* also exclude a bidder from the process in cases where certain grounds concerning the supplier's personal position are met (e.g. bankruptcy, professional misconduct, non-payment of social security or taxes). Under selection criteria in the narrow sense, bidders may also be assessed and excluded on the basis of their (a) suitability to pursue the professional activity, (b) economic and financial standing, and (c) technical and professional ability.

A new 'green' ground for possible exclusion has been included: in the performance of public contracts, enterprises have to comply with the applicable environmental obligations stemming from EU, international and national law (Article 18(2)), and an enterprise which does not respect these obligations may be excluded from the tender procedure (Article 57(4)(a)). Environmental law compliance may be used as a qualitative selection criterion.

Another way of defining the desired subjective quality of an economic operator is by using selection criteria in the narrow sense that mandate for example compliance with quality assurance standards and environmental management standards such as the ISO 14000 series or the Eco-Management and Audit Scheme (EMAS). To do so, contracting authorities shall refer to the EMAS or other relevant certificates (Article 62). Simply requiring such certification is not permitted under the Directives; requested certification must be linked to the subject of the contract in which case the certificate may serve as a proof (although other methods must be equally accepted). Other uses of suitability criteria are possible, and for example prior experience in 'green' contracts can be prescribed as an indicator of professional competence.

2.3. *Award Criteria (Articles 67–69)*

Award criteria are characterised by the fact that they are used in a specific stage of the formal procurement procedure. They lay down criteria and their weighting according to which the submitted bids are ranked. The subject of this type of criteria is therefore the individual bid that is put forward by a tenderer and the criteria express a preference of the contracting authority.

The process for the award stage of procurement procedures is laid down in Articles 67–69. The contract is awarded to the most economically advantageous tender, on the basis of price or cost. The costs are assessed on the basis of 'criteria, including qualitative, environmental and/or social aspects, linked to the subject-matter of the public contract in question' (Article 67). The relative weighting of the criteria chosen to determine the most economically advantageous tender must be specified, except in awards relying on price alone.

A particular novelty of Directive 2014/24/EU is that the MEAT can be defined on the basis of life-cycle costing (Article 68). This is a holistic approach to costs, covering the acquisition, use, maintenance and end of life phases of purchases. In addition they cover 'costs imputed to environmental externalities linked to the product, service or works during its life cycle, provided their monetary value can be determined and verified; such costs may include the cost of emissions of greenhouse gases and of other pollutant emissions and other climate change mitigation costs.' An example of an environmental externality is 'pollution caused by extraction of raw materials used in the product or caused by the product itself or its manufacturing, provided they can be monetised and monitored'.[16]

The new lifecycle costing approach taken by the Directive may be one of the most fundamental modernisation changes, and highly relevant to green procurement. It is a so-called horizontal provision with great application potential. At the same time, the approach is rather unspecified, and seems to legitimise a degree of experimentation with respect to green procuring. The contracting authority can simply find ways of accounting that better reflect underlying green policy concerns. 'Creative accounting' may be the most effective approach of influencing the outcome of procurement procedures. Additionally, the provision ties in the 'EU GPP criteria' soft law effort which drew up voluntary GPP criteria and life-cycle accounting methods for a number of product groups (see below). The lifecycle accounting reinforces this policy effort since it provides the few existing examples of how the lifecycle costing can be correctly undertaken.

2.4. Contract Performance Criteria (Article 70–73)

Contract performance conditions are specific requirements relating to the performance of a contract; they are pertinent in the post-award stage. They may not be disguised technical specifications, award or selection criteria and not be of a nature as to have changed the outcome of the procurement procedure.

A contracting authority can stipulate individual 'green' contract performance conditions, e.g. requirements 'intended to favour the implementation of measures for [...] the protection of the environment or animal welfare'.[17] These 'special conditions relating to the performance of a contract' must also be linked to the subject matter of the contract (Article 70). However, they may not extend to requirements referring to a general corporate policy.[18]

The Directive introduced a general duty on Member States to ensure economic operators' compliance with legal obligations, including environmental conventions listed in Annex X[19] (Article 18(2)). This can be seen as an implied mandatory contract performance clause that governs all contracts regardless of an explicit stipulation thereof.

16 Directive 2014/24/EU, recital (96).

17 Directive 2014/24/EU, recital (98).

18 Directive 2014/24/EU, recital (104).

19 Annex X lists the following Conventions: ILO Convention 87 on Freedom of Association and the Protection of the Right to Organise; ILO Convention 98 on the Right to Organise and Collective

3. Use of Eco-Labels

A particularly contested aspect, which has undergone significant change in the course of modernisation, is the use of eco-labels. This development is intrinsically linked to the distinction of the different types of procurement criteria listed above, and a deep controversy on how they can be used during procurement procedures in order to advance environmental concerns.

The original Directive 2004/18/EC contained a provision on labels that was then interpreted by the CJEU in the *Dutch Eco-Labels* case[20] (rendered in May 2012). In parallel, the procurement modernisation package in December 2011 proposed a substantially different provision on eco-labels.[21] Consequently, the proposal was amended, resulting in the current version of the provision in Directive 2014/24/EU.

The original Directive 2004/18/EC dealt with eco-labels solely under technical specifications. Contracting authorities were allowed to use the detailed specifications (or parts thereof) of specific labels and could indicate that the use of a certain label would create the presumption that the products bearing that label comply with the characteristics thus defined. Other means of proof had to be accepted. On a textual reading, it was quite clear that mere reference to a label was not sufficient if the specifications were not listed in the procurement documentation. Eco-labels then became an issue in the *Dutch Eco-Labels* case, which saw the Netherlands being brought in front of the CJEU by the Commission in 2010. The case concerned a procurement procedure in which EKO and Max Havelaar labels had been included without any reference to the underlying specifications.

In parallel, the proposal for a new directive was tabled in the modernisation package of 2011. On 15 January 2014, the European Parliament approved the proposal on first reading with far-reaching amendments. With respect to eco-labels the text was modified in order to allow eco-labels not only for technical specifications, but also for award criteria and contract performance conditions. According to the current Article 43 of Directive 2014/24/EU, contracting authorities may refer to eco-labels, but where they do not require all of the label requirements, they must indicate which label requirements are referred to. In addition, all labels meeting equivalent label requirements must be accepted. Although it is now possible for contracting authorities to refer to eco-labels, the provision requires an examination of a label's underlying specifications since those aspects which are not required by a contracting authority must be singled out. In addition, all of the

Bargaining; ILO Convention 29 on Forced Labour; ILO Convention 105 on the Abolition of Forced Labour; ILO Convention 138 on Minimum Age; ILO Convention 111 on Discrimination (Employment and Occupation); ILO Convention 100 on Equal Remuneration; ILO Convention 182 on Worst Forms of Child Labour; Vienna Convention for the Protection of the Ozone Layer and its Montreal Protocol on Substances that Deplete the Ozone Layer; Basel Convention on the Control of Transboundary Movements of Hazardous Wastes and their Disposal (Basel Convention); Stockholm Convention on Persistent Organic Pollutants (Stockholm POPs Convention); and the Convention on the Prior Informed Consent Procedure for Certain Hazardous Chemicals and Pesticides in International Trade (UNEP/FAO) (The PIC Convention) Rotterdam, 10 September 1998, and its 3 regional Protocols.

20 Case C-368/10 *Commission v Netherlands (Dutch Eco-Labels)* [2012], not yet reported.

21 Proposal for a Directive of the European Parliament and of the Council on public procurement, 20 December 2011, COM(2011)896 final.

required characteristics of the label must be linked to the subject matter of the contract, therefore the contracting authority must also analyse whether indeed all specifications of a referred label fulfil this criterion.

Given the timing of the *Dutch Eco-Labels* case, and since the legislative text has undergone significant changes, it is important to understand how far the case is still pertinent for GPP.

3.1. The Dutch Eco-Labels Case in the Light of the Procurement Modernisation Package

In terms of facts, the case concerned the requirement of two distinct eco-labels, namely EKO and Max Havelaar. As we will see, this makes the case more interesting, as the different specifications underlying a label were legally relevant and lead to important differences in the outcome.

The Commission alleged that the use of EKO and Max Havelaar labels in a tender notice was a breach of Articles 23(6) and 23(8) of Directive 2004/18/EC concerning the technical specifications and additionally did not constitute a permissible award criterion.

The CJEU held that under Article 23(6) Directive 2004/18/EC, the detailed specifications of an eco-label may be used to detail the technical specifications, but not the eco-label (here EKO) as such. Simply requiring the EKO label as a technical specification without referring to its underlying specifications was illegal, as it quite demonstrably went against the text of the Directive as it was then in force. The Court accordingly ruled that the Netherlands had breached the Directive. This ruling would now probably be different as the text of the Directive changed. In this respect, Directive 2014/24/EU reverses the outcome of *Dutch Eco-Labels*, as the case had interpreted a text that is now modified. According to the new Directive, if all label specifications were required, e.g. in this case 95% organic origin of produce, the mere reference to the EKO label in the tender documents would now be permissible. However, contracting authorities that do require a specific label must accept bids with labels confirming their equivalence to the required one.

The Max Havelaar label on the other hand describes products of fair trade origin, purchased at a price and under conditions more favourable than those determined by market forces from organisations made up of small-scale producers in developing countries. It is a fair trade label. The CJEU held that this label did not constitute a technical specification in the sense of Article 23 Directive 2004/18/EC. Instead, the Max Havelaar label fell under 'conditions for performance of contracts' under Article 26. The question is how a general fair trade label such as the Max Havelaar one would fare nowadays. Can a fair trade label be used as a technical specification?

The definition of technical specifications in the new Directive has changed. Article 42(1) of Directive 2014/24/EU reads: 'Those characteristics may also refer to the specific process or method of production or provision of the requested works, supplies or services or to a specific process for another stage of its life cycle even where such factors do not form part of their material substance provided that they are linked to the subject-matter of the contract and proportionate to its value and its objectives.'

Recital (97) explicitly states that fair trade conditions are an example of factors involved in the production or provision process. The recital in this context only refers to award and contract performance criteria (in line with *Dutch Eco-Labels*). The European Parliament, however, later amended the Directive to also include a reference to production processes for technical specifications. In this respect, the new Directive has changed the outcome of the *Dutch Eco-Labels* case. Arguably, Max Havelaar could now be used as a technical specification, based on the changed wording of the technical specifications definition.

Thirdly, the Commission had questioned whether it was permissible to establish an *award criterion* (Article 53 of Directive 2004/18) requiring that the ingredients to be supplied had to bear EKO and/or Max Havelaar labels. The CJEU confirmed that the most economically advantageous tender (MEAT) award criteria may be not only economic but also qualitative. The question whether there was a sufficient link to the subject matter of contract was answered in the affirmative, and therefore organic and fair trade origin labels could be used as award criteria. However, mere reference to the labels or equivalent without precision regarding the specifications underlying the labels was not permissible.

The Court held in the context of the contract performance criteria that both labels' requirements had a sufficient link to the object of the contract. Since fair trade conditions as set by Max Havelaar were judged by the court to have a sufficient link to the subject matter, it seems to follow that they must now also be assumed to be valid technical specifications by virtue of having a sufficient link to the contract. In this sense, the new Directive 'overrules' the *Dutch Eco-Labels* case by providing that process specifications can be allowed. Only where a label prescribes technical requirements that approach a general corporate policy, can this be questioned. In analogy to *EVN Wienstrom* this might be the case where a renewable energy award criterion for all electricity produced by an entity would be set, beyond that part of the electricity that is actually purchased by the contracting authority.

3.2. *Explaining the New Approach of Directive 2014/24/EU*

During the adoption process, environmental organisations lobbied for a 'functional' rather than an overly legal technical understanding of how environmental considerations could be included in procurement procedures. The adopted text of the Directive must be understood in this light and follows these calls.

After the publication of the initial modernisation proposal, the distinction according to the content between technical specifications, award criteria and contract performance conditions was criticised.[22] The key demand for changing the Directives was to abandon the artificial distinction aligning certain criteria with permissible content in favour of the broad 'link to the subject matter' rule. These suggestions have been taken on board by the amended proposal for the Directive and the adopted Directive.

22 See for example 'Distinguishing technical specifications and award criteria on the basis of role, not content', Client Earth, May 2012, available at www.clientearth.org/reports/role-not-content-distinguishing-technical-specifications-and-award-criteria.pdf.

So understood, contracting authorities have the possibility at all stages and in respect of all criteria to rely on an eco-label. The choice should ultimately be based on what they want to achieve. By relying on the *role* of the criteria, contracting authorities ought to decide whether a given environmental criterion is a minimum requirement or merely a preference that may be weighed against other criteria. True requirements are technical specifications, while preferences subject to weighting are award criteria. By their very nature, contract performance conditions are not verifiable at the tender stage, and therefore are a much more evasive kind of criteria than the previous two. It is based on these considerations, then, that the tender criteria ought to be classified. Instead of the content-based classification of criteria, the amended Directive supports the advocated role-based approach.[23]

4. Eco-Labels and their Significance for Green Public Procurement

The procurement modernisation package, one can observe, has greatly facilitated the ease with which contracting authorities can refer to eco-labels. Although this may be a desirable feature, one should not too easily forget the reason why the mere reference to labels was previously prohibited.

4.1. *Content Level Considerations*

A label is not just a label. Labels stand for different types of specifications and therefore it is important to look beyond the label at the underlying requirements. The old procurement regime was more favourable to that by requiring contracting authorities to explicitly state the specifications of a label. In addition, the *Dutch Eco-Labels* case was sensitive to the differences in labels, and distinguished a one-dimensional technical specification label such as EKO (95% organic origin) from the Max Havelaar general fair trade requirements. Although under the new regime, contracting authorities need to engage with the background specifications, it seems that it is easy for them to simply assume that they require all specifications of a given label. This may be warranted for simple one-dimensional labels, but the multi-dimensional labels are more difficult to justify.

Environmental concerns are but one facet of multi-dimensional sustainability standards. In particular, sustainability standards increasingly combine environmental, social, managerial, qualitative and ethical requirements. Coffee with the Netherlands as the destination market has at least 35 sustainability standards.[24] To illustrate the different specifications we will compare three main sustainability standards, namely the Fair Trade label (the Max Havelaar Foundation is Fair Trade Netherlands), UTZ Certified and EU Organic Farming.[25] The Fair Trade specifications are manifold, and for example grant a fair trade premium above the market price and guarantee a minimum price to producers.

23 Ibid.

24 See www.standardsmap.org, which provides a breakdown of different sustainability standards in five sustainability dimensions according to geographical origin, destination and product group.

25 This comparison is based on the results using the standardsmap tool. It identifies requirements ('hotspots') according to five sustainability dimensions, one of which is environment, the others being social, management, quality, and ethical requirements. For the results, see www.standardsmap.org/

UTZ Certified on the other hand adheres more to market principles and does not provide for an extra premium. EU Organic Farming on the other hand mainly contains environmental requirements, next to few quality and management criteria. This makes EU Organic Farming most akin to a one-dimensional standard. Of the three, Fair Trade covers the most environmental criteria (namely 53), EU Organic Farming follows with 47, while UTZ Certified includes 36 requirements. Comparing Fair Trade and UTZ Certified as multi-dimensional standards, Fair Trade includes a superior number of environmental and quality requirements while the other dimensions remain similar in quantity.[26] The degree of obligation is clearly highest for the EU Organic Farming scheme, in which all requirements are for immediate action and no recommendations are included. Fair Trade has a wider span for ultimate implementation of the specifications, but does not use recommendations, while UTZ Certified does handle mere recommendatory requirements (i.e. the weakest form of obligation that can be undertaken).

Figure 1. Hotspots per sustainability area

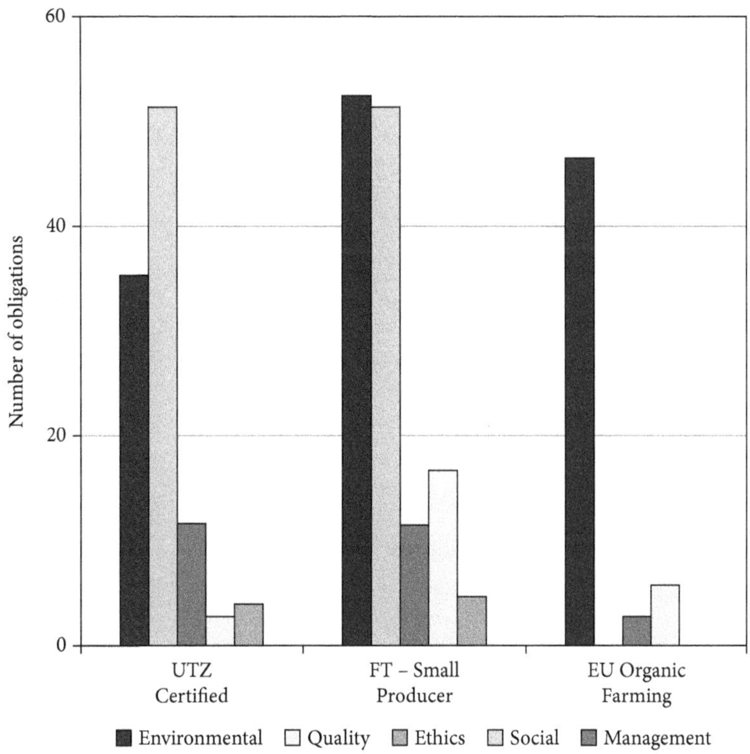

Source: www.standardsmap.org; comparison of three sustainability standards.

compare?standards=66,71,185&shortlist=66,71,185&product=Coffee&origin=Any&market=Netherlands&cbi=78:78:755.

26 Clearly, this quantitative comparison of requirements does not do justice to an in-depth comparison of the quality of the different requirements and is undertaken for illustrative purposes only.

Directive 2014/24/EU makes it possible to require specific (eco) labels. However, it is then on the contracting authority to ascertain that label requirements exclusively concern criteria that are linked to the subject matter of the contract. This is an obligation under Article 43(1)(a) of Directive 2014/24/EU. Where this is not the case, i.e. requirements not linked to the subject matter are set, contracting authorities may define the specifications by reference to those of the label (Article 43(2)).

The use of eco-labels places responsibility on contracting authorities to ascertain the quality of those labels they require in their procurement procedures. While the requirements as such are one aspect of the quality of labels, another one is linked to their governance and also legitimacy.

4.2. *Governance and Legitimacy*

Even where the technical specifications are the same, it is important to realise that labels are often private or mixed governance schemes. What is behind a label can hugely vary in terms of governance and also enforcement.

In fact, the text of the Directives has required contracting authorities in theory to go beyond the surface of labels. This is not only the case for substantive questions, e.g. what are the technical requirements underlying a label, but goes further to private governance questions. Labels need to satisfy the (now) five conditions, most of which were already laid down in the earlier Directive 2004/18/EC.

The conditions are listed in Article 43 of Directive 2014/24/EU; in particular, the last three conditions target the governance of labels:

> '(c) the labels are established in an open and transparent procedure in which all relevant stakeholders, including government bodies, consumers, social partners, manufacturers, distributors and non-governmental organisations, may participate;
> (d) the labels are accessible to all interested parties;
> (e) the label requirements are set by a third party over which the economic operator applying for the label cannot exercise a decisive influence.'

To this author's best knowledge, these conditions have not featured in public procurement litigation. However, if taken seriously, they could provide an indirect control of transparency and legitimacy on private standardisation bodies. Given the importance of the public demand for private initiatives, it is, at least in theory, an instrument of meta-governance on private standard setting governance.

Research points to the potential downsides of private governance schemes, such as the different quality of labels and certificates. Industry often responds to a specific prevalent standard by creating a competing more industry-friendly standard. Governance regimes of labels and certification vary, and stakeholder involvement is certainly not always guaranteed.[27]

[27] L. Gulbrandsen, 'Dynamic governance interactions: Evolutionary effects of state responses to non-state certification programs', *Regulation & Governance*, 2014, vol. 8, pp. 74–92, 86.

For example with respect to the timber certification, CPET (the UK government established body to assess certification schemes) concluded that the forest umbrella certification PEFC did not meet requirements due to 'unbalanced governance, inadequate public consultation during the certification process, and lack of public disclosure of auditing outcomes'.[28] In response, the PFEC modified its governance mechanisms. This illustrates on one the hand that public authorities by inclusion/exclusion can significantly influence internal processes of standardisation bodies. On the other hand, it also demonstrates that many countries quite willingly accepted a standard that was perhaps questionable on several grounds. It further points to the necessity for contracting authorities not only to engage with the substantive specifications set on specific products or production process, but equally to examine the governance of the private bodies that set standards and govern labels and certificates.

4.3. *Influence of Public Procurement on Private Purchases*

In particular in the light of this development, the influence on private purchasing and uptake beyond procurement ought to be highlighted. Empirically, research bears out an important influence of public demand on private standardisation and demand thereof. The effect of procurement policies in the Member States on certification schemes has been documented, describing how the active inclusion of certification labels in procurement procedures has drastically influenced the market for timber certification.[29]

By supporting specific certificates, or equally labels, that guarantee the compliance with eco-friendly standards, governments indirectly exert influence on private purchasing. It produces a signalling effect, and 'by approving specific certification schemes, governments signal that those schemes are credible governance systems on which private producers and other buyers can rely.'[30] In addition, it often engenders a whole chain effect, resulting in suppliers switching over to certified products for all of their customers.[31] Procurement practice therefore can have an important influence extending beyond contracting authorities' immediate purchases.

5. EU Green Public Procurement Framing Measures

While the prior discussion revolved around the facilitation of green procurement, it is important to note that there are also hard law *obligations* on contracting authorities to procure greenly. Apart from the EU public procurement directives themselves, a green procurement framing measures framework has been growing that is often neglected. These include hard law obligations, complemented by a number of timely soft law initiatives that target specific product groups and establish criteria for guiding contracting authorities in their green procurement.

28 Ibid, p. 83.
29 Ibid.
30 Ibid, p. 82.
31 Ibid.

5.1. *Analysis of the Framing Measures*

It is often forgotten that the EU has passed sector-specific mandatory GPP rules. These are hard law obligations on contracting authorities to follow green procurement contained in: the Energy Star Regulation (2008), creating an obligation on central contracting authorities to buy energy efficient IT office equipment; the Clean Vehicles Directive (2009) introducing the obligation to buy environmentally friendly vehicles for all contracting authorities; the Energy Performance of Buildings Directive (2010) introducing an obligation for new buildings owned and occupied by public authorities to be 'nearly zero-energy' by the end of 2018; and the Energy Efficiency Directive (2012) that contains a more 'soft' obligation to purchase energy efficient buildings and equipment of the highest energy labelling class.

The drawback of the regime is that it makes for a rather incoherent package, in terms of the kind of contracts covered, in terms of the strictness of the obligation and with respect to the level of government (i.e. federal or local).

In addition, the EU launched an EU GPP Support Programme, as outlined in the 2008 Communication *Public Procurement for a Better Environment.*[32] It encourages Member States to set up and revise National Action Plans for GPP, while setting political targets for the uptake of GPP in Member States; the current target is set at 50% of tendering procedures to be green. In the field of timber, for example, eight Member States (Austria, Belgium, Denmark, Finland, France, Germany, the Netherlands and the UK) have adopted national procurement policies for the purchase of sustainable timber.[33]

Furthermore, the Commission initiated action on the development of common EU GPP criteria for frequently procured products and services – not only selection and award criteria, but also specifications and contract performance clauses. The EU GPP criteria for product and service groups are supporting (voluntary) measures to assist contracting authorities in GPP and have been passed for the following target groups: copying and graphic paper; office IT equipment; transport; electricity; textiles; thermal insulation; wall panels; road construction and traffic signs; waste water infrastructure; imaging equipment; cleaning products and services; construction; furniture; food and catering services; gardening products and services; hard floor coverings; combine heat and power; street lighting and traffic signals; indoor lighting; and sanitary tapware.

With respect to the newly introduced lifecycle costing definition of the most economically advantageous tenders, we see that the EU GPP criteria initiative ties in increasingly with the procurement directives. New GPP criteria measures give first examples of lifecycle costing. For example, the GPP criteria for health care apparatus specify:

32 European Commission, *Public Procurement for a Better Environment*, COM(2008)400 final.

33 Standing Forestry Committee, *Public Procurement of Wood and Wood-Based Products* (November 2010), available at http://ec.europa.eu/agriculture/fore/publi/wg4-112010_en.pdf.

'Energy and water consumption can also be used in Life Cycle Cost (LCC) calculations. In this case, the public authority could calculate the water and energy spending over the expected lifetime of the equipment and include them in the price of the tender. Usually the cost of operation, maintenance, and disposal costs exceed all other first costs many times over (supporting costs are often 2–20 times greater than the initial procurement costs). If LCC is used in such a way, double counting must be avoided, i.e. that a lower energy and water consumption should not be awarded points twice but only in the framework of LCC or as an award criterion in addition to the price (without the costs for energy and water included).'[34]

We see that alongside facilitating Member State national policies on GPP, the EU is moving towards the creation of an EU-wide GPP policy by interlocking different hard and soft law instruments. While for the main part these are voluntary recommendations, the net of GPP measures is tightening, although the future of EU green public procurement will likely see a fragmented approach. In the presentation of the modernisation package, the Commission judged that:

'[I]t would however not be appropriate to set general mandatory requirements for environmental, social and innovation procurement [...] it therefore appears appropriate to continue on that path, leaving it to sector-specific legislation to set mandatory objectives and targets in function of the particular policies and conditions prevailing in the relevant sector and to promote the development and use of European approaches to life-cycle costing as a further underpinning for the use of public procurement in support of sustainable growth.'[35]

It can therefore be expected that timely EU green procurement policy will continue, perhaps leading in the very far future to a consolidation that makes up a general and overarching EU green procurement policy.

34 EU GPP Criteria for Electrical and Electronic Equipment used in the Health Care Sector, 22, available at http://ec.europa.eu/environment/gpp/pdf/criteria/health/Health%20Care%20EEE_en.pdf.

35 Directive 2014/24/EU, recital (95).

TRANSPARENCY OBLIGATIONS FOR PARKING SERVICES

Len Broeders*

1. Introduction

The parking sector is very popular in public procurement, at least in the Netherlands. One can only guess the reasons. As the investments regarding the building or renovation of parking facilities are high, the corresponding contracts are usually concluded for a longer period of time. This is appealing for operators who want to exploit parking facilities.

2. History

Even though (off-street) parking is big business nowadays, this has not always been the case. In the 1970s, the Dutch parking sector was generally controlled by local governments who considered it to be a money drain instead of an opportunity to make profits. Over time there has been a growing understanding of the value of land and space, specifically in countries with a high population density such as the Netherlands. Cities like Maastricht are not only in need of parking facilities for their own inhabitants, but also for the increasing number of tourists that visit the city by car.[1]

To meet this growing need, in the early 1970s the municipality of Maastricht built several (underground) car parks, such as the car park underneath the Onze Lieve Vrouweplein and the one underneath the Vrijthof, two of Maastricht's most beautiful and centrally located squares. Most of these car parks are accessible to the public at large which means that everyone is allowed to park there. Some parking facilities however are only open to designated persons who live or work in a particular quarter.

* Len Broeders is a partner at Broeders advocaten, Maastricht. She is member of the Dutch Committee of Public Procurement experts.

1 1.5 billion tourists visit Maastricht every year. Many of them come by car. See www.onderzoeksbanklimburg.nl/nieuws/categorie/gemeente-maastricht, last visited on 19 August 2014.

In 1979, the municipality of Maastricht closed a deal with a local firm, which later became known as Q-Park, which allowed Q-Park to exploit those car parks. Q-Park would lease, amongst others, the car parks underneath the Onze Lieve Vrouweplein and underneath the Vrijthof against a fixed rent – no indexation possible – for forty and fifty years respectively. The maintenance of the car parks would be done by the municipality.

Obviously, these contracts became more lucrative for Q-Park each passing year, as the rent to be paid did not increase, while (off-street) parking facilities significantly increased in value. As the years progressed, the parking deal proved to be not so good, as the municipality made little or no money on the off-street parking in Maastricht, but did have to pay for the maintenance.

The financial situation of the municipality was not that bright. A complete overhaul and face lift of the Vrijthof car park and the Onze Lieve Vrouwplein was absolutely necessary, but also very costly. The cost of the planned renovation works was considerable and it turned out that the municipality of Maastricht could not pay for it. It followed that between 1995 and 2002 the municipality and Q-Park negotiated on renewing their parking contracts and on changing the overall conditions. In 2002 a letter of intent was signed and in 2003 a contract was concluded for a period of thirty years. In the new contract it was stipulated that the previous lease contracts would come to an end. The contract provided for the ground rent (*erfpacht*) of the land owned by the municipality of Maastricht with the obligation for Q-Park to maintain the parking facilities and Q-Park had to pay for the upkeep. Q-Park furthermore agreed to renovate the car parks underneath the Vrijthof and the Onze Lieve Vrouweplein for an estimated total amount of €17.5 billion. €3.6 billion of the costs would be covered by Maastricht. Q-Park also had to pay a yearly (unfixed) contribution (canon) to the municipality while part of the parking revenues would go to Maastricht. It was agreed that in 2033, when the ground rent will end, Maastricht will get back the unburdened rights to the ground and the parking facilities. In return, the municipality will pay Q-Park €32 million and contribute to a possible fiscal claim up to €9.2 million.

Even though Maastricht and Q-Park were happy with this agreement, it does not come as a surprise that other market actors were not so pleased with it. In 2007 the municipality of Maastricht was challenged by P1, a Dutch company specialised in the parking sector, before the Court of First Instance of Maastricht. P1 argued that Maastricht had violated the EC Treaty and the principles of transparency and equal treatment by directly concluding a contract with Q-Park without publicising the tendering of the contract.[2] Before revealing the outcome of the case, some relevant judgments of the European Court of Justice will be discussed.

2 Court of First Instance Maastricht, 8 October 2008, 119309/HA ZA 07–419, LJN: BF7031. The facts that were discussed above can be found in the judgement.

3. The Court of Justice and the Transparency Obligation

Since the late 1990s, the Court of Justice has moulded and refined the principle of transparency in many public procurement cases. In *Unitron Scandinavia*,[3] a case in which the defendant was a concession holder (not a contracting authority), the Court focused on the non-discrimination principle. It held that this principle should not be interpreted restrictively and implied in particular, an obligation of transparency in order to enable the contracting authority to satisfy itself that it has been complied with.

This case was followed in 2000 by *Telaustria*[4] in which the Court held that:

> '[C]ontracting entities are bound to comply with the fundamental rules of the Treaty, in general, and the principle of non-discrimination on the ground of nationality, that principle implying in particular an obligation of transparency. This obligation of transparency which is imposed on the contracting authority consists in ensuring, for the benefit of any potential tenderer, a degree of advertising sufficient to enable the services market to be opened up to competition and the impartiality of procurement procedures to be reviewed.'

Next, in *Coname*[5] the Court held that:

> '[I]n the absence of any transparency, an undertaking has no real opportunity of expressing its interest in obtaining a concession. Undertakings located in the territory of a Member State other than that of the municipality in question should have access to appropriate information regarding that concession, so that, if such undertakings had so wished, would have been in a position to express their interest in obtaining that concession. It followed that unless justified by objective circumstances, a difference in treatment by which all undertakings located in another Member State are excluded, operates mainly to the detriment of these undertakings and thus amounts to indirect discrimination on the basis of nationality, prohibited by the Treaty.'

It is clear that the Court gave more weight to the transparency principle. A few months later the Court made the very important ruling in *Parking Brixen*[6] and held that 'the principle of equal treatment of tenderers is to be applied to public service concessions even in the absence of discrimination on grounds of nationality.' Accordingly, Articles 43 EC and 49 of the EC Treaty and the principles of equal treatment, non-discrimination and transparency preclude a public authority from awarding a public service concession to a certain company without putting it out to competition. The fact that all the parties in the case are based in the same country (Italy) was said to be of no importance as there is 'discrimination, at least potentially, against undertakings of other Member States'.

3 Case C-275/98 *Unitron Scandinavia* [1999] ECR I-08291, para. 31.
4 Case C-324/98 *Telaustria* [2000] ECR I-10770, paras. 60–62.
5 Case C-231/03 *Coname* [2005] ECR I-07287, paras. 17–22.
6 Case C-458/03 *Parking Brixen* [2005] ECR I-12057, para. 48.

This was confirmed by the Court in *APERMC*[7] and in *Wall.*[8] In this later case, the Court held that 'the obligation of transparency applies where the service concession in question *may* be of interest to an undertaking located in a Member State other that in which the concession is awarded'.

An Post[9] was about the direct award of a contract concerning B services. The Courts stated:

> 'It follows that the advertising arrangement, introduced by the Community legislature for contracts relating to services coming within the ambit of Annex I B, cannot be interpreted as precluding application of the principles resulting from Articles 43 EC and 49 EC, in the event that such contracts nevertheless are of *certain*[10] cross-border interest. [...] Also, in so far as a contract relating to services falling under Annex I B is of such interest, the award in absence of any transparency, of that contract to an undertaking located in the same Member State as the contracting authority amounts to a difference in treatment [...] In those circumstances, it is for the Commission to establish that, notwithstanding the fact that the contract in question relates to services coming within the scope of Annex I B to Directive 92/50, that contract was of certain interest to an undertaking located in a different Member State to that of the relevant contracting authority, and that that undertaking was unable to express its interest in that contract because it did not have access to adequate information before the contract was awarded.'

Since contracts relating to Annex I B are presumed not to have cross border interest, the Commission, who started proceeding on the basis of Article 226 EC Treaty (now Article 258 TFEU) had to prove that there was a certain cross border interest at the time. The Commission did not satisfy this burden of proof however.[11]

An explanation for the fact that in *Parking Brixen, APERMC* and *Wall* even potential discrimination was already enough to conclude that the non-discrimination principle was violated, while in *An Post* the Court demanded specific proof of the Commission, is related to the fact that the latter case was brought to the Court on the basis of Article 226–228 EC Treaty (Articles 258–260 TFEU) while the former case was decided after a preliminary question was asked by a national court. Of course one should always be careful not to interpret the transparency principle too broadly so as to render the distinction between services listed in Annex II A and Annex II B of Directive 2004/18/EC totally ineffective.[12]

7 This was confirmed in Case C-220/06 *APERMC* [2007] ECR I-12175, paras. 76–77.

8 Case C-91/08 *Wall* [2010] ECR I-02815, paras. 34–35.

9 Case C-508/03 *An Post (Commission v. Ireland)* [2007] ECR I-3972, paras. 29–32.

10 Emphasis added by the author.

11 A few months later, this was confirmed in Case C-119/06 *Commission/Italy* [2007] ECR I-00168, paras. 63–65.

12 Case C-95/10 *Strong Seguranca* [2011] ECR I-01865, paras. 40–41. Annex II B services are also called non priority services. Since they are presumed not to have any cross border interest, they are only subject to Articles 23 and 35(4) Directive 2004/18/EC. The distinction between Annex II A and Annex II B services is no longer present in Directive 2014/24/EU of the European Parliament and of the Council of 26 February 2014 on public procurement and repealing Directive 2004/18/EC.

4. The Judicial Procedure in the Netherlands

As noted above, in April 2007 the municipality of Maastricht was challenged by P1, a company specialised in the parking sector, before the Court of First Instance of Maastricht. P1 argued that Maastricht had violated the EC Treaty and the principles of transparency and equal treatment by not publishing a contract notice.[13] P1 demanded that the municipality of Maastricht be ordered to end the contract with Q-Park and to start a public procurement procedure for the award of the contract. It should be noted that the outcome of this case would not only have consequences for the parties involved: if P1 were to succeed, all parking contracts, and specifically those that were concluded before the transparency obligation gained more interest, were at risk.

The Dutch Court of First Instance held that the contract between the municipality and Q-Park should be qualified as a works concession as meant in Article 1(d) of Directive 93/37/EEC[14] which was in force at the time. This meant that the advertising rules as described in Article 11(3), (6), (7) and (9) to (13), and in Article 15 of the Directive were applicable to that contract when its value is not less than €5,000,000. The Court added that in case, the Directive would not be applicable to the contract, the municipality still had the obligation to respect the transparency obligations by verifying whether the contract had a certain cross border interest with the result that it had to be published. In this regard, the Dutch Court referred to *Telaustria* and *Unitron Scandinavia,* which were the only cases that were already decided upon by the European Court of Justice at the time that the contract was concluded. The Dutch Court added however that the contract could not be annulled. It stated that such possibility was not mentioned in the Directive. For this and some other reasons, P1 appealed the judgment and the case was brought before the Dutch Court of Appeal in 's-Hertogenbosch.

The Court of Appeal indicated that the contract should be qualified as a services concession and not as a works concession. This is in line with *Parking Brixen* which contained similar facts. Important to note however is that services concessions are not covered by Council Directive 92/50/EEC of 18 June 1992 relating to the coordination of procedures for the award of public service contracts, nor by any other Directive. The Court of Appeal decided nevertheless that the municipality of Maastricht still had to organise 'some kind' of public procurement procedure in light of the transparency principle if there was an actual cross border interest for the contract at the time.[15] The case was finally brought before the Supreme Court.

The Supreme Court confirmed in 2013 that the Court of Appeal had not erred by qualifying the contract as a services concession and by deciding that the transparency

13 It should be noted that the case also has a State aid dimension. This contribution only covers the procurement aspects of the case.

14 Council Directive 93/37/EEC of 14 June 1993 concerning the coordination of procedures for the award of public works contracts.

15 Judgments of the Court of Appeal in 's-Hertogenbosch of 23 June 2009, 8 December 2009 and 1 March 2011, HD 200.018.435.

principle should nevertheless be respected.[16] The Supreme Court confirmed the Court of Appeal's opinion that the services in question were Annex II B services with the result that there was a presumption that those services had no cross border interest. The Supreme Court indicated that the Court of Appeal had not erred by stating that P1 did not sufficiently prove the cross-border interest at the time. It followed that it left the verdict of the Court of Appeal intact.

5. Conclusion

On numerous occasions the Court of Justice has given guidance on the exact meaning and scope of the transparency obligation in public procurement law. Even though the legislator ruled out the application of the procurement directives if the thresholds were not reached or in case of service concessions or Annex II B services, the Court has made clear that the principle of non-discrimination and the transparency obligation have to be respected at all times. This means that in most – if not all – cases, 'some kind' of procurement procedure has to be applied. Undertakings should have access to appropriate information regarding projects planned by contracting authorities so that they can express their interest in obtaining a contract. Even if the thresholds are not reached, and even in cases of Annex II B services or social services,[17] the European transparency obligation has to be respected if there is a cross-border dimension. It follows that transparency has to be respected everywhere and at all times. It follows that in the future, the municipality of Maastricht will have to award a contract like the one concluded with Q-Park in a transparent way. As Maastricht is located near the Dutch borders with both Belgium and Germany that may not come as a surprise. Whether also municipalities which are located in the middle of the Netherlands will have to respect the European transparency principle when contracting on a service concession is another question and may even change if the new Directive is implemented in the Netherlands. In this regard, reference can be made to recital (1) of Directive 2014/24/EU which states:

> 'The award of *public contracts* by or on behalf of Member States' authorities has to comply with the principles of the Treaty on the Functioning of the European Union (TFEU), and in particular the free movement of goods, freedom of establishment and the freedom to provide services, as well as the principles deriving therefrom, such as equal treatment, non-discrimination, mutual recognition, proportionality and transparency. However, for public contracts above a certain value, provisions should be drawn up coordinating national procurement procedures so as to ensure that those principles are given practical effect and public procurement is opened up to competition.'

16 Supreme Court, 18 January 2013, ECLI:NL:HR:2013:BY0543.

17 As indicated before, Directive 2014/24/EU no longer makes a difference between Annex II A and Annex II B service. A special regime however still exists for social services. See Article 74 of the Directive.

This seems to indicate that the principle of transparency has to be respected at all times. It should be questioned, however, whether this is really what was meant by the European legislator, since reference is specifically made to the Treaty on the Functioning of the European Union which is in principle only applicable in cross-border situations. In this regard, it should be added that the fact that P1 did not satisfy its burden of proof regarding the actual cross-border interest of the parking contract even though the parking facilities were located in the heart of the Euregio will probably not encourage competitors that want to conclude contracts for facilities located in the middle of the country to raise their voice. It can be questioned whether the European Court of Justice would have taken the same stance.

IUS COMMUNE EUROPAEUM

A peer-reviewed book series in which the common foundations of the legal systems of the Member States of the European Union are the central focus.

The *Ius Commune Europaeum* series includes horizontal comparative legal studies as well as studies on the effect of treaties within the national legal systems. All the classic fields of law are covered. The books are published in various European languages under the auspices of METRO, the Institute for Transnational Legal Research at Maastricht University.

Recently published:
Volume 120: *The Effects of Judicial Decisions in Time*, P. Popelier, S. Verstraelen, D. Vanheule and B. Vanlerberghe (eds.)
Volume 121: *The Position of Small and Medium-Sized Enterprises in European Contract Law*, I. Samoy and M.B.M. Loos (eds.)
Volume 122: *Property Law Perspectives II*, B. Akkermans, E. Marais and E. Ramaekers (eds.)
Volume 123: *The Treaty on European Union 1993-2013 Reflections from Maastricht*, M. de Visser and A.P. van der Mei (eds.)
Volume 124: *Inside Police Custody. Training Framework on the Provisions of Suspects' Rights*, T. Spronken, J. Blackstock, E. Lloyd-Cape, J. Hodgson, A. Ogorodova, M. Vanderhallen
Volume 125: *Coordinating Ombudsmen and the Judiciary. A comparative view on the relations between ombudsmen and the judiciary in the Netherlands, England and the European Union*, M. Remac
Volume 126: *Legal Evolution and Hybridisation. The Law of Shares Transfer in England*, M. Solinas
Volume 127: *The Role of EU State Aid Law in Promoting a Pro-Innovation Policy. A Review from the Perspective of University-Industry R&D Cooperation*, M. Cisneros
Volume 128: *Tradition, Codification and Unification. Comparative – Historical Essays on Developments in Civil Law*, J.M. Milo, J.H.A. Lokin and J.M. Smits
Volume 129: *Nobody's Perfect. Comparative Essays on Appeals and other Means of Recourse against Judicial Decisions in Civil Matters*, A. Uzelac and C.H. van Rhee
Volume 130: *Legal Aid in the Low Countries*, B. Hubeau and A. Terlouw (eds.)

www.ingramcontent.com/pod-product-compliance
Ingram Content Group UK Ltd.
Pitfield, Milton Keynes, MK11 3LW, UK
UKHW051927100926
8556IPUK00022B/1425

9 781780 682747